Content's Dream

Books by Charles Bernstein

A Poetics (Harvard University Press, 1992)

Rough Trades (Sun & Moon Press, 1991)

The Absent Father in Dumbo (Zasterle, 1990)

The Nude Formalism, with Susan Bee
(Sun & Moon Press, 1989)

The Sophist (Sun & Moon Press, 1987)

Veil (Xexoxial Editions, 1987)

Content's Dream: Essays 1975–1984
(Sun & Moon Press, 1986; 1994)

Resistance (Awede Press, 1983)

Islets/Irritations (Jordan Davies, 1983;
reprinted, Roof Books, 1992)

Stigma (Station Hill Press, 1981)

The Occurrence of Tune, with Susan Bee [Laufer]
(Segue, 1981)

Disfrutes (Potes and Poets Press, 1981)

Controlling Interests (Roof Books, 1980)

Legend, with Bruce Andrews, Ray DiPalma,
Steve McCaffery, and Ron Silliman
(L=A=N=G=U=A=G=E/Segue, 1980)

Senses of Responsibility (Tuumba Press, 1979;
reprinted, Paradigm Press, 1989)

Poetic Justice (Pod Books, 1979)

Shade (Sun & Moon Press, 1978)

Parsing (Asylum's Press, 1976)

Editor

The Politics of Poetic Form: Poetry and Public Policy (Roof, 1990)

Patterns/Contexts/Time, with Phillip Foss (Tyuonyi, 1990)

L=A=N=G=U=A=G=E, with Bruce Andrews (1978–1981)

CONTENT'S DREAM

Essays 1975-1984

CHARLES BERNSTEIN

SUN & MOON
MOON

CLASSICS

49

SUN & MOON PRESS
Los Angeles

Sun & Moon Press
A Program of The Contemporary Arts Educational Project, Inc.
a nonprofit corporation
6026 Wilshire Boulevard, Los Angeles, California 90036

This edition first published in paperback in 1986 by Sun & Moon Press
10 9 8 7 6 5 4 3 2
SECOND PRINTING
Biographical information © Sun & Moon Press, 1986
All rights reserved

This book was made possible, in part, through a operational grant from the
Andrew W. Mellon Foundation and through contributions to
The Contemporary Arts Educational Project, Inc.,
a nonprofit corporation

Cover: Susan Bee, Detail of *Lighthouse in Black* (1981)

LIBRARY OF CONGRESS CATALOGING IN PUBLICATION DATA
Bernstein, Charles (1950)
Content's Dream: Essays 1975–1984
p. cm — (Sun & Moon Classics: 49)
ISBN: 0-940650-156-8
I. Title. II. Series.
811'.54—dc20

Printed in the United States of America on acid-free paper.

Contents

Six/ *Catechesis*

Preface

Night falls, is used to; when all the cues seem larks and
constancy's a brocade fan. Say, contentious, each becomes
logician of her argument, in turn a pearl, in turn appalled.
Or amelioration—when you ask the person next-of-door to
turn it down. Person? Personality is the production of a
social becoming; not yet being, all the quicker bodied. And
what of that undermass—as if flesh crawled or sucked—
since every idea of such is, as it is, retrospeculative. Yet these
conditions render a life its currency, like sugar with a spoon.
The punch is already in the sock.

"I'd rather be in meats than underwear." Then later, on
the news, "We have a right: Open up the process." For
which all are lined up the easier to knock down. Dumbly
mumbling the traces of conceptions, the trapezoids of
obligated catechism: a candle's chance in a blackout. To
protect against respect, cranked up and ready to show. But
the houses are straw and the angels are carting them to
Macy's. A loneliness of the long-distance small businessman.

Though there are stealthier things that egg, or fry: hidden
haciendas of deifications and defecations. Whatever purples
at times is pallid. Books like streets, designed for use of those
at hand; I have never been to Mannahatta but know the
trails. A friend disclaims an intent inferred—"the gossamer

9

wings of thought"; I would have said bats' waves of sound.
Such alternatives can seem more oracular, and exclusionary,
than "straight" talk, so that the very process of getting away
from authoritarian language use may be rejected for creating
its own occult authority. Still, you can't *dial* your way out of
a paper bag. The sooner we put up the pasta, the sooner we'll
eat.

Funny odd or funny peculiar? The clash of the flash—
plated desperation and carpeted distraction. For—from—
what?: hemorrhagic hootenannies, engrossment by engorge-
ment, adjectival remission? Somewhere there is a Pelopon-
nesus of the heart's own measure, which stops and stuns.
Other means are thus admitted to the circulation of the
nowhere seen, everywhere disturbed: variorums of variation
at the columns of the colorless. And *you*, always present in
the vanishing circuit of the neither here nor there, blow
booms to the tympanist's tweedy waltz. It gets better when
the counting stops.

Or wanders. Rumination is the soul's club foot, by which
it beats the rap. To tell some tales of terms, each the story of
its tug.

ONE/ THE SECRET OF SYNTAX

THREE OR FOUR THINGS
I KNOW ABOUT HIM

1. " ... the task of history, once the world beyond the
truth has disappeared, is to establish the truth of this world.
... "—Marx

2.   its like a living death   going to work
every day   sort of like being in a tomb   to sit
in your office   you close the door   theres the
typewriter   theres three or four maybe three hours of
work to be done   between that nine oclock and five
          maybe i listen to the news on wbai if i didnt get it
the night before that comes on at nine oclock
     i read the newspaper   i do anything to distract
myself   sometimes i sleep til around eleven   i
put both feet up on my desk   and i put my hand
against my head and i close my eyes   the time passes
if i listen to the radio   i type a letter   i write an
article   that would make the article that i wrote for
that medical newspaper seem like proust in comparison
          or sometimes i think   initially   the job
seemed more bearable   more to the point   of

just a diversion and source of income   for a while
            until i got unemployment   not now
        but   mostly its just that i'm taking things in a
bleaker way   i'm not quite sure why that is

                                                        of course
the writing   writing   even talking
like this   always seems to me   perfectly at
peace   so that   i was thinking i dont know
        this could be my own   you know   this
could be sort of the   the source of my crazy hood/ness
        that   the things that are really valuable dont so
much happen as you experience them   in the actual
present   a lot of what i experience   is just a
        tremendous sense of   space   and vacant
space at that   sort of like a stanley kubrick film
        sort of a lot of objects   floating separately
        which i dont   particularly feel do anything for
me   give me anything   make me feel good
            and when i do feel almost best   is
when i dont care   whether they make me feel good
        whether they have any relation to me   thats a
very pleasant   thats a real feeling of value in the
present moment   to just sit and do nothing
        and thats what writing is for me a lot   or just
sitting   sometimes when i   i sit in my office
    with my eyes closed   on my chair   and let
my mind wander   theres a certain   sense of
not caring   and letting it just go by   that i like
        and then there is actual relationships
            you know   sometimes   touching
        whether its listening to a piece of music sometimes

or talking to somebody a lot   being with
        certain people sometimes   but a lot of it has to
do with memory   & remembering   that it was
        it was something   that somehow the value
seems to lie   historically   i look back   and
see things that really do seem   worthwhile   and
worth it   for instance   the way i behave   if
i try to behave   well   decently   or
justly   or whatever it is   that we take to be
what we judge ourselves by   when we have a
conversation   and we say   thats fucked and
thats not   whatever we go by in that sense   i
mean   making that happen   building that
        it does seem   you know   worth
a value   funny refreshing   nice
wonderful   or a movie   sometimes
moments   hours   but   something
in   the   actual   experiencing   of
        it   that does seem   vacant   in
the way that a lot   is vacant   but   also
        the way   yeah   okay   new
mexico   is vacant
        really i'm   you know   completely gone
        just after working   by the time i get to this
        but i am able to concentrate and remember
        the different things ive said so far   that seem
disconnected   see i'm sort of condemned to be
disconnected and seem disjointed and sort of
        stupid   but really i can remember all the
different things ive said   i'm sort of   i dont
know   its almost a motif   thats a major

preoccupation with me   writing   the way a
relationship is   much the way my relationship with
susan or   or   my job   more than my
job   altho it creates an enormous number of hassles
for me   its really as bad as you would imagine it
would be to work for this mindless healthcare provider
bureaucracy   and the reason why you dont want to
work for it is because its exploitive of you   you are
used   your body is used   my writing
          and in that sense its an unsettling experience for me
          to have to sit   day after day in an office   and
be exploited   what really bothers me tho   in
addition   the rub   is the attitude of the other
people   that somehow they could do whatever it is
they had to do during the day   they could be
managers   they could be bosses   they could order
people around   let the women answer the phones
          and criticize me for typing   and say i should let
the secretaries do all the typing   they could basically
serve this large corporation   to the best of their ability
to serve it   and to further its particular interests
          this was actually a nonprofit corporation
and then sort of go out at lunch or   on the side
          and on a personal level say to you   that really
          who they were at the job   the way they
behaved at their job   what they did all day
          was not them   that the real them   the
real person   was   somebody different   who
went home at night and had liberal values   was
critical of what the company was doing   what the
job was making them do   that they really werent

what they did at the job   they were somebody else
        that the self that went home at night   and
watched television   and went to the movies
went out dancing   socialized   that was the
real   that was the real them   and that sort
of public self   the job self   was really just a
pretense that was necessary to secure a decent living
for their families   for themselves   or a chance
to have some kind of social power   here again that
tremendously distorted notion of what a person is
        and its this concept of a person which makes me
        question   the whole sense that we generally
have of what a person is   that you can imagine that
what you do socially   that the acts   you
perform   are not you youre really this private thing
that doesnt do anything   this sort of neutral gear
        but that whenever you put that gear into operation
        when you put yourself into gear   thats not you
        or thats only you under conditions when you want
to say well i like that and so i'll say well that is me
        but when youre actually doing things that have
some effect   that isnt you   the real you is this
personal self   and you even get this situation where
you have   colleagues or professional   work
        friends   as opposed to personal friends   well
he's a personal friend of mine   this person is simply
a job friend   this constant distortion   this
constant avoidance   that you are what you do
        that insofar as a self is anything its how it acts in a
social situation   what else is a person   anyway
        but a signifier of responsibility for a series of actions

if a self is anything it is what that self does with its
body   does with its mind   and that
responsibility is for what you do   not for what you
go home at night and think what you'd like to do if if if if
one day   some time   it creates at
the job place this tremendous vacancy of person   this
tremendous   lack of connection   with anybody
because if people dont really think theyre being
them all day long   in their suits and shaved faces
and their very reduced mild language   and
their reduced middle of the road opinions   which
they feel is the safest way   then theres no way to
get a connection with anybody   everything is just so
neutralized   that you can work in a place for years
and years   and really feel no   no clicking with
anybody else   no contact   with anybody there
you can go out to lunch at the same time   as
if with ghosts   there is no escape from what
you do   and even if you feel you dont mean what you
do   dont mean what you say   dont mean the way
you dress   dont mean the kind of business letter
language you use   dont mean the division of labor
you go along with   or that you institute
dont mean the kind of attitudes you have competitively
toward your coworkers   dismissingly to the
secretaries   that one does mean these things whether
one wants to or not   that they can be taken to be
intentional   to be you   are you   who
you are   and they can be read as being you
theres no escape from the nine to five

self by claiming that the five to midnight self   or the
midnight to eight self   is not really like this
            we become selves just because we do different
things   and its a very hard thing   hard to
accept that you are what youre forced to be when you go to
work   and not many feel that they want to get
behind   the products of their job   but we are
behind them   and i'm not saying
            well obviously   munitions workers are not
responsible for the war   but its this avoidance of
acknowledging the tracks of exploitation   and of
course for the ambitious   for the managers and
upper clerks   well   that conjuring trick of
projecting a self outside of ones own actions   is
practically a way of life

3. TOILET PAPER CONSCIOUSNESS
"Should never say should."
You're not responsible. You may be white. You may be
male. You may be heterosexual. You may be American. You
may be working for the government. You may be President.
But you are not responsible for anything but your own ass.
And if you keep your ass clean—to the best of your ability—
it's cool, it's groovy, it's okay.

4.   " 'Scientism' means science's belief in itself: that is, the
conviction that we no longer understand science as *one* form
of possible knowledge but rather must identify knowledge with science." —Jürgen Habermas

5. COMIC INTERLUDE

It is the imperialism of the bourgeois psyche that demands a
reduction in the number of words able to assume the weight
of depicting the world-picture. Nouns, because of their
proletarian pristineness as least distorted by the invasion of
bourgeois consciousness into the language, as, in fact, the
claim goes, repositories of the object residue of material
existence, are the principal word type favored under this
assumption. *Viz:* classism, ruling class, third world, exploitation, revisionist, capital, profit, worker, means of produc-
ion, alienation. 'Verb'al forms emerge mainly in the application of this—*uberhaupt*—principal structure—'exploiting',
'profiting', and also, 'struggling'*. Individual actions are
depicted as reified instantiations fixed by the intersection of
a variety of *theses*. It is, then, *our thesis* that political writing
becomes disoriented when it views itself as description and
not discourse: as not being *in* the world but *about* the world.
The hermeneutic indicts the scientistic with the charge that
it has once again subverted the dialogic nature of human
understanding with its behavioro-empiricism.

6.   a fun is what i want to avoid the work of sitting down &
m'um the cheezy. it's a hundred and forty five miles. you
don't go for no reason. couldn't stop thinking about it.
wanted to go to sleep so bad. under. stuff, thing. whats that
gnawing, keeps gnawing. switch, fug, cumpf. afraid to get

---

*'Struggle' retains the active principle and is thus undistorted by the noun
fetishism that marks infantile forms of Marxist thought. It is the 'verb'al
weight of 'struggle' as shift and dynamic that is the essence of a re-
hermeneuticized Marxism.

down to it. avoidances: movies. i think it's rather boring already dAncInG with LaRRy rIvers. marKINGs: not done by a machine. hAnDcRaFt. so you get into a scene and you say to y'rself—this is it, is outside it, & y'guys all know whats going on. Daddy-O you a hero. OHH. can't even get tired. what is it—dead—very wrinkled anyway. quiet ... i could hear the very 'utmost of m'heart. EEzzy. its fear eats away the ... i'm totally afraid of what it will sound like. flotsam. a $1 transcript. stomach sputters. noise, interference, & i can't work. TeAz tHE MeEk. we're'iz'iz puliticks? poised: there is no overall plan.

7.   In general I think I have since I was about 12 tended to subdue any sentimentality or strong emotional expressions of weakness, fear, etc., I might have expressed except in the cases of the women I was sexually relating to. At that time, I began to see how my parents demanded expressions of sentimentality, of commitment, of caring, of happy birthday anniversary chanukah, in a way that repelled me from *any* such expressions. In the family situation such expressions seemed oppressive, they served to lock me further into jealousy/possessiveness/control by my family. I completely lost trust in the natural place for depending on other people—because I knew I did not want to depend on my parents. I extended my feelings about my parents to others— which could show up as my seeming detached, cynical, cold, intellectual, cool. I learned that this distance from others was actually a tool for social power by manipulation. I learned to think that my only security was in what I could do by myself, alone—i.e., get good marks, do well at work, write a good proposal, do good writing. My security was in what I

personally had complete control over. (This is in general a "male class privilege" since, for example, a woman on her own with children is forced to depend on others just for survival while I could basically say fuck everyone else I'm in it for myself.) In fact, this keeping personal control of one's life, keeping distance, really does get social power—it's harder to pin such people down, it's harder to get to them. Anyway, even realizing this I found it hard to find security in relating to other people instead of by being in personal control of my life. I find it scary to give up that other security (which is power) by really trusting/needing/relating to others. The thing is that in making relationships my security/home I do lose my own control—because there are definite limits to my power, I may have to do something I don't want to or that isn't in my interest, I may get hurt, I may be powerless to prevent someone else from getting hurt. In other words, in relating to other people, I have to accept their needs/perceptions along with my own. Is this too abstract?

The thing is I still can feel my coldness/distance with other people. I find it hard to break that down. I become defensive (self-protective) or acerbic/witty (self-assertive). Some people get through that, see me through it. But I think it can be unnecessarily alienating. I don't think I give people comfort that much—that is, seem to them warm, nurturing, supportive. Don't, I sometimes feel, give people a feeling of getting "shelter from the storm/cold" but rather can be the cold that people seek the shelter from. I have a technique of bathing people in that cold, a puritan conviction that people should know the world is hard, and they should face it strong and stern. (& what happens to even good politics expressed this way?) And people should know that, but only sometimes can I transform that realization, go beyond it, and show that one shares that hardness with others, who care. That I am one of them. One of us.

8.   "There are those who worship loneliness—I'm not one of them; I've paid the price of solitude but at least I'm out of debt." A precursor here: the worship of loneliness, of being alone, as a way of being whole in the world that demands personal fragmentation as the price for fitting into society— the cult of Thoreau, Kierkegaard, etc., in the best and worst sense. So here the rejection, the realization that to worship being alone condemns one to isolation. *But:* the reward of solitude is yet to be out of debt; to owe no one anything, the self-made man, on your own and in control—the delusion of security in isolation, if you keep yr ass clean kid youll be okay, look out fer yrself, yr numero primo. And so the ravages of the world have forced us to be warriors, ravaged we take control of our individual lives fighting for the warmth of inside we've had to give up. "Come in she said I'll give you shelter from the storm." She she she, waiting: ready to comfort, to nurture, to support our shipwrecked egos. And so we take the comfort, but without transforming ourselves—she simply comforts, offers shelter, but we remain in the world of "steel eyed death" (a steely idea that)— exchange no words "between us". There is "little risk involved" because we have held fast to our isolation, simply allowing it to be warmed. "Come in she said I'll give you shelter from the storm." But there can be no shelter until we ourselves provide it each for the other together. Without that there will always be "a wall between us"; then the steely

idea triumphs: "Nothing really matters, it's doom alone that counts." *And yet?*: "Love is so simple, to quote a phrase, you've known it all the time I'm learning it these days." So simple and yet so seeming sentimental to say, as if sentimentality were the curse that prevented us from knowing how simple love is in our repulsion to its being demanded by our families/country/society at the price of self-abnegation. And so in the flight from the oppressive obligations of sentimentality; of polite hellos and demanded, guilt-ridden, love; in the retreat into the isolation and security of personal control, needing no one; a native sense was lost that love is so simple, to quote a phrase, that we are each for each other shelter from the storm, if we are not afraid to come in, or take another into where we are. But still all this while the secret has been known ("you've known it all the time") if only we had "spoken words between us", had taken that "risk". The words sound sentimental—I love you I miss you it hurts me so bad with a pain that stops and starts—words of separation, of closeness, of hurt, of joy—we choke on them: there is no depth here, no unique sensibility: everyone says them. But still the curse can be broken by their utterance. "I can change I swear." "It's the price I have to pay."—The commitment is to "cross the line" from the "foreign countries" each of us inhabits; *someday* to dissolve into a now.

9.   "It's like spelling. You know that whole sense that spelling things right in English is really sort of an aristocratic notion. You could tell the educated few by the fact that they spelled the same. Which I'm told is a lot of their system of education ... because in Shakespeare's time he spelled his

own name a lot of different ways, not to mention other words. You know, it was really like a body of material that would identify you as one of the educated people. Think of all the time we've spent in school spelling things right. Sort of a tremendous waste of time."—Clark Coolidge

10.   Ethics & aesthetics become increasingly "out there". Dress & syntax & right behavior are copied from presented models, a process of emulation rather than interpretation. Clerks & secretaries spend their time typing neatly, removing idiosyncracies from the language & presiding over a tan neutrality—"unobtrusive"—with the smoothness of flow allowed by explanatory transition.

Topic sentence. However; but; as a result. Blah, blah, blah. It follows from this. Concluding sentence.

Meaning, coherence, truth projected "out there" as something we know not for ourselves but as taught to us. (One day, maybe, we will be experts.)

It goes like this. "Clear writing is the best picture of clear thinking." Providing a clear view. (An imperial clarity for an imperial world.) An official version of reality, in which ethics is transformed into moral code & aesthetics into clean shaving, is labelled the public reality & we learn this as we would a new language. (Orthography & expository clarity are just other words for diction & etiquette.)

Imperial reality has as its essential claim not so much that it is *a* version of reality but that it is *the* version, i.e., (imperially) clear. That the composition of reality is supra-personal: the mistakes & plain takes of a person are not an essential part of reality's composition. Standardized spelling, layout, & punctuation enter into a world of standardization—clocks & the orbit of the moon & the speed of light. A social science epistemologically self-conceived on the model of the natural sciences becomes possible & grammar becomes a social science. Language is thus removed from the participatory control of its users & delivered into the hands of the state. Text is no longer regarded as requiring interpretation: rules for appropriate spelling & syntax are determined by consultation with generalized codes of grammar removed from their contextualized source in a text. (The Hebrew handwritten text required interpretation not only in respect to the meaning of its ethical & ritual tenets but even for the placement of vowels.) Decontextualized codification of the rules of language enforces a view that language operates on principles apart from its usage. These rules are not "picked up" but taught. Failure to produce appropriate language is regarded not as misperception but as error. The understanding begins to be lost that we are each involved in the constitution of language—that our actions reconstitute—change—reality.

It's a question of who controls reality. Is reality "out there" (as scientism tells us) or rather an interaction with us, in which our actions shape its constitution? Prescribed rules of grammar & spelling make language seem outside of our control. & a language, even only seemingly, wrested from our control is a world taken from us—a world in which language becomes a tool for the description of the world, words mere instrumentalities for representing this world. This is reflected by the historical movement toward uniform spelling and grammar, with an ideology that emphasizes nonidiosyncratic, smooth transition, elimination of awkwardness, &c,—anything that might concentrate attention on the language itself. For instance, in contrast to, say, Sterne's work, where the look & texture—the opacity—of the text is everywhere present, a neutral, transparent prose style has developed in certain recent novels where the words seem meant to be looked through—to the depicted world beyond the page. Likewise, in current middle of the road poetry, we see the elimination of overt rhyme & alliteration, with metric forms retained primarily for their capacity to officialize as "poetry". (That older texts are closer to handwritten & oral tradition is partial explanation for this, but having machines for uniform printing necessitates neither a uniform writing nor the projection of a suprapersonal world.)

Much of the spirit of modernism has been involved in the reassertion of the value of what has come to be fantasized as subjectivity. Faced with an imperial reality, "subjectivity" is first defined as "mere idiosyncrasy", that residue of perception that is to be discounted, the fumbling clouds of vision that are to be dissolved by learning. But in just this is the ultimate *subjectivity* of a people: stripping us of our source of power in our humanness by denying the validity of our power over the constitution of our world through language. The myth of subjectivity and its denigration as mere idiosyncrasy—impediments to be overcome—diffuses the inherent power in the commonness of our alienation:

that rather than being something that separates us, alienation
is the source of our commonness. I take it that this is why
Marx saw as inevitable that a proletariat conscious of its
alienation would be able to develop human relations—
solidarity—which would be stronger than any other human
power.

The poetic response to the imposition of an imperial
reality has been to define subjectivity, by a kind of
Nietzschean turn around, not as 'mere' but as exalted. The
image of the poet as loner & romantic continues to condition
this response. An unconscious strategy of contrariety devel-
ops—that the official manners & forms are corrupt &
distorted & only the private & individual is real. Beat—to
abstract & project a stance, acknowledging the injury this
does to the actual poetry—is an obvious example, as is
Surrealism, itself & as an influence. These two modes—for
the moment letting them stand for a much wider variety of
literary response—are grounded in reaction. Beat poetry, as
such, could go no further than the dramatization of alienation; the genesis of much of its considerable & indispensable
formal innovation is (quite justifiably) epaté la bourgeoisie.
(The rhapsodic other side was, at the least, pastoral romanticism; at its best it put off the theater of vision for the
language of presence.) Likewise, Surrealism, in itself, could
do little more than theatricalize our alienation from official
reality, since it is completely rooted in bourgeois spatiotemporal perception: it simply distorts it. Both Beat &
Surrealism are essentially poetries of gesture, viz: Reality is
different from our schooled conceptions of it, more fantastic,
more————. In these modes, to use Stanley Cavell's

phrase, the moment is not grounded but etherialized: alienation is not defeated but only landscaped.* What is needed, now, is not the further dramatization of far-outness but the presence of far-inness. These modes have shown a way. Surrealism & Beat broke open syntax & placement of words on the page, they widened the range of content & vocabulary, they allowed shape & texture & hover of consciousness to become more important than description. Unfortunately, much current poetry goes no further, fixated on the idea of establishing the value of the interior world of feeling, irrational (whimsical) connections, social taboos, the personal life—over & against "official" reality.† As if we didn't already know that "bad grammar" can speak more truthfully than correct grammar, that learning & expertise don't really impart knowledge, that private fantasies don't coincide with public property. It's not that we don't need to hear these things again & again, any more than that that is the objection to socialist realism, but that there is so much more we can do than simply underline the fact—& describe the conditions—of our alienation, of the loss of the world's presence to us. (As if it were enough to simply mourn & not organize.) The promise of the return of the world can (& has always been) fulfilled by poetry. Even before the process of class struggle is complete. Poetry, centered on the condition

*Likewise, this is true of the avant-gardism & conceptualism, taken for themselves as a stance, which pervade much of the seventies art scene.

†This helps to explain the almost ideological anti-intellectualism—"dumbness"—that runs through some poetry circles.

of its wordness—words of a language not out there but in here, language the place of our commonness—is a momentary restoration of ourselves to ourselves.

11. "At home, one does not speak so that people will understand but because people understand."

—Eduard Fuchs

12. & obviously we're committed to political struggle, to the necessity of changing current capital distribution, to making the factories & the schools & the hospitals cooperatives, to finding a democracy that allows for the participatory authority of each one to the extent of the responsibility we place on her or him. there are no prefixed means & the answer is in struggling & discussing & deciding as groups & acting. & it troubles—isn't this incessant writing & questioning writing a diversion? isn't *the* business . . . ? well, but language *is* our business, fully as much as 'acting'. anyway, how do you pre-suppose to separate out the deed & the reflection? you might say we've got dual responsibilities, & one doesn't take us off the hook of the other. writing, by itself, does not further class struggle. "it is a fertilizer not a tool." pound's politics don't in any way diminish the power & significance of his writing. nor do they limit the aesthetic/political value of the work. but that in no way absolves the man from his own political responsibilities. social credit—to be a little silly & talk about measuring it—is really a multiplication of the "dual" responsibilities. & a zero multiplied by even an astronomical figure doesn't get

you very far. i'm not saying the "private" literary activity is separable from the "public" conduct. i'm saying a person's got a variety of responsibilities (if to say 'dual' then only when speaking of a particular conflict)—& it's not okay to be a bully just because you're wearing a pretty dress. there's no end to responsibilities. & poetry, well, it's in a sense an additional responsibility—as a woman or a man you'd not lose 'credit' for not doing it. it's not that aesthetic conscious-ness & political consciousness are essentially different, quite the opposite, but really this is the goal: reunification—in practice—of what we now face as multiple demands. the power of poetry is, indeed, to bridge this gap—for a moment—by providing instances of actualization. it is a glimpse. but, sadly, for us, now, no *maker* is able to reap the legitimate rewards of his or her labor. & so our responsibilities remain multiple & we are called on to fulfill all of them.

13. We imagine there is a gap between the world of our private phantasies & the possibilities of meaningful action. & so it becomes easy to talk & talk on what is lacking, to discourse on end, & yet feel impotent. 'What's to do.' But this gap is the measure not so much of our desires or depression or impotence but of our*selves*. It has been the continual failure of Marxist aesthetics to insist that this gap is simply another illusory part of our commodity lives. It is at the root of our collectivity.

14. The essential aspect of writing centered on its language is its possibilities for relationship, *viz*, it is the body of 'us'ness, in which *we* are, the ground of our commonness.

Language is commonness in being, through which we see
& make sense of & value. Its exploration is the exploration
of the human common ground. The move from purely
descriptive, outward directive, writing toward writing centered on its wordness, its physicality, its haecceity (thisness)
is, in its impulse, an investigation of human self-sameness, of
the place of our connection: in the world, in the word, in
ourselves.

15. The situation, the relations, the conditions under which.
The task of unchaining & setting up. They hankered to &
the people proclaimed an abbreviated stroke no more than a
ruffling of the surface. An entire people: that by means of a
revolution had imparted itself a power of motion suddenly
finds itself back to the old dates the old names a dim burning
lamp fastened to the head behind a long whip. Men & things
seem set in sparkling brilliance till a pale casts over. The
riddle is not solved by turns of speech, the fixed idea of
making gold, which in the press fall victim to the courts &
even more equivocal figures. An array of passwords maintained against a wider one. Placards are posted on all street
corners. The priests appear & wail about the necessity of
moral reform. A drive against the schoolteachers. (Even
bourgeois liberalism is declared socialistic.) Its gladiators
find their ideals wholly abosrbed in products & Caesar
himself is watching over. Antediluvian colossi disappear into
sober mouthpieces with suitable up to date manners knock-
ing feudal manners like someone who has just learned a new
language always translating back into the first. "Property,
Family, Religion, Order." The bureaucracy is well gal-
looned & well fed. The individual turns in stupefied

seclusion & the peasants dwell in hovels. A bunch of blokes push their way forward. —*When the real aim is achieved & society is accomplished. As when we find our way in it without thinking in terms of the old. The event itself appears like a bolt from the blue.*

SEMBLANCE

It's as if each of these things has a life of its own. You can stretch them, deform them and even break them apart, and they still have an inner cohesion that keeps them together.

Not "death" of the referent—rather a recharged use of the multivalent referential vectors that any word has, how words in combination tone and modify the associations made for each of them, how 'reference' then is not a one-on-one relation to an 'object' but a perceptual dimension that closes in to pinpoint, nail down (*this* word), sputters omnitropically (the in in the which of who where what wells), refuses the build up of image track/projection while, pointillistically, fixing a reference at each turn (fills vats ago lodges spire), or, that much rarer case (Peter Inman's *Platin* and David Melnick's *Pcoet* two recent examples) of "zaum" (so-called transrational, pervasively neologistic)—"ig ok aberflappi"— in which reference, deprived of its automatic reflex reaction of word/stimulus image/response roams over the range of associations suggested by the word, word shooting off referential vectors like the energy field in a Kirillian photograph.

All of which are ways of releasing the energy inherent in the referential dimension of language, that these dimensions are the material of which the writing is made, define its medium. Making the structures of meaning in language more tangible and in that way allowing for the maximum resonance for the medium—the traditional power that writing has always had to make experience palpable not by simply pointing to it but by (re)creating its conditions.*

Point then, at first instance, to see the medium of writing—our area of operation—as maximally open in vocabulary, forms, shapes, phoneme/morpheme/word/ phrase/sentence order, etc., so that possible areas covered, ranges of things depicted, suggested, critiqued, considered, etc., have an outer limit (asymptotic) of what can be

---

*Alan Davies has objected that language and experience are separate realms and that the separation should be maximized in writing, in this way questioning the value of using language to make experience palpable.— But I don't mean 'experience' in the sense of a picture/image/representation that is calling back to an already constituted experience. Rather, language itself constitutes experience at every moment (in reading and otherwise). Experience, then, is not tied into representation exclusively but is a separate 'perception'-like category. (& perception not necessarily as in perception onto a physical/preconstituted world, as "eyes" in the Olson sense, that is, not just onto a matrix-qua-the world but as operating/ projecting/composing activity.) The point is, then, that experience is a dimension necessarily built into language—that far from being avoidable, or a choice, it is a property. So this view attempts to rethink representational or pictorial or behaviorist notions of what 'experience' is, i.e., experience is not inextricably linked to representation, normative syntax, images, but rather, the other way around, is a synthetic, generative activity—"in the beginning was the word" & so on, or that's our 'limit' of beginnings.

thought, what can (might) be. But then, taking that as zero degree, not to gesturalize the possibility of poetry to operate in this 'hyperspace', but to create works (poems) within it.

The order of the words, the syntax, creates possibilities for images, pictures, representations, descriptions, invocation, ideation, critique, relation, projection, etc. Sentences that follow standard grammatical patterns allow the accumulating references to enthrall the reader by diminishing diversions from a constructed representation. In this way, each word's references work in harmony by reinforcing a spatiotemporal order conventionalized by the bulk of writing practice that creates the 'standard'. "The lamp sits atop the table in the study"—each word narrowing down the possibilities of each other, limiting the interpretation of each word's meaning by creating an ever more specific context. In a similar way, associations with sentences are narrowed down by conventional expository or narrational paragraph structure, which directs attention away from the sentence as meaning generating event and onto the 'content' depicted. By shifting the contexts in which even a fairly 'standard' sentence finds itself, as in some of the prose-format work of Barrett Watten, the seriality of the ordering of sentences within a paragraph displaces from its habitual surrounding the projected representational fixation that the sentence conveys. "Words elect us. The lamp sits atop the table in the study. The tower is burnt orange...." By rotating sentences within a paragraph (a process analogous to jump cutting in film) according to principles generated by and unfolding in the work (rather than in accordance with representational construction patterns) a perceptual vivid-

ness is intensified for each sentence since the abruptness of
the cuts induces a greater desire to savor the tangibility of
each sentence before it is lost to the next, determinately
other, sentence. Juxtapositions not only suggest unsuspected
relations but induce reading along ectoskeletal and citational
lines. As a result, the operant mechanisms of meaning are
multiplied and patterns of projection in reading are less
restricted. The patterns of projection are not, however,
undetermined. The text operates at a level that not only
provokes projections by each sentence but by the sequencing
of the sentences suggests lines or paths for them to proceed
along. At the same time, circumspection about the nature
and meaning of the projections is called forth. The result is
both a self-reflectiveness and an intensification of the
items/conventions of the social world projected/suggested/
provoked. A similar process can also take place within
sentences and phrases and not only intersententially. Syntactic patterns are composed which allow for this combination of projection and reflection in the movement from
word to word. "For as much as, within the because, tools
their annoyance, tip to toward."—But, again, to acknowledge this as the space of the text, and still to leave open what
is to be said, what projections desire these reflections.

The sense of music in poetry: the music of meaning—
emerging, fogging, contrasting, etc. Tune attunement in
understanding—the meaning sounds. It's impossible to
separate prosody from the structure (the form and content
seen as an interlocking figure) of a given poem. You can talk
about strategies of meaning generation, shape, the kinds of
sounds accented, the varieties of measurement (of scale, of

number, of line length, of syllable order, of word length, of phrase length, or measure as punctuation, of punctuation as metrics). But no one has primacy—the music is the orchestrating these into the poem, the angles one plays against another, the shading. In much of my own work: working at angles to the strong tidal pull of an expected sequence of a sentence—or by cutting off a sentence or phrase midway and counting on the mind to complete where the poem goes off in another direction, giving two vectors at once—the anticipated projection underneath and the actual wording above.

My interest in not conceptualizing the field of the poem as a unitary plane, and so also not using overall structural programs: that any prior principle of composition violates the priority I want to give to the inherence of surface, to the total necessity in the durational space of the poem for every moment to *count*. The moment not subsumed into a schematic structure, hence instance of it, but at every juncture creating (synthesizing) the structure. So not to have the work resolve at the level of the "field" if this is to mean a uniplanar surface within which the poem operates. Structure that can't be separated from decisions made within it, constantly poking through the expected parameters. Rather than having a single form or shape or idea of the work pop out as you read, the structure itself is pulled into a moebius-like twisting momentum. In this process, the language takes on a centrifugal force that seems to trip it out of the poem, turn it out from itself, exteriorizing it. Textures, vocabularies, discourses, constructivist modes of radically different character are not integrated into a field as part of a predetermined planar architecture; the gaps and jumps compose a space within shifting parameters, types and styles of discourse constantly crisscrossing, interacting, creating new gels. (Intertextual, interstructural . . .) (Bruce Andrews has suggested the image of a relief map for the varying kinds of referential vectors—reference to different domains of discourse, references made by different processes—in some of his work in which words and phrases are visually spaced out over the surface of the page. However, the structural dissonance in these works is counterbalanced by the perspicacious poise of the overall design, which tends to even-out the surface tension.)

Writing as a process of pushing whatever way, or making the piece cohere as far as can: stretching my mind—to where I know it makes sense but not quite why—suspecting relations that I understand, that make the sense of the ready-to-hand—i.e. pushing the composition to the very limits of sense, meaning, to that razor's edge where judgment/aesthetic sense is all I can go on (know-how). (Maybe what's to get beyond in Olson's field theory is just the idea of form as a single web, a unified field, one matrix, with its implicit idea of 'perception' onto a given world rather than, as well, onto the language through which the world is constituted.) So that the form, the structure, that, finally, is the poem, has emerged, is come upon, is made.

STRAY STRAWS AND STRAW MEN

1. "I look straight into my heart & write the exact words that come from within. The theory of fragments whereby poetry becomes a grab bag of favorite items—packed neatly together with the glue of self-conscious & self-consciously epic composition, or, lately, homogenized into one blend by the machine of programmatic form—is a diversion. The eye is not split open in such work. There are structures—edifices—wilder than the charts of rivers, but they are etched by making a path not designing a garden."

"Natural: the very word should be struck from the language."

"... but what the devil *is* the human?"

2. Ron Silliman has consistently written a poetry of visible borders: a poetry of shape. His works are composed very explicitly under various conditions, presenting a variety of possible worlds, possible language formations. Such poetry emphasizes its medium as being constructed, rule governed, everywhere circumscribed by grammar & syntax, chosen

vocabulary: designed, manipulated, picked, programmed, organized, & so an artifice, artifact—monadic, solipsistic, homemade, manufactured, mechanized, formulaic, willful.

3. Work described as this may discomfort those who want a poetry primarily of personal communication, flowing freely from the inside with the words of a natural rhythm of life, lived daily. Perhaps the conviction is that poetry not be made by fitting words into a pattern but by the act of actually letting it happen, *writing*, so that that which is "stored within pours out" without reference to making a point any more than to making a shape. The thing is not to create programs to plug words into but to eliminate such imposed interferences.

An influence of work that appears to be of this (other) type is the sanctification of something that gets known as its honesty, its directness, its authenticity, its artlessness, its sincerity, its spontaneity, its personal expressiveness; in short, its *naturalness*. (As the pastoral was once the natural, & likewise the romantic.)

I would point to Bernadette Mayer's *Memory* as a work that seems rooted in some of these ('natural') assumptions, as well as to much of Kerouac. In a different way, & the look of the work is the measure of how different, Frank O'Hara's poetry is relevant. The achievement of these three poets has much to do with how they have fronted these assumptions.

4. Personal subject matter & a flowing syntax, whatever those descriptions mean to a particular writer, are the key to the natural look. (Though it needs to be said that the variety

of writing that relies on some sense of natural for its inspiration & domain is infinite.)

5. The sexual, for example, has much the pull of the natural. For some it poses as the most intimate subject matter. Others have it as the energy that drives their writing, or else its source.

Edward Dahlberg (sexistly) describes Word as Cock. "Masculine fiery particles", "motions of will", he says, animate the great writing of the past. He rebukes American literature for not being grounded in the Flesh, describing it as stagnant, dehumanized, & frigid. "Esoteric artificers" & "abstruse technicians", our writers—Poe, Dickinson, Thoreau, Hawthorne, Melville & those before & after— have led away from "the communal song of labor, sky, star, field, love."

6. There is also an attraction toward looking for the natural in 'direct experience', both in terms of recording the actual way objective reality is perceived (the search for the objective) & making the writing a recording instrument of consciousness.

"This work I experience as an instance of the writer's fantasy & imagination & vision & not as a construction. I feel immersed in it. It seems seamless to me. I am carried along by it. The experience is present to me. Shifts in tone, place occur as inevitable sequences: inevitable because they cohere, because they allow me to experience them, because they seem to happen."

7. 'Technical artifice' they scream, as if poetry doesn't

demand a technical precision. ("That poetry is an art, an art with technique, with media, an art that must be in constant flux, a constant change of manner.") Technicians of the human.

8. A sign of the particularity of a piece of writing is that it contains itself, has established its own place, situates itself next to us. We move up close, stare in, & see a world. It has moving parts, accountable & unaccountable recurrences, a particular light, a heavy dense odor. "But can I actually experience it?" Yes. But it reveals the conditions of its occurrence at the same time as it is experienced. So I don't feel a part of it as much as facing it.... Of course at times you forget. All of a sudden a few hours, a week, flash by before you actually notice, & you say to yourself "how the time slips—"

9. "*Next* to us the grandest laws are continually being executed. *Next* to us is not the workman whom we have hired, with whom we love so well to talk, but the Workman whose work we are."

Next to. Fronting the world with a particular constellation of beliefs, values, memories, expectations; a culture; a way of seeing, mythography; language. But we are "beside ourselves in a sane way" for what is beside us is also ourselves. At the same time in & beside.—The signs of language, of a piece of writing, are not artifical constructions, mere structures, mere naming. They do not sit, deanimated, as symbols in a code, dummies for things of nature they refer to; but are, of themselves, of ourselves, whatever is such. 'Substance.' 'Actuality.' 'Presence.' The

very plane through which we front the world, by which the
world is.

10. Compare / these two views / of what / poetry / is:

In the one, an instance (a recording perhaps) of reality or
fantasy or experience or event is presented to us through the
writing.

In the other, the writing itself is seen as an instance of
reality or fantasy or experience or event.

11. Another example.

The sanctification of the natural comes up in terms of 'voice'
& has been extended by various excursions into the oral. On
the one hand, there is the assumption that poetry matures in
the location of "one's own voice" which as often as not is no
more than a consistency of style & presentation. "The voice
of the poet" is an easy way of contextualizing poetry so that
it can be more readily understood (indiscriminately plugged
into) as listening to someone talk in their distinctive manner
(i.e., listen for the person beyond or underneath the poem);
but this theatricalization does not necessarily do the individual poem any service & has the tendency to reduce the
body of a poet's work to little more than personality. (This
contrasts with that major preoccupation in American poetry—
the investigation of the grammar of talking, of speech, both
by traditional poetic technique &, lately, by tape transcription.) On the other hand, there is a growing use of voice in a
variety of sound poetry. Some performance & audiotape
works use voice as essentially a vocabulary to be processed by
techniques such as cut-up, consonant & vowel intonation,
simultaneity, etc. Others, searching for the "natchuralness"

of an oral liturgy we've lost, & influenced by tribal & religious & bardic—communal—poetic practice, make use of vocalizations related to the human breath (e.g., chanting & other assorted organic-sounding tones).—Voice is a possibility for poetry not an essence.

12. I am not making a distinction, there is no useful distinction to be made here, between making the poem a subject or an object. Nor is it necessary to choose up among the personal desire to communicate, tell what has been seen, share a way of seeing, transmit some insight or irony, or simply give a feeling for texture.

What I want to call attention to is that there is no natural writing style; that the preference for its supposed manifestations is simply a preference for a particular look to poetry & often a particular vocabulary (usually perceived as personal themes); that this preference (essentially a procedural decision to work within a certain domain sanctified into a rite of poetry) actually obscures the understanding of the work which appears to be its honoured bases; & especially that the cant of "make it personal" & "let it flow" are avoidances—by mystification—of some very compelling problems that swirl around truthtelling, confession, bad faith, false self, authenticity, virtue, etc.

13. The considerable achievement of Frank O'Hara is to have built a form of poetry largely within the domain of the personal. Note, however, that O'Hara's word 'personism' is not 'personalism'; it acknowledges the work to be a fronting of another *person*—another mind, if you will, as much as another nature. O'Hara's work *proposes* a domain of the

personal, & not simply *assuming* it, fully works it out. His remarkable use of voice, for example, allows, through a musing whimsy in that voice, for fantasy as wild as any surrealist imagines, contained, still, within his proposed boundaries.

14. There is no automatic writing. It is a claim that has had to be made to the detractors of modernism again & again (an early article by B. F. Skinner attacked "Stein's little secret") & must now be made another time to avoid accepting as a value an analysis generated out of misunderstanding & animosity.

Not that the followers of the natural, or the organic, or the personal, would necessarily have work that looks automatic. But it seems to me that this is at the heart of the strongest claim to natural spontaneous writing—the impulse to record or transcribe the movements & make-up of one's consciousness. The modernist assumption. What's to note is that in practice, projectively, that impulse transposes itself to something like a search for a method of "syntacticalizing consciousness", i.e., ordering one's consciousness into language, as if consciousness existed prior to—aside from—language & had to be *put into* it; as if consciousness were not itself a syntacticalization—a syntaxophony.

Every phrase I write, every juxtaposition I make, is a manifestation of using a full-blown language: full of possibilities of meaning & impossibilities of meaning. It can't be avoided. Whatever comes out comes out on account of a variety of psychological dispositions, personal experiences, & literary preoccupations & preconceptions. The best of the writing that gets called automatic issues from a series of choices as deliberate & reflected as can be.

15. Whatever gets written gets written in a particular shape, uses a particular vocabulary & syntax, & a variety of chosen techniques. Whether its shape, syntax & vocabulary result from an attraction (or ideological attachment to) the organic & spontaneous, or to some other look, it is equally chosen. Sometimes this process takes place intuitively or unconsciously (the pull of influence comes in here since somewhere in the back of your mind are models for what looks natural, personal, magical, mystical, spontaneous, automatic, dream-like, confessional, didactic, shocking). Sometimes it is a very conscious process. Any way, you're responsible for what turns up. Free association, for example, is no more inherently 'natural' than cutting up: & neither is in any sense 'random'. One technique may be used because a decision is made to use subconscious material. Another may be used to limit the vocabulary of the poem to words not self-generated. In either case, various formal decisions are made & these decisions shape the work.

16. Okay, given that, it's given, is it possible to continue under conditions set up before? Or is everything, every instance, a new decision at each moment? & recklessly charging forward it appears to copy some other thing, or be beholding, or under. What happens when the images cease, when there are no more images confronting the eye of imagination & still the signs, the written traces of activity, continue to be produced. Music sounds. It too must pass. A

syntactical exploration of consciousness becomes very explicitly the concern, so embedded even in a subject matter of boundaries & possible worlds, that it ceases to be, or only diverts. The subject matter simply all that is inside, given rhythm, different cadences, the punctuation in typing of each letter as separate unit, the propulsion of a comma. Is it possible, for example, to allow typographical errors, mistypings, to remain integral? Typing itself then becoming a condition. It becomes part of the temptation. Or perhaps it's just my fear that when I tap what I find inside myself I will find that it is empty & insist that the scratchings must account for something.

17. Writing necessarily consists of attaching numerous bits & pieces together in a variety of ways. & it comes to a point where you feel any composition is an artifice & a deceit. & the more "natchural" the look the more deceptive. That any use of language outside its function of communicating in speaking is a falsehood (cf. Laura [Riding] Jackson). Or even, that language itself—everywhere conditioning our way of seeing & meaning—is an illusion (as if there were something outside language!).

Or take it this way: I want to just write—let it come out—get in touch with some natural process—from brain to pen—with no interference of typewriter, formal pattern. & it can seem like the language itself—having to put it into words—any kind of fixing a version of it—gets in the way. That I just have this thing inside me—silently—unconditioned by the choice I need to make when I write—whether it be to write it down or write on. So it is as if language itself gets in the way of expressing this thing, this flow, this movement of consciousness.

But there are no thoughts except through language, we are everywhere seeing through it, limited to it but not by it. Its conditions always interpose themselves: a particular set of words to choose from (a vocabulary), a way of processing those words (syntax, grammar): the natural conditions of language. What pulses, pushes, is energy, spirit, anima, dream, fantasy: coming out always in form, as shape: these particulars, "massed at material bottoms" in hum of this time—here, now—these words, this syntax & rhythm & shape. The look of the natural as constructed, programmatic—artful—"lying words" as the most abstract, composed or formal work.

18. There is no natural look or sound to a poem. Every element is intended, chosen. That is what makes a thing a poem. Modes cannot be escaped, but they can be taken for granted. They can also be meant.

Work like Silliman's explicitly acknowledges these conditions of poetry, language, by explicitly intending vocabulary, syntax, shape, etc.; an acknowledgement which is the actual prerequisite of authenticity, of good faith. The allure of the spontaneous & personal is cut here by the fact of wordness: reproducing not so much the look of the natural as the conditions of nature—autonomy, self-sufficiency. In this light, a work like Mayer's *Memory* can be seen to be significant not on account of its journal-like look alone but also on account of its completely intended, complex, artifactual style. Heavy, dense, embedded. "The essential thing is to build a world." Energy & emotion, spontaneity, vocabulary, shape—all are elements of that building. It is natural that there are modes but there is no natural mode.

A PARTICULAR THING

I was determined to know beans.
                                    —THOREAU

These words, or those in poems, are not used to describe
events in the world that have already occurred, in life or in
fantasy, or intended to be about some thing else; it being
primarily a question of attention, of not wanting to attend to
bringing forward a memory or an idea or an event, all
external to the poem itself (to the act of writing), but to
attend to the internal event that is taking place in it. What is
come upon as this, lived and lived out, need not be
deciphered or uncoded but simply let be, having become, in
itself, for itself.

I want in my writing a texture of wordness opaque and alone
separate untouched   of particularity and presentness
        intended and specific   unadulterated and so made
whole   complete   of stillness
        from a sense that my most particular/private/unique
                insistence, way of seeing, aesthetic sense, dream

50

              is the most completely
                   collective—public—knowable
         that when language is at the threshold of its
                        coming to mean   at the border of
                                    sense and
                                              sound
                   we find a scripture
                          open to
more than finite
              interpretations, that reveal
                          the form and
                          mythography
                            of the (a)
                            world.

Part of what happens is play with
possibilities the concreteness of
arrangement, ways of intending
                                   (& not only
                                    line as
                                    breath
                                    but
                                    word, syllable
                                    whatever measures
                                    stops or starts)
              figuring it out
              or letting it come of itself
              ways of
                  (never known prior, always coming out
                      in the com(*op*)posing,
                          it going on).

So a poem as discrete field of meaning, trying not to echo externally explicated grammars but rather to discover (come upon) the limits that make up meaning, which is the human; that is, the grammar that is shared, lived within. (Why do precisely these words make up a world?) In this sense, poems become less a matter of personal expression as they attend to enactments of meaningfulness. The intention not to show myself "but that order that of itself can speak to all". . . .

STYLE

COAUTHOR: SUSAN BEE

It is said that one can tell during a conversation that lasts no longer than a summer shower whether or not a person is cultivated. Often it does not take even so long, for a raucous tone of voice and grossly ungrammatical or vulgar expressions brand a person at once as beyond the pale of polite society. As one goes forth one is weighed in the balance and if found wanting he is quietly dropped by refined and cultured people, and nearly always he is left wondering why with his diamonds and his motors and his money he yet cannot find entree into the inner circles. An honest heart may beat beneath the ragged coat, a brilliant intellect may rise above the bright checkered suit and yellow tie, the man

Sources include Follett's *Modern American Usage*, Kittridge's *Advanced English Grammar*, Stein's *How to Write*, Modern Language Association's *In-House Style Sheet*, Hagar's *The English of Business*, Martin and Ohmann's *Logic and Rhetoric of Exposition*, Raleigh's *Style*, and Eichler's *Book of Etiquette*.

53

in the shabby suit may be a famous writer, the woman in the untidy blouse may be an artist of great promise, but as a general rule the chances are against it and such people are dull, flat, stale and unprofitable both to themselves and to other people. In the end, coherence is always a quality of thought rather than a manner of expression. The confused mind cannot produce coherent prose. A well-proportioned letter is the product of a well-balanced mind. The utterance of the single word "Charles!" may signify: "Hello, Charles! are you here? I am surprised to see you." Language, however, is not confined to the utterance of single words. To express our thoughts we must put words together in accordance with certain fixed rules. Otherwise we should fail to express ourselves clearly and acceptably, and we may even succeed in saying the opposite of what we mean. Since language is the expression of thought, the rules of grammar agree, in the main, with the laws of thought. Even in matters of divided usage, it is seldom difficult to determine which of two forms is preferred by careful writers. Everything is taken care of in the most orderly fashion: terms are defined, possible ambiguities eliminated, implications and assumptions explained, proofs adduced, and examples provided. On the whole it is safe for the writer to leave semantic theory unexplored. We favor the standards of the more precise stylists if only because we cannot be more permissive without risking their disapproval, whereas those who do not object to less exacting usage are not likely to be offended by the correct usage. A good expository sentence does not call attention to itself, although Strunk comments that an occasional loose sentence has its virtues. No one who speaks and writes can expect his audience to respond to connotations

that arise from his own purely personal experience. Some
people associate colors with numbers, but orange is not a
connotation of "four". The trouble with Humpty Dumpty's
stipulative definitions, if they can be dignified by such a
word, is that they are entirely capricious and absurd. For
sentences must measure up to standards: it is always fair to
ask of a sentence, "How *good* is it?" Among the qualities that
contribute to an effective impression, the five most essential
are clearness, correctness, conciseness, courtesy, and character. For style is ingratiation; negative ideas, as a rule, should
not be developed at length. And constructions to be shunned
include those that are vague, abstract, equivocal, slanted,
misleading, exaggerated, understated, loose, abbreviated,
oversimplified, obvious, irrelevant, oblique, figurative, re-
dundant, empty, impossible, or obscure. It would be a
curious state of affairs if only those who seldom think about
the words they use, who read little and who "cannot be
bothered" with distinctions should be the only ones with full
powers over vocabulary and syntax. Even on the grounds of
free democratic choice the hands-off attitude about language
receives no support. These assumptions further suggest that
the desire for correctness, the very idea of better or worse in
speech, is a hangover from aristocratic and oppressive
times....The young foreigner who apologizes for the fact
that the chocolates he has bought as a gift are *molten* is told
with a smile that that is not English: the right word is
melted.—We talk to our fellows in the phrases we learn from
them, which seem to mean less and less as they grow worn
with use. The quiet cynicism of our everyday demeanor is
open and shameless, we callously anticipate objections
founded on the well-known vacuity of our seeming emotions,

and assure our friends that we are "truly" grieved or
"sincerely" rejoiced at their hap—as if joy or grief that really
exists were some rare and precious brand of joy or grief. A
sentence says you know what I mean, dear do I well I guess
I do. Grammar does not mean that they are to limit
themselves. More and more grammar is not a thing. Grammar does not make me hesitate about prepositions. I am a
grammarian I do not hesitate I rearrange prepositions.

THE DOLLAR VALUE OF POETRY

Social force is bound to be accompanied by lies. That is why all that is highest in human life, every effort of thought, every effort of love, has a corrosive action on the established order. Thought can just as readily, and on good grounds, be stigmatized as revolutionary on the one side, as counter-revolutionary on the other. In so far as it is ceaselessly creating a scale of values 'that is not of this world', it is the enemy of forces which control society.

—SIMONE WEIL, *Oppression and Liberty*

So writing might be exemplary—an instance broken off from and hence not in the service of this economic and cultural—social—force called capitalism. A chip of unin-fected substance; or else, a glimpse, a crack into what otherwise might ...; or still, "the fact of its own activity", "in itself and for itself" such that ... In any case, an appeal to an *other* world, as if access is not blocked to an experience (experiencing) whose horizon is not totally a product of the coercive delimiting of the full range of language (the limits of language the limits of experience) by the predominating social forces. An experience (released in the reading) which is noncommoditized, that is where the value is not dollar value (and hence transferable and instrumental) but rather, what is from the point of view of the market, no value (a negativity, inaudible, invisible)—that nongeneralizable residue that is specific to each particular experience. It is in this sense that we speak of poetry as being untranslatable and unparaphrasable, for what is untranslatable is the sum of all the specific conditions of the experience (place, time, order, light, mood, position, to infinity) made available by reading. That the political value of poems resides in the concreteness of the experiences they make available is the reason for the resistance to any form of normative standardization in the ordering of words in a unit or the sequencing of these units, since determining the exact nature of each of these is what makes for the singularity of the text. (It is, for example, a misunderstanding of the fact of untranslatability that would see certain "concretist" tendencies as its most radical manifestation since what is not translatable is the experience released in the reading while in so far as some "visual poems" move toward making the understanding independent of the language it is written in, i.e., no longer requiring translation, they are, indeed, no longer so much writing as works of visual art.)

Certainly, one method is the restoration of memory's remembering on its own terms, organizing along the lines of experience's trace, a reconstruction released from the pressures of uniform exposition—"the only true moments" the ones we have lost, which, in returning to them, come to life in a way that now reveals what they had previously concealed—the social forces that gave shape to them. So

what were the unseen operators now are manifest as traces of
the psychic blows struck by the social forces (re)pressing us
into shape (i.e.: "a Sigh is the Sword of an Angel King").
"What we do is to bring our words back"—*to make our
experiences visible*, or again: to see the conditions of experience. So that, in this way, a work may also be constructed—
an "other" world *made* from whatever materials are ready to
hand (not just those of memory)—structuring, in this way,
possibilities otherwise not allowed for.

Meanwhile, the social forces hold sway in all the rules for
the "clear" and "orderly" functioning of language and
Caesar himself is the patron of our grammar books.
Experience dutifully translated into these "most accessible"
codes loses its aura and is reduced to the digestible contents
which these rules alone can generate. There is nothing
difficult in the products of such activity because there is no
distance to be travelled, no gap to be aware of and to bridge
from reader to text: What purports to be an experience is
transformed into the blank stare of the commodity—there
only to mirror our projections with an unseemly rapidity
possible only because no experience of *other* is in it.—Any
limits put on language proscribe the limits of what will be
experienced, and, as Wittgenstein remarks, the world can
easily be reduced to only the straight rows of the avenues of
the industrial district, with no place for the crooked winding
streets of the old city. "To imagine a language is to imagine a
form of life"—think of that first *imagine* as the active word
here.

"Is there anybody here who thinks that following the
orders takes away the blame?" Regardless of *what* is being
said, use of standard patterns of syntax and exposition

effectively rebroadcast, often at a subliminal level, the basic
constitutive elements of the social structure—they perpetuate
them so that by constant reinforcement we are no longer
aware that decisions are being made, our base level is then an
already preconditioned world view which this deformed
language "repeats to us inexorably" but not *necessarily*. Or
else these formations (underscored constantly by all "the
media" in the *form* they "communicate" "information"
"facts") take over our form of life (see *Invasion of the Body
Snatchers* and *Dawn of the Dead* for two recent looks at this),
as by posthypnotic suggestion we find ourselves in the grip
of—living out—*feeling*—the attitudes programmed into us by
the phrases, &c, and their sequencing, that are continually
being repeated to us—language control = thought control =
reality control: it must be decentered, community controlled, taken out of the *service* of the capitalist project. For
now, an image of the antivirus: indigestible, intransigent.

THOUGHT'S MEASURE

1. WRITING (AS) (AND) THINKING

> To my lot fell
> By trust, false signs, fresh starts,
> A slow speed and a heavy reason,
> A visibility of blindedness—these thoughts—
> And then content, the language of the mind
> That knows no way to stop[1]

Language is the material of both thinking and writing. We think and write in language, which sets up an intrinsic connection between the two.

Just as language is not something that is separable from the world, but rather is the means by which the world is constituted, so thinking cannot be said to 'accompany' the experiencing of the world in that it informs that experiencing. It is through language that we experience the world, indeed through language that meaning comes into the world

---

1. Laura (Riding) Jackson, "By Crude Rotation", in *The Poems of Laura Riding* (New York: Persea, 1980), p. 107.

and into being. As persons, we are born into language and
world; they exist before us and after us. Our learning
language is learning the terms by which a world gets seen.
Language is the means of our socialization, our means of
initiation into a (our) culture. I do not suggest that there is
nothing beyond, or outside of, human language, but that
there is meaning only in terms of language, that the
givenness of language is the givenness of the world.

An analogous idea to that of language not accompanying
but constituting the world is that language does not
accompany 'thinking'. "When I think in language, there
aren't 'meanings' going through my mind in addition to the
verbal expressions: the language is itself the vehicle of
thought."[2]

"What does language communicate? It communicates the
mental being corresponding to it. It is fundamental that this
mental being communicates itself *in* language and not
through language. Languages therefore have no speaker, if
this means someone who communicates *through* these languages.... All nature, insofar as it communicates itself, communicates itself in language, and so finally in [persons]."[3]

2. Ludwig Wittgenstein, *Philosophical Investigations*, trans. G. E. M.
Anscombe (New York: Macmillan, 1958), §329. See also §§330, 331, 332,
335, and 336.
3. Walter Benjamin, "On Language as Such and the Language of Man", in
Reflections, trans. Edmund Jephcott (New York: Harcourt Brace Jovano-
vitch), pp. 315-16 and 318-19. Benjamin here understands language as more
than simply a verbal entity. "There is a language of sculpture, of painting,
of poetry.... We are concerned here with nameless, nonacoustic languages,
languages issuing from matter; here we should recall the material
community of things in their communication" [p. 330].

As the body is to a person, so language is to the world; to speak of a 'soul' is then to speak of a projection cast by the body. In this sense, to discount the pervasiveness of language—to be so accustomed to its presence that its constituting power over the values and objects of the world is disregarded—is to avoid the body and with it the materiality of time and space.

> He is gone now
> Taking his body with him
> When all the time
> I thought it was
> The beauty of his mind
> I loved[4]

In talking about language and thinking I want to establish the *material*, the stuff, of writing, in order, in turn, to base a discussion of writing on its medium rather than on preconceived literary ideas of subject matter or form. And I want to propose 'thinking' as a concept that can help to materially ground that discussion. 'Thinking' as the conceptual basis of literary production suggests the possibilities for leaps, jumps, fissures, repetition, bridges, schisms, colloquialisms, trains of associations, and memory; as a literary mode it would rely on concepts related to spontaneity, free association, and improvisation.

Many writers have wanted to plug into the stream of thinking that seems to be constantly going on in the head, or have wanted to cast an image or make a picture of what thinking is like, or to actually embody thinking in writing.

---

4. Ted Greenwald, "Off the Hook", in *Common Sense* (Kensington, CA: L, 1978), p. 190.

Some have used thinking as the content of the work, as in genres such as the meditation or contemplative poem. This involvement with thinking is a basic passion, a basic desire, in writing. It is one of the attractions to writing poetry and reading it.

The power of hearing a person think out loud is tapped by such relatively recent works as Lenny Bruce's later spontaneous talks, Kerouac's transcriptions of conversations in *Visions of Cody*, and David Antin's talking pieces. Talking improvisationally—"from the top of one's head"—can be a way of putting thinking into words, with the dynamics of words organized by extemporaneous thought and speech rhythms allowing the terrain of the mind at work to open wide. In contrast, polite discursive conversation is more a form of mannered behavior than thinking; and similarly, extemporaneous debate, like oratory, is more a replica of formal written exposition and doesn't draw as directly on a semblance of 'thinking' for its literary mode. In Antin's work, while the stylistic movement is paratactic and guardedly rambling, the tight rein of the raconteur is present, keeping the discursiveness of what Antin calls discourse foregrounded.[5] The talking monologue, a form that is largely based on the model of thinking in public, can also be seen in the "Talks" issue of *Hills* magazine.[6] Both these examples use transcription of tapes to try to capture the style of live talk. Of course, the limitation of talks as a model for written thinking is that they tend to be organized in part by expository and rhetorical techniques. A work such as Lenny

5. See David Antin, "Real Estate", in *Tuning* (New York: New Directions, 1984).
6. *Hills* Nos. 6-7, ed. Bob Perelman (San Francisco: 1980).

Bruce's "Live at the Curran Theater" is perhaps least invested in such techniques primarily because of Bruce's concern with bringing out his 'private' obsessions and trains of associations, prompted by his conviction that these are *social* contents. Whether transcripts of unguarded or private conversation record (portray? depict?) the thought process more accurately is more likely to be glimpsed from the intensive rapping in *Visions of Cody* than in the generally anecdotal tone of the phone call transcriptions in Ed Friedman's *Telephone Book*, a work that suggests that informal conversation is more behavior than thinking, or makes you wonder if there's a difference.[7] Perhaps the most attractive model is talking to oneself: the soliloquy being a primary example of a literary formulation for thinking, with the exception that its dramatic structure may be seen as theatricalizing thought rather than exhibiting it.

Certainly "stream of consciousness" writing satisfies the desire for thinking in writing with maximum exhilaration, and as such is a primary example of writing as thinking. Hannah Weiner, in her journal, carries this mode to a contemporary literalness, finding a way to record the continually interruptive quality of her thinking, the mind intruding on itself as one worry breaks off and another image takes hold.[8] Yet these examples, as well, can seem limited by their stylistic casts, throwing them into the realm of literary forms more than manifestations of thinking. But that would take this investigation down the path of looking for the chimerical private experience that cannot be shared.

7. Ed Friedman, *The Telephone Book* (Guilford, CT: Telephone/Power Mad, 1980).
8. Hannah Weiner, *The Clairvoyant Journal* (New York: Angel Hair, 1978).

Thinking is certainly a private experience; the problem is that if we try to pin 'thinking' down we project an image of it as an *entity* rather than, indeed, the very content of language. Like with a dream, the experience slips through our fingers if we try to recount it: we know that the telling of a dream is a quite different matter than dreaming itself.

Dreaming and thinking are primary subjects for René Descartes in his *Meditations*. The form of meditation, of contemplation, so vividly realized 300 years ago by Descartes, is picked up in uncannily similar ways in a number of recent poetry texts.[9] Descartes uses the written meditation to make you feel you are with him in his study, the effect is to identify with his thinking so that you feel as if you're thinking it too. But despite Descartes' remarkable perspicuity in charting the process of thinking through a problem, his meditations are more a formal representation of the thinking process than an immersion in it; and this idealization of reasoning and clarity tend to mediate the pull of thought's idle energy. Robert Creeley, sharing the conceit of meditation—thought presented and examined, weighted and measured—is more involved with the texture of the process itself, less with a representation than an enactment. In "The Measure", the form of the meditation is used to create a *music of thought*, where thinking becomes the material in which the measure is found.

> I cannot
> move backward
> or forward.
> I am caught

9. David Antin's *Meditations* (Santa Barbara: Black Sparrow, 1971) is an explicit instance.

in the time
as measure.
What we think
of we think of—

of no other reason
we think than
just to think—
each for himself.[10]

With Ted Greenwald, as with Creeley, the mind thinking
becomes the active force of the poem—

Stand next to my head
Examining long and deeply
Each particle that's designing
It's own, ah!, good impression

More than I thought I
Could handle without
Knowing exactly where to
Locate the *thought* handle . . .

Take puffs of links . . .
The thought of what's coming . . .
Thinking to find a way
To put myself back together[11]

The music and rhythm of contemplation become the form
of the life, a life, as it is being lived in a body. Indeed with
Greenwald, the viscosity of thought is no less than the sheer

10. *Words* in *The Collected Poems of Robert Creeley* (Berkeley: University of
California, 1982), p. 290. In "I keep to myself such/measures as I care for
. . ." [p. 297]: "There is nothing/but what thinking makes" immediately
modified by "it less tangible. The mind . . ." and then finally the recurring
Creeley image of sitting and thinking, here the pose of the thinker holding
head: "I hold in both hands such weight/it is my only description."
11. Ted Greenwald, *You Bet!* (San Francisco: This, 1978). pp. 19, 20, and
22.

physical presence of the body in that thought. In Michael Gottlieb's *Local Color/Eidetic Deniers*, the thinking stands up out of the chair of meditation, merging with perception (as emphasized by the collage-like photos that are juxtaposed with the text). We are looking at thinking as it moves through him/us and dazzled by the sheer beauty of the process so articulated, the measure found.

> afternoon in mind   how   a giant swap nearly
> a new wind and talked off onto ...
> Like a rock slide ...   Perfected rift logic ...
> Gloved positions   the actuarial synapses   hesitation[12]

The motivation in this—to see how the 'world' would/will come into view, how it works: the investigation/creation of human culture. So not just an interest in expression of 'my' thoughts, thoughts think the world. In this way, too, the mapping of the free-associative 'thinking' process, the *ordering* internal to the movements of the mind/perception, provides a model for writing in sharp contrast to common expository and representational modes by focussing in on other types of movements from one thing to the next, allowing for writing to be put together in continuously 'new' ways—how various shapes and modes and syntaxes create not alternate paraphrases of the same things but different entities entirely. Grains of mind. The desire for writing to be the end of its own activity, its very thatness.

In looking at Creeley's "A Piece" ("One and / one, two, / three")[13] or Brian McInerney's "The World", the articu-

---

12. Michael Gottlieb, "Local Color", in *Local Color/Eidetic Deniers* (Brooklyn: Other, 1978), sec. 4.
13. *Words*, in Creeley, p. 352.

lation of contemplation is an example of how *(a technique)* words can be brought into one's more total awareness in reading, where in reading you are brought up short to the point of the text becoming viscerally present to you, the 'content' and the 'experience of reading' are collapsed onto each other, the content being the experience of reading, the consciousness of the language and its movement and sound, the page.

> outside
> is
>
> a thought,
>
> a consecutive thought
> laid down,
> written on a page—
>
> the idea of a room.
>
> for you,
> to you alone
>
> I am alone,
> a leading into
>
> thought, a
>
> solution
>
> laid down, reading
> on this page[14]

Perhaps the quintessential poem of this type is Louis Zukofsky's "Anew" #20:

14. Brian McInerney, "The World", in *Changing Accounts* (Boston: Origin, 1978).

> The lines of this new song are nothing
> But a tune making the nothing full
> Stonelike become more hard than silent
> The tune's image holding in the line.[15]

Similarly, in Zukofsky's "It's a Gay Li‑ife" the wordness of the poem is foregrounded, as a way of concretizing the language, making it visible on the page, sounding it at the level of each phoneme, so that the phonemes turning to morphemes turning to words turning to phrases turning to 'poem' is felt, heard, made tangible, palpable.

> There's naw—thing
>   lak po—ee try
>   it's a delicacy
>   for   a horse:
>
> Dere's na—thing
>   lak pea- nut-brittle
>   it's a delicacy
>   for   the molars[16]

Rather than making the language as transparent as possible, where these other qualities are repressed as a matter of technique (by creating, stylistically, the illusion of the invisibility of wordness and structure), the movement is toward opacity/denseness—visibility of language through the making translucent of the medium. To actually map the fullness of thought and its movement. Cut of mind/perception/grain of mind ... to ... the factness of the world in the factness of the poem. Poem becoming a perceptual field/experience 'independent' of 'author'. (Cf: Olson's

---

15. Louis Zukofsky, *ALL: The Collected Shorter Poems* (New York: Norton, 1971), p. 97.
16. "Twenty-Nine Songs", #5, in ibid., p. 48.

"Projective Verse" essay: each perception instanter on the next: the form of the poem charts the perception so eliminating of traditional 'inherited' forms which strip poetry of this active power.) The antihabitual ordering of attentions so that attention can be vivid—the intending rather than assuming of order, including order of sound/syllable/ phonemes. So to go from 'thinking' as an activity of 'self' to a world creating/perceiving idea. *Thinking things the world.* So that in the end the poem stands as another particular being, hence object, like myself, in the world, and I beside it. And I return not to myself "as some egocentric center, but experience myself as *in* the world", that with the meaning and limits therein revealed I have also placed myself.

"Limits / are what any of us / are inside of" [Olson]. "...that order that of itself can speak to all" [Zukofsky].

I'm talking here not so much about a motivating theory but a desire: To make language opaque so that writing becomes more and more conscious of itself as world generating, object generating. This goes not only for making palpable the processes of the mind and heart (inseparable) but for revealing the form and structure in which writing occurs, the plasticity of form/shape. So that writing may be an experience in which the forms and objects of the world may seem to be coming into being. The making invisible—inaudible—of these forms/structures/ shapes gives the sensation of a world beyond the page/the language that is already given, assumed; whereas the acknowledgement of these forms as materials to be worked with, as an active part of the writing, suggests 'our' participation in the constitution of nature and meaning.

There is no escape in writing (or 'elsewhere') from struc-
tures/forms, they are everpresent—'de'forming and 're'forming. To *see* them—to *hear* them—as inseparable from
'content'.

2. STRUCTURE AND CONSTRUCTION

I have been talking about 'thinking' as a means of locating
the materials of language and writing. This is partly to
contrast with literary and expository forms that tend to
channel writing—and so feeling/thinking/expression—into
certain set routes. By imagining the free-associative order
and relations in 'thinking' as a mode, new domains of
compositional possibility can be located, ranges of content/
expression/meaning can be reached. I want also to suggest
that an obverse way of looking at writing, in which one
starts from an external rather than an internal approach, is a
method of getting to this as well: the use of structures
(constructions, programs) as a way to get the dimensions of
meaning necessary to put forward the fullness of my
experiences and perceptions. —But what is the value of
breaking away from habitual psychological or literary
tracks, from automatic or predetermined patterns? For one
thing, such patterns can make us blind to what is going on
with our feelings/consciousness and with the world, with
others. But more than this the desire is to reveal the
specificity, the tone and texture as much as 'content'
'summary' (of experience). Making writing, the activity
itself, an active process, the fact of its own activity,
autonomous, self-sufficient. That in this way, one becomes
more responsible to and for the work, for more dimensions
of the meaning. I am certainly not, however, advocating

gesturalizing the ways language can make meaning; as if to dramatize the capacities of language were enough, as if poetry wasn't just as much as ever the revelation of meaning, an active process with language as the medium, requiring an acknowledgement that language always occurs in forms and structures. "Form is never more than the extension of content"—no bodiless souls or soulless bodies. It is by and through structurings that the world gets revealed; they cannot, any more than the body can, be avoided. But there is no given (set of) structures(s) for all cases; they must always be generated [(re)discovered] anew.

In constructive writing, the outer structure or parameter, or the method by which a work is generated, is made visible, for example by its 'typographicity', or audible, for instance by its 'syntaxophony', or both. By 'constructive' partly I'm trying to point to certain radicalities or extremes of compositional strategy that tend to increase the artifactual, non-naturalistic sense of the poem—a project that includes a wide range of recent work including Jackson Mac Low's chance-derived architectural poems; Clark Coolidge's restricted and repetitive lexicon in *Polaroid*; Ron Padgett's "Haiku"— "First: five syllables / Second: seven syllables / Third: five syllables"; Paul Violi's "Index" to an imaginary vocabulary or Terry Winch's equally imaginary resume; Lyn Hejinian's alphabetically-placed lines creating a lyric intensity in *Writing Is an Aid to Memory*; Kit Robinson's *Dolch Stanzas*, composed entirely from the Dolch list of common words, or James Sherry's use of a similar list as part of a dance score; Tina Darragh's demonstration of the interdependence of sounds, clichés, and place in *Pi in the Skye*; David Bromige's "My Poetry"—a weaving of excerpts of reviews of his work;

to name just a few. Historically, the *gematria* and other
"word events" documented in Jerome Rothenberg's *A Big
Jewish Book* are relevant; more crucial to the current context
is the work of such early modernist Russian writers as
Viktor Shklovsky and Velimir Khlebnikov—for example
Khlebnikov's "zaum" (astandard-word) poems as well as his
"Incantation by Laughter" which is entirely based on
prefixes and suffixes of the root word for laughter.[17]
(Compare also: Steve Reich/Philip Glass/Charlemagne
Palestine; Michael Snow; Ad Reinhardt; Malevich, El
Lissitzky, Moholy-Nagy.) (Expository writing as constructive, e.g., Francis Bacon, since exaggeratedly visible para-
digmatic syntax and sentence and paragraph order?!) —In
the end, a result of this conscious constructing is that of
'making strange', the 'alienation effect': To be able to see
and feel the force and weight of formations of words,
dynamics that otherwise go unnoticed; to feel it as stuff, to
sound the language, and in so doing to reveal its meanings.

In the visual arts the constructive base is perhaps more
apparent than in writing, where we are seduced more readily

17. Jackson Mac Low, *Stanzas for Iris Lezak* (Barton, VT: Something Else,
1971); Clark Coolidge, *Polaroid* (Bolinas, CA: Adventures in Poetry/Big
Sky, 1975); Ron Padgett, *Tulsa Kid* (Calais, VT: Z, 1979); Paul Violi,
"Index", in *None of the Above*, ed. Michael Lally (Trumansburg, NY:
Crossing, 1976), pp. 208-9; Terry Winch, *"Resume"*, in *None of the Above*,
p. 129; Lyn Hejinian, *Writing Is an Aid to Memory* (Berkeley: The Figures,
1978); Kit Robinson, *Dolch Stanzas* (San Francisco: This, 1976); James
Sherry, "Integers", in program notes for Nina Weiner and James Sherry at
American Theater Laboratory, May 8-11 (New York: 1980), II:6; David
Bromige, "My Poetry", in *My Poetry* (Berkeley: The Figures, 1980);
Jerome Rothenberg, ed., *A Big Jewish Book* (Garden City, NY: Anchor/
Doubleday, 1978); Velimir Khlebnikov, *Snake Train*, ed. Gary Kern (Ann
Arbor: Ardis, 1976).

into accepting a natural 'speech'-derived syntax or 'logic'-derived discursiveness. For one thing, construction is assumed to be an integral part of visual work, or even, in the case of sculpture, its essence. Yet, just as fundamentally, construction is at the heart of writing. Anyone who has ever learned to write a newspaper article (who, what, when, where, why) or taken a course in expository prose is taught about outlines that enable parameters and codes to be set up that the reader will notice and decipher. The front page of *The New York Times* is, in a sense, a collage or simultaneity with a clearly structured hierarchic meaning to its placements and orderings over the page and in each article. *Ordering and sequence express values.* If, in poetry, we wish to take responsibility for the work, the text, then we must intend the order, take the order as a crucial part of what we are doing. The idea of order suggests sequence but I also want it to suggest the mode/shape/form/structure in which the ordering occurs. The question also arises as to what is the *unit* of ordering—phoneme, morpheme, word, phrase, sentence, etc. (Syntax is the ordering of strings of words.) What, then, is the *measure*, measure being the unit or ordering? The measure being something we discover in writing poetry not something we assume. This would almost distinguish what I mean by poetry as a type of writing, though that would exclude a common characterization of poetry as that writing which uses a measure handed down by tradition, e.g., iambic pentameter. But I am putting forward a poetry that does not assume a measure but finds it, articulates it. In this context, a value in constructive work is that it lays the measure bare to the ear and eye, so that we can hear and see the structuring and how it creates (conditions) meaning by its structuring. So actively displays how meaning in the world comes to be. It is a method that shows how ordering and sequence assert values, how form limits/conditions what you can say in it. Which also suggests that all writing exists in form, in shape, as mode, in a style, in genres. Some writing may make you more or less conscious of this fact—this is indeed a compositional vector in writing. In starting out talking about 'thinking' as a kind of genre of recent poetry I was citing examples of an idea of ordering based on the 'spontaneous' movements of the mind. This type of 'natural' 'free-associative' mode I would like to collapse onto the artifactual, 'constructive' mode: both are valuable in that they call the 'measure' into question, take as part of the project finding the measure. Any given presentation of order, realization of measure, suggests a world view. In the act of writing, order and structure become integrated into the 'text', into the experiential realm, where they exist as a part of that totality.

> She measured to the hour its solitude.
> She was the single artificer of the world
> In which she sang. And when she sang, the sea,
> Whatever self it had, became the self
> That was her song, for she was the maker. Then we,
> As we beheld her striding there alone,
> Knew that there never was a world for her
> Except the one she sang and, singing, made. [18]

18. "The Idea of Order at Key West" in *The Collected Poems of Wallace Stevens* (New York: Knopf, 1954), pp. 129-30.

3. PRIVACY

I want to keep circling—from structural and constructive perspectives on poetry back around to a seemingly more 'internal' starting point for writing, back, for this moment, to the picture of Descartes sitting alone in his study, so as to think about 'privacy' as a central aspect of writing. Poetry is a private act in a public place—the public place being both 'the language'—which is shared by all—and the page, open as it is to reading and rereading (by oneself and others). For some the search for the private—that which is true to oneself and for oneself on one's own terms—has taken the form of breaking away from highly standardized and institutionalized forms—indeed, from any previously realized forms—whether they be literary forms that prize evenness and pentameter and high tone, or dry descriptiveness, or airy wittiness floating through beautiful mannered stanzas, or quasilogical 'non-fiction' expository forms of argument, or . . . — from automatic or prescribed patterns. The tangibility of perception or thought, of experience—how you can get to that. The weight and density of the language *entoned*—the ear—that allows for the specificity, the particularity, of a composition to be felt. The order being the order that comes from one's 'private' *listening*, hearing—which in its privacy seems to be the order of the world, even without 'me'. That this measure, these syllables so ordered, this phrase after this thought after this word, brings the world onto the page, allows its meanings to be discovered. "The aspects of things that are most important to us are hidden because of their simplicity and familiarity. (One is unable to notice something—because it is always before one's eyes.) The real foundations of his enquiry do not strike a person at all.

Unless *that* fact has at some time struck him. —And this means: we fail to be struck by what, once seen, is most striking and powerful."[19]

That writing is in some senses the exploration and revelation of that which is private seems the heart of the desire to write poetry. A person, alone with their thoughts, takes pen in hand . . . Indeed the social conditions of writing poetry—that it is not generally work performed for another in exchange for money—tend to put it, sociologically, in the private (personal) sphere, an avocation performed for 'pleasure'. The final judgments for what is written and how it is written are made, privately, by the writer (although this is often the robotized privacy of the consumer choosing among brands—social norms can exert a stronger influence in a personal choice than in a collective one). The very terms that are often used to characterize positive values in poetry—personal, confessional, moving, etc.—present a picture of poetry as a private expression made public. Literary writing has in fact been a place where the 'private' secrets of 'our' lives have been laid bare(r)—where taboos about what was improper to say have been broken, where the seemingly most intimate secrets of desire and behavior have been spelled out. Even, in fact, where the most commonplace insecurities and egotisms—"masked in public"—have shown their "all-too-human" faces. Yet, strangely, the more deeply personal a writer's revelation, the more the writing itself comes to be taken as evidence of a shared truth, not unique to the writer at all. It is almost like the myth of psychoanalysis—that our most private fantasies and dreams hold the key by which our behaviors become 'publicly' comprehensible.

19. Wittgenstein, §129.

Rousseau's *Confessions* is an obvious place to look back to
for a text that shatters the public illusions (i.e., hypocrisies)of
both behavior and desire in its quest for 'honesty' ('truthfulness', 'authenticity'). (The work itself—the genre is memoir
—is no more a private expression than a public accounting.[20]) Certainly, at the time, this type of work was both
courageous and outrageous. People evidently had, as they no
longer do, the capacity to be shocked by the details of a
person's private life. By now, such details flood the market-
place of literary artifact—the confessions of the most repul-
sive to the most angelic are a daily part of what we read and
hear, seemingly no personal fact about 'public' figures is left
private. More recently, the experience of many people
otherwise inaudible and invisible to the culture at large—
black people, gays, women—have been recognized as an
important part of literary production, allowing the emer-
gence into the public light of what had been methodically
privatized, silenced. The extent of this outpouring of the
'private' has made the confessional mode more and more

20. "Although I abandoned the field of the world to my enemies, I left in
the noble enthusiasm which has inspired my writings and in the steadfast-
ness with which I had adhered to my principles a testimony to my qualities
of soul, corresponding to that which my whole conduct adduced to my
natural qualities. I had no need of any other defence against my calumnators
. . . . I could leave them my life to criticize from one end to the other, in
the certainty that, notwithstanding my faults and weaknesses, notwithstanding my ability to tolerate any yoke, they would always find me a just and
good man, free from bitterness, hatred and jealousy, quick to recognize
when I was in the wrong, even quicker to excuse the injustices of others,
seeking my happiness always in the gentle emotion of loving, and behaving
on all occasions with a sincerity verging on rashness and with a dis-
interestedness that was almost past belief. I was in a manner, therefore,
taking leave of my age and my contemporaries and, by confining myself to
that island for the rest of my life, was bidding the world farewell." —from
The Confessions (1795), trans. J. M. Cohen (Baltimore: Penguin, 1965),
pp. 590-91.

rhetorical (less and less intimate). Using various 'taboo' contents can read at this point as only a literary device to give the semblance of intimacy and authenticity. To such an extent that anecdotally personal content has to overcome its manipulative charge in order to in any significant way tap into the power that privacy has previously enjoyed. It's not that one doesn't believe the confessions of the private life to be true, but that such confessions take on a style and content largely predictable, largely, in a sense, already 'publicized'. So what, then, could the 'private' be anymore?

One power of the concept of privacy for writing is that of an address of intimacy ('truthfulness' rather than 'truth' to use Wittgenstein's distinction[21]) that allows the formal requirements of clarity and exposition to drop away. To speak intimately is to be free to speak as one will, not as one should. Confusion, contradiction, obsessiveness, associative reasoning, etc., are given free(er) play. A semblance of coherence—or strength or control—drops away. In contrast to this, or taking the idea further, the private can also seem to be the incommunicable. As if I had these private sensations (or thoughts or feelings) that no one can truly know as I know them. As if my thoughts and feelings are hidden

---

21. "The criteria for the truth of the *confession* that I thought such-and-such are not the criteria for a true *description* of a process. And the importance of the true confession does not reside in its being a correct and certain report of a process. It resides rather in the special consequences which can be drawn from a confession whose truth is guaranteed by the special criteria of *truthfulness*. (Assuming that dreams can yield important information about the dreamer, what yielded the information would be truthful accounts of dreams. The question whether the dreamer's memory deceives him when he reports the dream after waking cannot arise, unless indeed we introduce a completely new criterion for the report's 'agreeing' with a dream, a criterion which gives us a concept of 'truth' as distinct from 'truthfulness' here.)" Wittgenstein, pp. 222-23.

from everyone else—that I remain in some crucial way an enigma to others, or that others seem in some fundamental way enigmatic or closed to me (since I can't feel what they feel, see as they see, etc.). That one's private thoughts are in some ways incommunicable would, perhaps, provide an explanation for the 'obscurity', the difficulty, of reading some poetry. As if it were a matter of writing in a 'private language' that no one else could be anything but external to, an outsider. The idea of a private language is illusory because language itself is a communality, a public domain. Its forms and contents are in no sense private—they are the very essence of the social. One's 'private' writing is partly the result of a traditional and contemporary practice of such works, always mediated by a larger social production. The investigation or revelation of meanings, relying only on one's own private convictions and insistences, one's ear and the measure one finds with it, is not an isolating activity but its opposite—the exploration of the human common ground. "For what is hidden, for example, is of no interest." [22]

The intense experience of separation that is a part of a continuing power of privacy in writing can make tangible what otherwise seemed invisible: the world made strange so that we can see it, as in a dream of the familiar become foreign. "One is unable to notice something because it is always before one's eyes. . . . We fail to be struck by what, once seen, is most striking and powerful." It is measure that we have seen, that language is measure. And it is with this that we make our music—by ourselves, privately (if so that

22. Ibid., §126. Private language is, of course, a recurring issue in the *Investigations*. See also Alan Davies's related discussion in "Private Enigma and the Open Text" in *L=A=N=G=U=A=G=E* No. 13 (New York: 1980).

the measure's heard)—a private act, a revelation of the public. So that that writing that had seemed to distance itself from us by its solitude—opaque, obscure, difficult—now seems by its distance more public, its distance the measure of its music. A privacy in which the self itself disappears and leaves us the world.

4. IDLENESS AS THE POLITICAL VALUE OF POETRY

In Rousseau's *The Confessions* he writes of his "great scheme" for a life of privacy and idleness, far from that other kind of idleness of society's parlors. "Idleness is enough for me and, provided I do nothing, I prefer to dream waking than sleeping . . . to live without constraints and eternally at leisure. . . . The idleness I love is not that of an indolent fellow who stands with folded arms in perfect inactivity and thinks as little as he acts. It is the idleness of a child who is incessantly on the move without ever doing anything, and at the same time the idleness of the rambling old man whose mind wanders while his arms are still." [23]

Idleness is a primary desire in poetry—of a writing that is just for itself, not to be used for some other thing, this or that, not to serve up some ideas or tell you a story about what

23. Rousseau, p. 591. "I had got the habit of going in the evenings to sit on the shore, especially when the lake was rough. It gave me a strange pleasure to watch the waves break at my feet. I made them a symbol of the tumult of the world and of the contrasted peacefulness of my home; and so moved was I at times by this delightful thought that I felt the tears flow from my eyes. This repose, which I so passionately enjoyed, was only disturbed by the fear of losing it; but my feeling of uneasiness was so great as quite to spoil its charm. I felt my situation to be so precarious that I dared not count on it. 'How gladly', I used to say to myself, 'would I exchange my liberty to leave this place for the assurance that I could always remain here' " [pp. 595-96].

is happening over there, but just in here, in it, content to sit and make a virtue of that, call it noninstrumental (a writing that does not carry a meaning along with it as information to take away, which would make the writing there primarily to serve up this information, a shell in itself) where language is not in gear, is idling. Laziness as a kind of stubbornness—at one's own pace, my own measure, and not doing any*thing*, just doing (cf: the lilies of the field, etc.). Instrumentality in contrast is labor done to produce a product, the means for an end. (The model of the factory system of production.) The language *used* to communicate, rather than itself being the communication.

> The measure all use is time congealed labor
> In which abstraction things keep no resemblance
> To goods created; integrated all hues
> Hide their natural use to one or one's neighbor. [24]

A system of abstraction: the particular, the discrete occurrence, merely a shell, the value residing in (underlying in) that which exists as a result of the occurrence, valued only as a means toward a goal of a process. Valued only for what a thing produces, its product.

24. Louis Zukofsky, *"A"*-9, in *"A"* (Berkeley: University of California, 1978), p. 106. All use the measure of abstraction, which assumes value as the end product of an equation (surplus value = rate of profit x cost of labor/material) rather than inhering in particular occurrences (i.e., labor itself). All use, that is, instrumentality, is thus alienating (estranging), having as its goal the extracting ("extorting") of value (profit). So labor is removed from its "loci" as maker and turned into a "token" which "Flows in unbroken circuit and induces/ Our being" to its decentering. "Bought, induced by gold at no gain, though close eye/ And gross sigh fixed upon gain have effected/ Value erected on labor, prevision/ Of surplus value, disparate decision" [pp. 106-7].

> Bought to be sold things, our value arranges . . .
> But see our centers do not show the changes
> Of human labor our value estranges. [25]

Writing as stupor, writing as out-to-lunch. Writing as vacation. Writing degree zero. Idleness as antistatic (functionless, it becomes estranged). Writing as idled thinking (not just the means to a displaced end, becomes world revelation).

Investigation/restoration/vision of the world as self-sufficient.

> . . . how song's exaction
> Forces abstraction to turn from equated
> Values to labor we have approximated. [26]

And how does poetry idle itself? It is the product of the most intensive labor, concentration, attention. Attention to measure, to the ordering of occurrences, that such occurrences are instances of how the world itself comes to mean.

> There are things
> We live among 'and to see them
> Is to know ourselves'.
>
> Occurrence, a part
> Of an infinite series . . . [27]

The language itself idled—layed-off—so that even to read a text as 'poetry' would mean to see its language as citational—at minimum doubly valent, both acting to convey information and sounded for its qualities of tone, rhyme, partic-

25. Ibid., p. 106.
26. Ibid., p. 108.
27. George Oppen, *Of Being Numerous*, in *Collected Poems* (New York: New Directions, 1975), p. 147.

ularness/peculiarness of expression, oscillations, vibrations, bands of intensity, *resonance*, i.e., not just *what* it means but *how* (a doubleness that can be more or less apparent— another technical vector of the medium). That: hearing how this meaning formation occurs, is occurring ("the music of poetry is just the experience of sound coming to mean something", [28] a music of content) is necessary if we are to 'value' other than the value *of* abstraction, instrumentation, alienation.

Hands, heart, not value made us [29]

The ability to let language resonate absolutely. The sound of the world we (would) inhabit. Poetry the testament of these singularities—testimony.

> Which is ours, which is ourselves,
> This is our jubilation
> Exalted and as old as that truthfulness
> Which illumines speech. [30]

28. Don Byrd, "Getting Ready to Read '*A*'", in *boundary 2* X:2 (Binghamton, NY: 1982).
29. Zukofsky, "*A*"-9, p. 127.
30. Oppen, *Of Being Numerous*, p. 173.

Ron Silliman comments: "You make out of idleness and privacy the image of the poem & poet at work in all times and within all classes of the production of the same ideological message, wch is an idealization at the very least. The fact that poetry is so uneconomic does not alter its economic determination, but merely demonstrates its weakness as a determination, hence the contradictions that arise & the inevitable overdeterminations. . . . Poetry is not produced within the personal sphere by those who publish—this is a major distinction between those who consume what they produce & those who exchange, as we do, their productions. . . . What we finally get is an image of the poet, not a particular one or even of a particular school or generation, wch I don't believe. . . . Partly, the problem is dehistoricization—you generalize the word poem to such a degree that it seems timeless & (as bad) almost without meaningful distinctions at any given point in time—the section on construction notwithstanding. . . . My sense is that you have to concede the primary socialness of literary production (that poetry exists first as a totality wch then breaks down into structured groups & that the individual poet comes at the end of the chain & is far from the center). [However], that you shd deal with the poet as (transhistorical, transaesthetic) individual as the center is . . . true to the emphasis you give in your poems to vulnerability, doubt & the wrong end of manipulation as language codes. . . . "

—I don't particularly disagree with the view you put forward about the social preceding the individual, but my sense of using 'privacy' as an issue was to eschew the possibility that language or expression could be 'private' except in an uninteresting way (i.e., hidden) since language is essentially a social medium and poetry a social (i.e., group) expression. Even the idea of 'idleness' is related to the fact that a *method* of attention/critique of the social/conventional language forms rather than rote operations within them leads to a deeper social revelation—I don't mean to suggest that this *method* is 'private' or 'individual' in its 'essence' but also a socially conditioned one, 'group practice' as you say, & yet this 'group' practice still differs from normative language practice of a larger group configuration, and individual practices, of course, differ often radically within any grouping. (Language is held in common but we each must learn it—speak it, act it—for ourselves.) In a sense, the 'individual' you suggest I am positing needs to be defined not as a single isolated Romantic individual but as a methodological practice learned in active collective work with other's reading and writing. I do not accept a psychocentric view of persons and, indeed, question whether there are preconstituted 'persons' at all in the primary instance (though 'person' may be the most fundamental projection we make). It is to bring back a visceral understanding of the collective nature of consciousness and world that I suggest the things I do. The centrality of the inscription is 'our' investigation. The power of the projection of separateness from the collectivity has to be acknowledged and worked through, it is the historical situation, the body. So I do maintain the value of the perspective of broken-off-ness (inherent in aspects of both 'privacy' and 'idleness') as central to a genuine social revelation. If I rest on a term like 'poetry' it is to allow for the (talismanic? ecnoid?) power the medium itself has acquired through its history to emerge: revealing the adherence of individuality and collectivity, binding and unbinding and rebinding. —C.B.

Two/ Film of Perception

FRAMES OF REFERENCE

We wait, all, for a story of us that shall reach to
where we are. We listen for our own speaking; and
we hear much that seems our speaking, yet makes us
strange to ourselves.   —LAURA (RIDING) JACKSON

1. THE UNWILLING SUSPENSION OF DISBELIEF

Behind the film's credits, Mad Max of the MFP (Maximum
Force Patrol) is chasing—what? a truck, a motorcycle gang?
He switches into superspeed, I sink back into my seat, body
dropping into a pose pleasantly between slumber and stupor.

What is it that attracts me to this movie, to the movies?
Not, that is, any particular movie, not movies of special
aesthetic value, but the movies at hand, on the block? I want
to understand film from the point of view of the consumer:
not the connoisseurship of cuisine but the gluttony of the
ravenous.

It starts by making a fast exit from the street, the job, the
apartment—worlds of potential sociability—and ducking
into the darkened cocoon of the movie house (no appearance
au théâtre this), in search of the anonymity of the darkness,
the absence of distraction ("Please be quiet!").

Max's vehicle (it's something beyond a mere car, although it does resemble a standard issue police coupe) has just flown straight through a 25 foot truck and hit the ground running. Nothing works so well to catch the attention, and I don't mean this scene or this film but movies in general. What's involved doesn't feel like a *willing* suspension of disbelief, as if I actually had to work at conjuring the images, as you do in reading this sentence: Max's world imposes itself on me, all I have to do is slip into neutral. *Absorption:* the unwilling (that is, passive) suspension of disbelief. Not imagination (the act of forming a mental image out of something not present to the senses) but *im-position* of the image on the mind—*imagabsorption.*

Mad Max is a revenge film in which Max's wife and children have been brutally (how else) killed by a scum-of-the-earth motorcycle gang, the members of which Max eventually hunts down and kills. The fast action violence of this film works to rivet my attention, its excesses (don't worry—I'm not going to quote Blake on excess, yet) glue me ever more fixedly to the screen, allowing for what amounts to a coercive domination of attention, albeit a coercion I choose to submit to and can lessen at any moment by closing my eyes.

Films like *Mad Max*—I call them terror films—are not my favorite kind of movie but rather represent the heart of the experience of film that I find compelling. Their explicitly frightening nature is an extreme literalization of a basic experience of all movies—basic because of the apparatus of film making and the conditions of film viewing. Science fiction or supernatural horror films, with notable exceptions, work less well for me than films that turn on the psychopathology (a.k.a. evil) of ordinary life. I am more captivated by *The Texas Chain Saw Massacre* or *The Naked Kiss* than by *Halloween* or *Alien.* But this is overly simplistic, since what makes horror films great is their ability to find external—alien—bodies for human psychopathology, or, perhaps more remarkable, to humanize what first appears alien and evil, as for example Klaus Kinski does in Werner Herzog's *Nosferato.* In any case, what makes movies work for a person is more largely a product of his or her own gullibilities and culpabilities than any sort of hierarchy of the quality of the individual films or genres.

The pleasure that comes from watching movies, especially terrorizing ones, is of an unselfconscious voyeurism. The need to respond to situations seen is numbed, satisfying an intense craving for passivity. Film is infinitely more technically adept at defeating self-consciousness than theater.[1] In the theater, the artifice of theatricality and the mechanisms of illusion cannot be effaced, and, combined with the sociality of a live performance event, distract from an anonymous and private consumption of image. The screened distance from the scenes represented in a movie intensifies the objectification of voyeurism. To see a live human sacrifice in an arena would bring into play active responses to the scene and to the audience largely obliterated in seeing a movie of such an event. It is the difference between being a spectator and being a voyeur; the former is a passive participant who is present, the latter is an absent viewer. Cinema is capable of making the spectacle of drama a *plastic*

---

1. See "On Theatricality" in this collection.

art, combining in this way the power of the theater with the power of painting.

Sex and violence may be the heavy metal of the erotics of voyeurism, but they are by no means its only subjects. The essence of cinematic voyeurism involves the power derived from looking at an *other* situation that is self-contained and unaffected by me, and toward which I am invisible, irrelevant. In simplest terms, I watch, unseen, the performance of everyday life. This is the power of the great stars, who allow us to have a sensation of intimacy with them—Brando in *On the Waterfront*, or Powell and Loy in *The Thin Man*, or Messina in *La Strada*, or Falconetti in *The Passion of Joan of Arc*. Recently, *My Dinner with André* played extensively on this simulacrum of intimacy, being composed of an extended conversation, which partly worked the way that overhearing the next table's conversation might work at a restaurant—a mixture of titillation and scorn.

The cinema is the unparalleled technology for the imposition/consumption of image, in contrast to the free play of imagination. For these purposes, the novel, which fulfills many of the same functions as the movies, most obviously in the serial novels and *feuilletons* of the 19th century, cannot compete on a "candy's dandy but liquor's quicker" scale. In terms of fulfilling the desire for obliteration of self-consciousness and the fantasy of voyeurism, the motion picture is the heroin(e) of the arts, the greatest image-is-junk food, brain candy. Or so it is for me; that's why I go. Its great rival, television, is burdened with the role of the modern hearth-fire, symbol of home and family, as Roland Barthes has pointed out. Not only is the movie theater potentially more conducive to absorption, but so is the quality of the image in terms of size and resolution. Movies partake of the aura of the mechanically reproduced, in contrast to the blander appearance of the newer electronic reproduction. Oddly, in the electronic age, mechanical reproduction takes on the aura that handcraft had in the mechanical age; witness the antique shop fetish for old photographs or old labels, which when they first appeared seemed free of this type of nostalgia (much as xerox copies are free of any such aura at the present time).

2. TRANSPARENCY

The movie screen becomes, through the magic of cinema, a window onto a world behind it. This illusion of the transparency of the screen is the result of a particular set of technological procedures involving an ideology of spatial depth derived from Renaissance perspective, in which there is a convergence, via lens and focus, onto the single point of an observer or subject. This type of perspective supposedly simulates "normal" perception. In fact, perspective idealizes one aspect of perception—a fixed, forward gaze onto an object in the near distance—and disregards other types of perception, including the fragmentation of scattered and mobile focus (employing the whole of the retina not just the fovea). Ironically, the motion in conventional motion pictures is based on an immobile point of perception, the stationary viewer as camera/eye, while technologies involving mobile points of perception, such as Michael Snow's *La Région Centrale* and ↔, abandon Renaissance perspective and the related dynamics of "deep focus". The type of perspective often employed by commercial movies embodies a metaphysical view of the primacy of solid figures (a.k.a.

objects) set against grounds, in contrast to a non-Euclidian sense of space as discontinuous and heterogenous.

Two-dimensionality is another property of films that seems to enhance the transparency effect. In contrast, 3-D undercuts the illusion of a world in back of the screen by making the image appear in the spatial area between the viewer and the screen, that is, in the space of the proscenium theater stage, *in front of* the screen. The resulting claustrophobia conflicts with the possibility for a sensation of horizon *behind* the screen possible in 2-D. Although, for example, Alfred Hitchcock uses this shut-in-ness of the 3-D space to magnificent effect in *Dial M for Murder.*

It may seem odd that what I find so compelling in film is what, in writing, I am most prone to distrust: the disappearance of the word / the appearance of the world; that is, writing in which the words are made as transparent as possible to allow a sensation of wordless images to be conjured up by them.[2] But there is no easy analogy between writing or poetry that brings the conditions of language into audibility, and film that brings the apparatus of cinema into visibility.

Stan Brakage, for example, relies, in part, on the metaphor of eye, and on film disclosing what the eye sees; although he breaks with the conventional patterns of representing the eye = camera equation. The result is, for him, a more authentic, literally, surreality: the world as viewed by an eye unbounded by habitual patterns, a Romantic Native Eye.

2. See Bruce Andrews and my "Pacifica Interview on Politics" and Ron Silliman's "Disappearance of the Word, Appearance of the World" in $L=A=N=G=U=A=G=E$ Supp. No. 3 (New York: 1981).

Even when the objects which that eye sees break down, as in *The Text of Light,* there is still some sense of the world before us to behold beyond the screen. We are still looking through a window out onto the world, imaged as a pristine visual "reality" unmediated by "words". The claim is not of a celluloid artifice of composition but of a glimpse of a world beyond the screen; the experience of looking is not onto the surface of the screen, as Jackson Pollock's drips exist on the surface of the canvas, but beyond it, in back of it. The metaphor is perception, not structure:

> Imagine an eye unruled by man-made laws of perspective, an eye unprejudiced by compositional logic, an eye which does not respond to the name of everything but which must know each object encountered in life through an adventure of perception. How many colors are there in the crawling grass to the baby unaware of "green"? How many rainbows can light create for the untutored eye? . . . Imagine a world before the "beginning was the word."

> Forget ideology, for film unborn as it is has not language and speaks like an aborigine. . . .

> To search for human visual realities, man must, as in all other homo motivation, transcend the original physical restrictions and inherit worlds of eyes.[3]

Brakage, like other film artists as different from him as Ernie Gehr, has not abandoned the transparency effect but re-envisioned it.

3. Stan Brakage, *Metaphors on Vision* (New York: Film Culture, 1963), pp. 25-28.

There are, nonetheless, films that are a direct counter to
the transparency effect, most obviously any lensless film—
where it is impossible to set up an eye=camera analogue:
photograms, animation, the scratch films of Len Lye, Peter
Kubelka's *Arnuf Ranier*. Snow's work, while often utilizing
the sensuous thrill of the transparency effect, subverts it by
foregrounding the architecture of the method, framing the
framing so that it is as much on view as what has been
framed. Some of Jean-Luc Godard's work provides other
examples counter to the transparency effect, despite his
heavy reliance on sexual voyeurism as a *leitmotif* to illustrate
the commodification of reality through the imagimposition
of the movies.

In a more commercial context, Herbert Ross's *Pennies
from Heaven* also goes against the grain of a voyeurism that
transports the viewer into a world beyond the screen.
Unrelentingly theatrical, Brechtian in its self-consciousness,
it is brilliantly played for the "alienation effect" by Steve
Martin, who always keeps you aware of the put on. Refusing
to allow for a saturation in the experience, each scene, each
musical number in the movie is cut up short rather than
being allowed to "take off", the distance function working
to make the spectacle feel hollow, the gestures empty. There
seems to be a refusal to facilitate the suspension of disbelief,
so the film is uncomfortable to watch; self-conscious of itself
in a way that makes the viewer self-conscious. When Martin
and Bernadette Peters, in color, dance in front of a giant
black and white backdrop of Astaire and Rogers dancing,
the effect is to bring home the simulacrum of theatricality, as
opposed to cinematic transparency, that is central to the
film. This is achieved by a *trompe-l'oeil* in which Martin and

Peters do not dissolve into the world behind the screen but
pop out in a way suggesting 3-D, appearing to dance in front
of the screen, that is, on the audience's side of the screen.

3. THE FRAME

It had always seemed to me that the bigger the movie screen,
the greater would be the transparency effect. Thomas
Nicholson, Director of the American Museum of Natural
History, makes just this point in reference to the new
"Naturemax" theater at the museum, which has a screen
four stories high. The film "To Fly", which features
spectacular aerial shots, has been the main attraction at the
theater.

> Naturemax is simply an extension of the diorama
> presentation for which the museum is most famous.
> Our dioramas are recreations of the natural habitats in
> which animals and people live. With Naturemax, we
> use the film medium to produce the same effect. I've
> seen "To Fly" over a dozen times, and yet when we
> balloon over the waterfalls, emotionally I still feel like
> I'm there. I'm not looking at a picture, I'm in it.[4]

In contrast, Naturemax has convinced me of the diminishing
returns of size (beyond full 70mm projection) and the crucial
role of having the frame in view.

The limitedness of the movie screen is central for the
capacity of film to present a world screened off from me into
which I look passively, the space and meaning of the scene
upon which I gaze already constituted: the ultimate experi-

4. Richard Schwartz, "Westsider Thomas Nicholson" (interview), *West Side
TV Shopper*, April 3-9, 1982 (New York), p. 21.

ence of the consumption of the world as image. By image I
mean a reduction of epitomization of the otherwise untotal-
ized and uncharacterized expanse of the visual field. In this
sense, an image has as its upper limit object idealization and
its lower limit blankness. The power to so circumscribe the
visual field in film is the function of the frame; its reduction
and delimitation provide, in collaboration with the transparency effect, a singled perspective or view of the world
projected.

> The camera, being finite, crops a portion from an
> indefinitely large field. . . . When a photograph is
> cropped, the rest of the world is cut *out*. The implied
> presence of the rest of the world, and its explicit
> rejection, are as essential in the experience of a photo-
> graph as what it explicitly presents. . . . The camera
> has been praised for extending the senses; it may, as
> the world goes, deserve more praise for confining
> them, leaving room for thought.[5]

As the screen becomes bigger, it diminishes the sense of
looking through a hole and begins to feel like the very
immersion—thrownness—into sensation from which film
offers relief/release.

4. METAPHYSICS

Movies fulfill my desire to witness the world as already/
always constituted. I view a world enbubbled and so became
a tourist of experience rather than a participant in it or a
constituter of it. In this way, films put me in an ontological
position of a subject, giving sway to the Cartesian split

5. Stanley Cavell, *The World Viewed* (New York: Viking, 1971), p. 24.

between my subjectivity and the externality of a world
which exists without me. By this fact, movies simulate the
conditions for Cartesian uncertainty in respect to the veridi-
cality of my experience.

If the movies did not exist, Western metaphysics would
have had to invent them. "The mere fact that our world is
set forth in the frame of a film forces that world into the
sphere of what you call objectness," says Martin Heidegger's
Japanese interlocuter in "A Dialogue on Language". "The
photographic objectification is already a consequence of the
ever wider outreach of Europeanization."[6] That is to say, the
dualism of Western metaphysics is already present in the
film image: the real as sensuous appearance (filmic reality)
and the ideal as nonsensuous form (verbal or ideological or
logico-conceptual structure).

What becomes of people on film? They are behaviorized,
object-ified. What becomes of people at films? No longer in
the world, they become witness to it. What becomes of
things on film? They are fixed, perspectivized, categorized,
viewed. What becomes of people and things on film? They
are transformed into appearance, phenomenalized, dematerialized.[7] In these ways, film plays out the Kantian
account of human knowledge—knowledge not of "things-
in-themselves" but of things as mediated by the conditions
of knowledge, that is, time and space. Like in the movies,
the Kantian world is not apprehended directly but is viewed

6. Martin Heidegger, *On the Way to Language*, trans. Peter D. Hertz (San
Francisco: Harper & Row, 1982), p. 17.
7. Compare Stanley Cavell's "What Becomes of Things on Film?" in his
Themes Out of School: Effects and Causes (San Francisco: North Point, 1984),
pp. 173-84.

as phenomena. We are sealed off from the world and not, as Heidegger would have it, indwelling within it—the great fantasy, and half-truth, of being outside the world and looking in.[8]

It is this fantasy that Edgar Allan Poe turns outside in in "Descent into the Maelstrom", a work that anticipates the metaphysical implications of transparency and voyeurism in respect to film while exploding the terms of the discourse. What begins as the presentation of the outer appearance of a graphic and horrifying scene cascades into a surfaceless vortex without any outside or boundedness, so that what started as a classic "disaster" narrative turns into an experience of sheer thrownness inside the world, where any possibility or semblance of a fixed viewpoint from outside the maelstrom becomes impossible, the dynamic of terror being redoubled in the process of the enactment of depthlessness and "deterritorializing flows".

> Well, so far we had ridden the swells very cleverly; but presently a gigantic sea happened to take us right under the counter, and bore us with it as it rose—up—up—as if into the sky. . . . And then down we came with a sweep, a slide, and a plunge that made me feel sick and dizzy, as if I were falling from some lofty mountain-top in a dream. . . . The boat did not seem to sink into the water at all, but to skim like an air-

8. This fantasy is played out in a marvelously frontal way in Robert Altman's *Popeye*. Popeye's home island is one of the most magically enbubbled worlds ever imagined. Everything about it is set slightly off expectation, the film embodies its own not-quite-earthly physics. It's even hard to understand the words the characters are speaking until gradually your ears become attuned to their sound.

bubble upon the surface of the surge. Her starboard side was next to the whirl, and on the larboard arose the world of ocean we had left. It stood like a huge writhing wall between us and the horizon. . . . Never shall I forget the sensation of awe, horror, and admiration with which I gazed about me. The boat appeared to be hanging, as if by magic, midway down, upon the interior surface of a funnel vast in circumference, prodigious in depth, and whose perfectly smooth sides might have been mistaken for ebony, but for the bewildering rapidity with which they spun around. . . . Round and round we swept—not with any uniform movement—but in dizzying swings and jerks. . . .

Poe's epigraph for this story (from Joseph Glanvill) suggests that inadequacy of our frames of reference to do any more than skim on the surface of phenomena.

The ways of God in Nature, as in Providence, are not *our* ways; nor are the models that we frame in any way commensurate to the vastness, profundity, and unsearchableness of His works, *which have a depth in them greater than the well of Democritus.*

An analogue in film to Poe's "Descent into the Maelstrom" might be the 360° vertigo-inducing pans/spins that Brian DePalma uses in *Carrie* or *Obsession*, or, where they originated, in the works of the master of turning surface into dizzy depthlessness, Hitchcock. But while such effects are a standard enough in Hollywood film, it might be more fruitful to look for an analogue in the descent into light itself in *The Text of Light*, or Gehr's flippings of surface and inside space in *Serene Velocity*, or Snow's vortex machines, ↔ and *La Région Centrale*. As Abigail Child writes of her films:

". . . not to hold onto the image, or as one might exist on a line edging chaos and this without dissolution. . . . [A] landscape of vortices, constant corners, contrast switching. . . . There's a continuity of line through motion, a piling up of image and affect in the steady accretion of vortices, stops, starts, sharps. . . ." [9]

5. REALISM

In a sense, the conditions of film parody the subject/object split, indulge the fantasy that, for instance, the human world is like a bubble separable—severed—from me. (This may account for the special fascination of seeing human beings rather than landscapes in movies, since nature, unlike society, may be something it is second nature to regard with the eye of a tourist.) By using the frame as a window which crops *a* view, cut-off and partial, the dominant practice of commercial film has accelerated this possibility of cinema. Specifically, the emphasis of "deep focus", in contrast to Eisensteinian montage, has made films look more "real" than reality—I'm thinking of the trippy space in Stanley Kubrick's films or the acidy lighting in Steven Spielberg's *Close Encounters.*

This is André Bazin speaking:

> [Deep focus promotes a respect for] the continuity of
> dramatic space and its duration. . . . Considered in
> terms of narrative, Wyler's deep focus is almost the
> cinematographic equivalent of what Gide and Martin
> du Gard declared to be the ideal in writing fiction:

9. Abigail Child, program notes for "Ornamentals" and "Prefaces", Millenium Film Workshop, December 18 (New York: 1982).

> perfect neutrality and transparency of style which
> must interpose no coloration, no refraction between
> the realism and the story.[10]

It is not that deep-focus films are actually realistic, since the reality constructed is a very partial and contrived one, but that the power of certain filmic conventions for totalization and idealization of the visual field evoke the kind of response Bazin's remark illustrates. "The result", says a review of *Citizen Kane* in *American Cinematographer*, referring to Gregg Toland's cinematography, "is a realism in a new dimension: we forget we are looking at a picture, and feel the living, breathing presence of the character."[11] What's been created is not a classic reality so much as a classic unreality, based on the so-called realism of the nineteenth century novel. The eye does not see in framed deep-focus images; but this intensification and restriction of ordinary seeing is what makes some movies look more real than reality. As for realism, from the point of view of reproducing the material conditions of seeing—including diffusion, distraction, fragmentation, blurring—works by Snow or Brakage, and the like, are probably more deserving of the term.

6. IDEOLOGY

The effect of what is conventionally called cinematic realism is to maximize the subjectification of the viewer. By this process, movies reinforce what Louis Althusser has described

10. André Bazin, *What is Cinema?* trans. Hugh Gray (Berkeley: University of California, 1967).
11. Quoted by Christopher Williams, ed., *Realism and the Cinema* (London: Routledge and Kegan Paul/British Film Institute, 1982).

as the ideological construction of the subject as a passive recipient of perceptions. At the same time, the visual and social realms viewed in films by the subject are totalized and idealized in accordance with bourgeois ideological conceptions of the continuity of space (deep focus) and time (continuity) and the predominance of plot and character (adapted from the conventions of the nineteenth century "realist" novel). As Barthes puts it, "Ideology is, in effect, the imaginary of an epoch, the Cinema of a society."[12] Film blithely and deceptively shows ideology as the hypnogogic underpinning—the language—of experience. A particular ideology is a way a collectivity experiences the world. Realist films picture something essentially mythologic: an unfragmented, territorialized, monolithic social-cum-visual world.

Certainly a legitimate argument can be made against much commercial film practice. Perhaps it's more accurate to say not that movies are the heroin of the arts but the soma; for instance, that the social sanctioning of sex and violence in movies is an instrument of social stabilization (but then, films might be that, only appreciated, in a society in which one believed). While films are a possible vehicle for the flight from individual self-consciousness, they markedly exacerbate the level of self-consciousness within human society. Looking at ourselves has increased the awareness of the effect of gesture, of gesture as detachable from the bearing of a meaning—gesturalized gesture. (*Gest*ure: the body becomes gestural only when it is noticed.) With its

12. Roland Barthes, "Upon Leaving the Movie Theater", in *Appartus*, ed. Theresa Hak Kyung Cha (New York: Tanum, 1980), p. 3.

mirroring feedback mechanism, movies have contributed to
a greater anxiety over the effect of one's bearing and
diminished irreparably the possibility for unselfconscious
being-in-the-world. Film (along with video and photography) fixes, blocks, scleroticizes—which is to say, reifies—
behaviors, styles, mannerisms in the process of holding
them up to view. It fuels the split between our outer
behavior and inner feeling (the public and the private, the
soul and the body, self and identity). Movies are all about the
creation and consumption of fashion and in that process they
turn human gestures into fashions: no longer the welling of
expression or meaning—a discourse of exchange—they
become instrumentalities for effect. On the one hand, this
makes possible the understanding of systems of gesture as
forms of ideology; but on the other hand, this possibility for
critique is subverted in commercial films by their use of this
split as the motor for gesture as style. (One could imagine
work, call it dance, that would attempt to reclaim the body
by externalizing gesture, in effect exaggerating and hence
exposing it: a process of deeroticization by remateriali-
zation. [13])

Nonetheless, the desire to experience idealized and totalized visualizations is not abated by critique. Life experience
is so often up-in-the-air, in process, indefinite, that the
experience of a defined place and time and duration and
meaning offers a fantastical relief. Movies can be a sym-
phonic realization of the constituting powers of the ideologies within which we are enveloped from birth to death.

13. See, for example, Sally Silvers's dance work, presented in the same
series as this essay.

They provide the opportunity not simply for a hint or glimpse of the flesh and blood of ideological inscription but its most full-blown envisionment. Movies satisfy a longing to see exemplary depictions of the repressive unreality to which we are subject(ed), in an otherwise oblique or invisible fashion. They satisfy a longing to sit back and look at our encapsulated ideological lives.

> In the final analysis, stars are created by the need we have for them, and not by talent or absence of talent or even by the film industry or advertising. Miserable need, dismal, anonymous life that would like to expand itself to the dimensions of cinema life. [14]

Writing about these features of the cinema, Jean-Louis Baudry accounts for the special power of film in terms of both regression and dream. Regression: the conditions of viewing mime the darkness and immobility of the womb. Dream: the experience of the projected images suggests a return to a condition, prior to the ideological construction of the self, in which hallucination and externality have not been differentiated by the "reality test"; film, that is, invokes a period of immobile immersion in perception similar to the dream state and fulfills a desire, governed by the pleasure principle, to return to this period of "archaic satisfaction".

> Dream is "an hallucinatory psychosis of desire" [Freud]—i.e. a state in which mental perceptions are taken for perceptions of reality. Moreover, Freud

14. Guy Debord, "On the Passage of a Few Persons Through a Rather Brief Period of Time" in *Situationist International Anthology*, ed. Ken Knabb (Berkeley: Bureau of Public Secrets, 1981), p. 33.

> hypothesized that the satisfaction resulting from hal-
> lucination is a kind of satisfaction which we knew at
> the beginning of our psychical life when perception
> and representation could not be differentiated, when
> the different systems were confused, i.e. when the
> system of consciousness-perception had not differen-
> tiated itself. The object of desire (the object of need), if
> it happens to be lacking can at this point be hal-
> lucinated. It is precisely the repeated failure offered by
> this form of satisfaction which results in the dif-
> ferentiation between perception and representation
> through the creation of the reality test. [15]

This account compellingly suggests the source of the power
of movies as an apparatus of psychic captivation. Films, like
dreams, tap a desire for an experience that annuls the
differentiation between externality and internality, so evok-
ing early childhood experience, before the self has been
segmented out from its surrounding (via the mirror stage)
and become autonomous. (For Jacques Lacan, the mirror
stage—*stade du miroir*—occurs when the infant "misrecog-
nizes" his or her image in the mirror, forming a totalized,
biomorphic conception of *I* from earlier sensations of
fragmentation and diffusion of the body. "The formation
of the *I* is symbolized in dreams by a fortress, or a stadium
(stade)—its inner arena and enclosure, surrounded by mar-
shes and rubbish-tips, dividing it into two opposed fields of
contest where the subject flounders in quest of the lofty, re-
mote inner castle whose form . . . symbolizes the id. . . ."[16]

15. Jean-Louis Baudry, "The Apparatus", in *Apparatus*, p. 52.
16. Jacques Lacan, "The Mirror Stage", in *Ecrits*, trans. Alan Sheridan
(New York: Norton, 1977), p. 5.

But it seems to me that films have precisely the power to dramatize the mirror stage itself: to externalize rather than to internalize the world, projecting it as separate, as other (Other?!). I am *in* my dreams; I *watch* a film. Movies do not collapse the distinctions between "active and passive, between acting and suffering experience, between eating and being eaten" as Baudry suggests, but rather they accentuate the latter terms of these pairs. Rather than being a "mode which is anterior to the 'stade du miroir,' to the formation of the self, and therefore founded on a permeability, a fusion of the interior with the exterior", [17] movies seem grounded in an irrevocable rending of the two. If this is true, then the power of movies is not a function of regression (to the so-called oral stage) but of reinforcement by reenactment of the transitional phase of the establishment of the self as subject (the problematically-called genital phase). The desire fulfilled by movies, then, is for *social power*, the manipulation of the external requiring separation from it.

Jean Piaget's research adds another dimension to this consideration. He has found that the child learns to perceive the visual field as a unitary representational space ("an objectified and spatialized causality") correlatively to the development of object relations, that is, to the experience of other persons as separate from oneself. [18] Thus, the development of what Piaget calls logico-mathematical concepts are a necessary prerequisite for the ability to perceive the representation of the "objectified" space of conventional films.

17. Baudry, p. 54.
18. Jean Piaget and Bärbel Inhelder, *The Psychology of the Child* (New York: Basic, 1969), p. 26.

7. LOOKING BACKWARD

The desire to see the world spectacalized, to become a nonparticipating viewer of it, of course predates film, and perhaps predates all the arts, or to say it another way, is simultaneous with the origin of art.

Many "anticipations" of film, from the Greeks onward, have been commonly cited. And no doubt today's movies are anticipations of some other, grander, Diorama of the Imaginary. (Certainly, the fare on my neighborhood's twenty screens suggests more than is ever delivered. But that brings up my inital question again: What is it about movies that makes "quality" (though not "craft": invidious distinction!) a secondary issue, that allows anticipation to take the place of fulfillment?) Movies, as part of the history of visualizations, have origins going back 50,000 years. Indeed, painting and sculpture predate architecture of the crudest post-and-lintel type. That is, painting and sculpture emerged in full-blown, "advanced" form not only tens of thousands of years before what we now call writing, but before the earliest construction of shelters. Cave paintings testify to an ancient longing to *look at*, to BEHOLD visualizations of the world. Typically, the scene beheld was epical, involving warriors and hunts and dogs and multitudes of people, in a scale attempted by D. W. Griffith's films, for example.

Thinking in terms of the history of visualizations, it may be that the motion in motion pictures, at least the *continuity* of movement standardized by a fixed number of frames per second, is less central to the effectiveness of the medium than might be supposed. Consider that rock painting, as well as many of the artifacts of primitive societies (cultures outside the occidental/oriental historical framework) were

apparently used in ritual performances, which may have
been frightening to experience. These objects were probably
not statically contemplated but moved around, shaken,
suggesting the power of an invocation of objectness that
might usefully be related to Ken Jacobs's stereo projections
and to films like Gehr's *Reverberation*. In contrast, the
idealized, seamless motion of commercial films, especially
insofar as they employ deep focus over and against montage,
seems static, dematerializing the physical obtrusiveness and
conspicuousness of objects by making invisible the transition
of frame to frame. Jacobs and Gehr have found an archaic
power in cinema not adequately tapped by commercial
films. Jacobs's interest in picking up on some of the
abandoned directions in early cinema suggests that commercial movies might have adopted very different conventions for motion and objectness than they so far have. Since
cave art and associated rituals developed over a period of time
more than ten times as long as the entire period subsequent
to the inception of writing, it is reasonable to expect that
cinema, still in its perinatal epoch, will not be fixed to the
predominant modes of contemporary practice.

8. FEAR

Many of the cave wall paintings have dark solid figures set
against white fields, inducing a sensation of illumination or
projection of the image onto a screen. In their conditions of
viewing, they seem to share some of the features of watching
"terror" films: "The caves are not only dark and gloomy,
but there is about them something eerie and fear-inspiring.

Shut off and separated from the outside world, the caves suggest secrecy." [19]

Brakage:

> The earliest cave paintings discovered demonstrate that primitive [people] had a greater understanding than we do that the object of fear must be objectified. The entire history of erotic magic is one of possession of fear thru holding it. The ultimate searching visualization has been directed toward God out of the deepest possible human understanding that there can be no ultimate love where there is fear. Yet in this contemporary time how many of us even struggle to deeply perceive our own children. [20]

There is a deeply satisfying, sensuous experience of fear that films can provide over and above a frightening subject matter. Indeed, the ontological conditions of film create their own ministry of fear regardless of the subject matter. These conditions include the largeness of the image and the darkness of the theater (some movie houses have the annoying habit of leaving on dim lights to better control the situation). But most scary of all is being split-off from the world screened, which induces a sensation of outsideness, paranoia. The more horrible and terrorizing, the more visceral is the voyeuristic thrill of not being touched, not being a part of the perceived world—invisibility, marginalization, transparency; deep fear of being unwanted, unnoticed, alone in the world and irreparably other than it. All

19. Erwin O. Christensen, *Primitive Art* (New York: Thomas Y. Crowell, 1955), chapter 6.
20. Brakage, p. 25.

fears that are exhilarating to live through under the controlled conditions of the movie house.

I have found that the ideal time for going to a movie is
during lunch on a full-time job. I remember seeing *Who'll
Stop the Rain* one lunch time, and the terrific charge I got
going from the robotized bureaucracy of the workplace to
this world of buildings blowing up and so forth. Most
exciting was how my disconnectedness from the people on
the screen mimicked my disconnection from the people at
the office. The movie played out my fear of atomization in a
masochistic way. There was the separation anxiety, but
there was also the wish-fulfillment of being free from the
need to respond to others, to act rightly or wrongly or at all.

By saying that fear is at the heart of my attraction to
movies, I mean to include all types of films—comedy, for
example, my own favorite kind. Any film can induce a mild
response of outsideness, although habitual viewers probably
aren't conscious of it, especially if the film is "funny". Like
some drugs, a tolerance for the effects of movies builds:
Children are usually awed by any movie; in contrast,
frequent viewers crave more and more sensationalism, as is
indicated by the spiraling technology of science fiction and
horror films over the past few years. With whatever fear
may be associated with movie viewing, there is the correlative pleasure of being unselfconscious and feeling free to
enjoy or be distracted by other people's troubles (at least
they're not your own). The Christians and the lions of the
Roman circus probably provided many of these same oppor-
tunities; so did their buffoons and clowns. (Catharsis—
release—to cry; violence and sex, horror and pleasure;
comedies and tragedies: but these have never changed
anything.)

My fascination with movies is caught up with the great pleasure of seeing terrifying things screened, experiencing them in a controlled situation. Pier Paolo Pasolini's *Salo* is an illuminating exploration of the sadomasochism of viewing, of voyeurism, in terms of the *competing* realm of aesthetics and ethics (the sensuous and the ideational, experience and ideology), or, more disturbing to admit in this connection, their inextricability. But what is the desire to reexperience fears, paranoias, humiliations (the essence of the filmic for both Herzog and R. W. Fassbinder)? I want to relive my fears because they give me pleasure. Fanning my fears, I am able to expel them, play them out, "the satisfaction of their exhaustion splits of an indissoluble incongruity". That would be a contact with death: touching the limits, ends, of life, for it is only in death that in fact one is severed from the world.

The earliest cave art consists simply of hand prints—the first evidence of a human need to erect the stadium of the mirror, to construct spectacles. By spectacalizing the world, we domesticate it, get (by making) a view of it, create the diachronic and diatropic distance that allows for the manipulation of the projected things of the world as signs and symbols. By totalizing the world—and thereby *mis*representing it—we are able, nonetheless, to get a handle on it, on our own immersion in it. Subduing the truth of our being-in-the-world, and being overcome by the world, is not only exhilarating but liberating (or shall I say, gives the illusion of liberating—what else could it do?) from the chains of insideness.

WORDS AND PICTURES

I have sometimes thought that the story of Homer's
blindness might be an artistic myth, created in critical
days, and serving to remind us . . . that the great poet
is always a seer, seeing less with the eyes of the body
than . . . with the eyes of the soul. . . . When Milton
became blind he began to compose as everyone should
compose, with the voice purely . . . that mighty,
many-stopped organ. —OSCAR WILDE

1. INTRODUCTORY
   What is the relation between pictures and
   writing? My first answer is no—
   no relation—they are as different
   as sky and earth, nothing in
   common. This would be to imagine
   pictures to be experience, the subjectivity
   I am always seeking and being rebuffed
   by—or that there is any other, above
   or beside.

114

What is the relation of the visual to
the verbal? Are they not separate
realms—races—each with their own civilization?
And what more can we do then
pay each tribute at the temples
which are their Art? Difference
is power, but it is also regret.
The bird sings as sourly at noon
when accosted by wolves as she does
in famine's moonlight.

2. SILENCE

The visual image overwhelms: erecting itself foresquarely
before the eyes—as trees, sky—looming and total, assuming
acquiescence in its presence. Unlike the visual arts, the
verbal arts can never achieve the *trompe-l'oeil* of "sensuous
appearance". As Jean Piaget notes, in terms of the difference
in the perception of space and time, a picture seems to be
apprehended *all at once*, a geometric simultaneity, while
words are experienced in pieces, a duration that never
transcends its utter sequentiality.

> Knowledge of space is therefore much more direct and
> simpler from the psychological point of view than
> knowledge of time. . . . We can perceive a whole
> geometric figure . . . simultaneous[ly]. A temporal
> duration, however, no matter how short it is, cannot
> be apprehended *all at once*. Once we are at the end of it,
> the beginning can no longer be perceived. In other

words, any knowledge of time presupposes a reconstruction on the part of the knower. [1]

Film, because it is the visual art most dependent on
duration, shares a unique kinship with writing. I do not
mean by this that writing provides much of the content for
movies in the form of *mise-en-scene* and dialogue; I refer to
the formal affinities between the two mediums. Understanding film provides a method for understanding language,
since in its nonlexicality, its grammar of shots and angles, it
may contain the essence of the linguistic. No doubt writing
and painting also share a common origin; aren't, after all,
the cave paintings the first known form of inscription,
recording: lines on the wall. But while the ideogram retains
a relation to the individual word, it took moving pictures to
find the most striking visual equivalent of a sentence: a shot,
as Ron Silliman, for instance, has shown in *Tjanting*. [2] Film,
that is, helps to conceptualize the plasticity of language, the
intrinsicness of ordering and editing to meaning.

For these reasons, silent film—by virtue of its silence—
may have the most intimate connection with writing. In the
early silent films, we can see language as pure gesture in the
sense that Heidegger speaks of gesture as the "gathering of a

1. Jean Piaget, *Genetic Epistemology* (New York: W. W. Norton, 1970),
p. 61. Italics added. Psychological research has also shown that complex
visual images are read, or scanned, in somewhat predictable sequences. The
experience of the simultaneity of the visual is the *product* of a multilevel
series of operations that constitute the human perceptual field, as described
below.
2. Ron Silliman, *Tjanting* (Berkeley: The Figures, 1981). See, for example,
p. 63.

bearing". [3] This silence of the world—"all eyes, no tongue"—
is echoed in Apollinaire's poem "Annie", which was written
in 1912, just seventeen years after Lumiere's *Arrival of a
Train at a Station* was first shown in Paris, and in the same
year as Gertrude Stein's *Tender Buttons* and shortly after
Pablo Picasso's *Les Demoiselles d'Avignon*.

> On the coast of Texas
> Between Mobile and Galveston there is
> A grand garden all full of roses
> It contains also a villa
> Which is a grand rose
>
> A woman walks often
> In the garden all alone
> And when I pass on the route bordered by limes
> We look at ourselves
>
> Like this woman is mennonite
> Her roses and her clothing have not buttons
> There are of them lacking two on my vest
> The lady and me follow the same rite. [4]

What is invoked here is the silent objecthood of the world:
an objecthood perfected in the imaging of the world in films
that are silent and which is disrupted by the introduction of
sound into them. An objecthood Stanley Cavell finds most
fully realized in Keaton's films:

> What Heidegger calls Being-in-the-World is the basic
> state of what he calls *Dasein* (which is what we call the
> human). In the third chapter of *Being and Time* (the

3. Martin Heidegger, "A Dialogue on Language", *On the Way to Language*,
trans. Peter D. Hertz (San Francisco: Harper and Row, 1971), p. 18.
4. Guillaume Apollinaire, "Annie", in *Alcools*. My translation.

chapter entitled "The Worldhood of the World") he makes Being-in-the-World first visible—as a phenomenon for his special analysis—by drawing out, in his way, the implications of our ability to carry out certain simple forms of work, using simple tools in an environment defined by those tools (he calls it workworld). . . . It is upon the disturbing or disruption of such carryings on. . . above all in the disturbing of the kind of perception that these activities require . . . that . . . a particular kind of awareness is called forth . . . [which] turns out to be *of* . . . the worldhood of the world . . . an awareness that prior absorption was already directed toward a totality with which, as Heidegger puts it, the world announces itself. By the time Heidegger characterizes the supervening awareness as a mode of sight that allows us to see the things of the world in what he calls their conspicuousness, their obtrusiveness, one may sense an affinity with some of the principal topics of film comedy. . . . It is in Keaton's silent absorption with things (not, say, in Chaplin's) that what is unattended to is the worldhood of the world announcing itself (in the form, for example, of entire armies retreating and advancing behind his just turned back). [5]

3. A SCHOOL FOR SENSES
What is this silent totality of obtruding objects, conspicuously present to the eyes? "The senses have . . . become *theoreticians* in their immediate praxis. They relate to *thing*

5. Stanley Cavell, *Pursuits of Happiness* (Cambridge: Harvard University, 1982), pp. 271-72.

for its own sake, but the thing itself is an *objective human* relation to itself and to man and vice versa" [Marx]. The object-ive spatial field is a projection from the eyes outward, met with a force always at the least its equal.

"We see only what we know", said Goethe; and Emerson, "That only can we see which we are, and which we make." Language is the lens of sight.

I use the term "language" for all forms of socially exchangeable meaning—visual, verbal, gestural, or tactile. In this sense, verbal language includes both speech and writing, and visual language both perception and painting (architecture, sculpture, drawing, etc.). The equivalent of speech in verbal language is seeing in visual language: perception is a sight act. I consider language to be both what Piaget calls "logico-mathematical" organizing processes, which are very early conceptual constructions formed by the child, as well as what he calls "semiotic or symbolic functions", which Piaget has defined as developing at a later stage of childhood. Allowing for this significant difference, Piaget has found that there is no direct perception of objects but that such perception "incorporates specific constructions of a more or less complex nature. [These] logico-mathematical concepts presuppose a set of operations that are abstracted not from the objects perceived but from actions performed on these objects, which is by no means the same." [6] That is, perception is always mediated (but *not* determined) by socially developed paradigms that act on and so transform the things perceived. "Perception . . . is

6. Jean Piaget and Bärbel Inhelder, *The Psychology of the Child* (New York: Basic, 1969), p. 49.

subordinate to action."[7] This ideological construction of the human visual sphere is comparable to the construction of the human internal sphere, the subject or self. The formation of both the subject and the object are the result of constructed organizing processes; neither is present to begin with. Piaget has shown that the conception of permanent external objects occurs reciprocally at the time the child is learning to idealize and totalize space in conventional "logico-mathematical" manner. This is the inception of what is sometimes called "object relations":

> The universe of the young baby is a world without objects, consisting only of shifting and unsubstantial "tableaux" which appear and are then totally reabsorbed, either without returning, or reappearing in a modified or analogous form. . . . [T]here exists neither a single space nor a temporal order which contains objects and events in the same way as containers include their objects. There are, however, several heterogenous spaces all centered on the child's own body—buccal, tactile, visual, auditory and postural spaces . . . but without objective coordination. . . . These different spaces are then gradually coordinated [under] the scheme of the permanent object . . . into a fundamental structure which constitutes the framework of practical space. This structure will later serve as the foundation, once it has been internalized, for the operations of Euclidian geometry . . . and will permit a general representation that is simultaneous and increasingly extra-temporal. [8]

7. Piaget in an interview. Richard I. Evans, *Jean Piaget* (New York: E.P. Dutton, 1973), p. 39.
8. Piaget and Inhelder, pp. 14-17. For a discussion of the reciprocal

Perhaps the most far-reaching neurobiological study of
this "scheme of permanent objects" is *Vision* by David
Marr.[9] Marr argues that three-dimensional object-centered
adult vision is a "construction of descriptions" [p. 354]; that
is, a model resulting from an extremely complex multilevel
information processing system. The initial stages produce
representations derived from groupings of retinocentric
input. First, there is a 2-D "primal sketch" of image
intensities and geometric organization. Next, transformed
from the 2-D sketch, comes a "2½-D sketch" of the
geometry of the visible surfaces within a viewer-centered
frame. "The final step consists of transforming the viewer-
centered surface description into a representation of the
three-dimensional space and spatial arrangement of an object
that does not depend upon the direction from which the
object is viewed. This final description is object centered
rather than viewer centered" [p. 37]. In Marr's analysis, the
"main job" of sight is to tell about "shape and space and
spatial arrangement, . . . to derive a representation of

formation of the "self", see pp. 25-27. Compare Virginia Woolf's recollec-
tion of her earliest visual experience: "If I were a painter I should paint
these first impressions in pale yellow, silver, and green. There was the pale
yellow blind; the green sea; and the silver of the passion flowers. I should
make a picture that was globular; semi-transparent. I should make a picture
of curved petals; of shells; . . . I should make curved shapes, showing the
light through, but not giving a clear outline. Everything would be large and
dim; and what was seen would at the same time be heard; sounds would
come through this petal or leaf—sounds indistinguishable from sights. . . .
sight was always then so much mixed with sound that picture is not the
right word. . . . " "A Sketch of the Past" in *Moments of Being* (New York:
Harcourt Brace Jovanovich, 1976), pp. 66-67.
9. David Marr, *Vision* (San Francisco: W. H. Freeman, 1982). This
discussion of Marr originally appeared in *Sulfur* No. 8 (Pasadena: 1983).

space"—even in certain cases (say, optical illusions) when "there is not direct visual evidence" [pp. 36 and 51]. Insofar as this is true, an object-centered bias appears to be built into adult visual processing systems that create, maintain, and *read* representations [p. 330]. Marr goes on to suggest that the 3-D model of sight, which is, after all, developed within a social context, may be usefully conceptualized as a *semantic* process [pp. 354-61]. "The perception of an event or of an object must include the simultaneous computation of several different descriptions of it that capture diverse aspects of the use, purpose, or circumstance of the event or object" [p. 358].

4. THE OARS OF PERCEPTION

Perception is totally subscribed to the population of the social body; there is no native sense. It is impossible to fully comprehend the degree to which our perception is habituated by social being, a social being that is reflected in language, which is, in itself, properly speaking, the social body. An idea of perception can seem to posit an eternality upon which we look, our senses five becoming portals onto a centric field of the world. There is always the possibility of this projection of a sight unmediated by the conditions of human being, or an unalloyed substance external to our processing of it. But this projection of a native site from which we are barred (or to which we have only occult access) is a product of a discourse of perception that itself is responsible for its own shortcomings. The strange and simple fact is that this so-called eternality is none other than the processes of conditioning that form the core of a material, historical, spatial existence. So that rather than being cut off (by language) from native sight and sound, what is native is the very conditions of human being. The center does not hold because there are only sights—cites of our enclosures in infinitude, these enclosures themselves the very substance that seemed denied to us.

This place we have never found audible is always in our hearing, but a multiplied hearing in reflection in which the membrane through which we perceive is sounded, the possibilities of its structure heard. These structures are not universal—that would be to substitute one metaphysical absolute (of content) for another (of the model); what might be said to be "universal" is the *possibilities* of structures. My quarrel with the structuralists is just this—it is from the heteroclites, the anomalies, the historical accidents that the genus arises. Rules are always secondary to the irregularities from which they are extracted; except that they too have the denseness of the peculiar, are instances of it. The reality we seek is not underlying, beyond the phenomenal level. In that sense alone I would agree with Jacques Derrida—no "real" that is hidden or disguised by custom, which can be unmasked by the analytic moment to the point of deep structure, say the truth of Oedipus, or the Raw and the Cooked and the Rotten, or nature versus culture. Although there are masks that can be unmasked in a process, serial through time, of an exchange of interpretations, each reflecting truths of its own and disguising or repressing other truths, in turn themselves to be critiqued, and so on. The "truth" lies in none of these but in all of them, in the process of aspects itself: the thing-in-itself is the materiality of the gaze, the possibilities of phenomena. Phenomena, in this sense, do not approximate a displaced "physical reality".

They are the product of a mediation by the membrane of consciousness, which is language, and hence actualizations of such a reality. [10]

5. VISUAL LITERACY

According to the Hebrew myth, light was the first act of creation. That is probably the most famous hierarchization of sight among the human senses: the Bible creates the conditions for using eyes before it creates eyes. Eyes, at least in our culture, are the most prized of the human sense organs; assumed to be responsible for processing the most information about the world, eyesight is the sense most associated with survival. Presumably, the evidence is that most people would give up limbs or tongue, ears or nose— though such choices are usually hypothetical—before they would cede sight. The problem with these formulations is that sight is imagined to be split off from the other senses and from language, and assumed to be an autonomous realm, the *sine qua non* of truth, its own evidence—ocular proof. Evidence of the eyes is more believable than the ears, nose, hands, heart: "Show me." Because the eyes are seen as incorrigible, our metaphors of belief, like "are seen as", are often visual: "I've seen the light", "it's plain to see", "use your eyes", "seeing is believing". It should be no surprise, then, that something so accepted at face value, so rarely questioned in everyday contexts, might be the product of a profoundly naive empiricism, as if we value highest what we know least about. Like a woman in the sexist world view,

10. This section originally appeared in *O.ARS/Perception*, ed. Don Wellman (Cambridge, MA: 1982).

sight is put on the pedestal of a respect that masks a deeper scorn. It may be taken for granted as the queen of the senses, but—and here's the twist—when push comes to shove, visual experience is only validated when accompanied by a logico-verbal explanation.

Within the context of a Western educational system, there is a cultural bias toward verbal over visual language as the currency of intellect as well as commerce. Rewards are high for those able to develop elaborate verbal skills, to write expositorily, to recognize verbal behavior in terms of rhetorical forms and to respond in kind. In contrast, there is less reward for developing comparable visual skills such as rendering, recognizing, and naming visual structures, or learning the names of colors. While it is reasonable to imagine a "well-educated" person not knowing the basic concepts of color theory, it is less imaginable that she or he would not know the basic concepts of grammar; verbal syntax is basic knowledge, visual syntax esoteric.

Certainly, there are many people who develop expertise in the visual realm and through the graphic arts of advertising and packaging they exert as great an influence on our ideological preconceptions as do the verbal manipulators of the law courts and the news media, etc. But even highly adept manipulators of the visual are forced to learn some verbal skills, while the reverse is not necessarily the case. Simultaneously, there is a tacit acceptance of the visual as brute reality: the objects that we apprehend appear to make a claim to exist outside of language, silent exemplars of physical fact.

In contrast, verbal training has the effect, at least to some degree, of making identifiable the rhetorical, the constructed, component in verbal presentations (writing, talk). There is a widespread suspicion of the truth-value of verbal discourse; it is not uncommon to question the form of a verbal presentation as biased—to ask what viewpoint determines the choice of words, and if (or how) this choice of words is giving a partial view of the matter under discussion. This is not to say that no one takes newspaper reports at face value, as neutral pictures of reality. But there is a greater tendency to think of pictures, worth all those thousand words, as neutral. The bias in a news report may be easier to spot at the verbal than at the visual level; while a visual critique, although possible, is still less common. After all, the argument might go, the verbal critique is more important, since it is at the verbal level that the real ideological manipulation is taking place, whereas pictures are just representing the visual world.

What is difficult to see is that the visual realm is as fully constructed, as fully a syntax, a rhetoric—a language—as is the verbal. The ability to differentiate objects and colors, figure from ground, is based on a set of biological and cultural conditions that circumscribe into a language what the eyes see.

The stereoscopic simulation of the two eyes is a particular and partial scanning mechanism that produces a constructed and partial visualization. If our visual processes prejudice toward finding shapes, as Marr suggests, the situation is compounded by an inherent bias in Western metaphysics toward reifying objectness. One effect has been the development of innumerable technologies for fixing surfaces and edges. Photography, mimicking some aspects of the human ocular apparatus, has in turn affected the perception of visual phenomena by encouraging a picturing of reality as surface appearance, dematerialized outward shells, delineated volumes. ("The camera is outside its subject as I am outside my language."[11]) Alternative imaging techniques—x-ray, computer scanning, ultrasound—provide very different pictures than either the eyes or the photography of normalized sight. (Radiologists talk about "reading films" not viewing them.) Like photography, such methods of scanning provide different kinds of covers. This search for, and hence production of, boundaries, membranes, limits, stoppages, and territorializations idealizes fixed, static objects: they protrude. In the process, movement, flux, and shift are derealized. Which is not to say that there aren't things that stop us, that we have to look out for; the objects of meaning are sometimes seen and sometimes heard and sometimes responded to, or not. The world is continually made actual by our apprehensions.

Apparently, not all cultures share our bias for the visual among the senses. David Guss reports, in conversation, that in the heavily shaded world of the upper Orinoco (Venezuela), all life forms are oriented more toward sound than light. He suggests that while the horizontal space of sight distances in its objectification, the shaded world of sound permits an intimacy of interconnectedness.

Walter J. Ong traces the "visualist" bias in contemporary Western society in terms of a shift from oral-aural cultures to ones in which verbal language is itself visualized by alphabetization and printing.

---

11. Stanley Cavell, *The World Viewed* (New York: Viking, 1972), p. 127.

The Hebrews tended to think of understanding as a
kind of hearing, whereas the Greeks thought of it
more as a kind of seeing, although far less exclusively
as seeing than post-Cartesian Western [civilization]
generally has tended to do. . . . Basically, the Greek
word *idea* means the look of a thing. It comes from the
same root as the Latin *video* (I see), which yields the
English "vision" and its cognates. [Plato contrasts
ideas and shadows.] . . . Far more than the ancient
Greeks, [medieval civilization] heightened the visualist, quantified quotients of awareness. . . . The
ensuing [struggle], in which the disputatious oral
approach to existence and knowledge lost much of its
hold, was a struggle between hearing and seeing.
Seeing won. With the shift in the sensorium [from the
dominance of oral-aural to the dominance of sight],
the large-scale campaign for the "clear and distinct"
soon began, led by Ramus and focused by Descartes—
a campaign for visually-conceived cognitive enterprise.
. . . Intellectual knowledge was henceforth, more
than ever before, conceived almost solely by analogy
with vision. [12]

12. Walter J. Ong, *The Presence of the Word* (New Haven: Yale University,
1967), pp. 3, 35 and 221. Ong's very insightful book is burdened by his own
oralist-auralist hierarchization, which makes out of the human *voice* (but *not*
the human language, as I use that term here) an animist metaphysics of
"presence" at the same time as obscuring, for example, economic factors
within his practically media-determinist historicity. Ong is so completely
words-as-voice oriented in his interpretation of the oral-aural that he does
not once mention music (and even more oddly song). Like St. Augustine,
and perhaps out of similar religious impulses, he seems to be saying *in
interiore homine habitat veritas*, to which Merleau-Ponty has replied (to the
citation of this quote that ends Husserl's *Cartesian Mediations*): "Truth does

Indeed, the criteria of "clear and distinct" was to operate within the visual metaphor of "observation" toward the devitalizing fixation on objects in the atemporal "single space" to which Piaget refers. Newton's rationalized sight—*Opticks*—was a result.

In the pictorial arts of the West, the representation of objects within a "single space" made a great advance in Italy in the fifteenth century with the invention of perspective. "The system of central perspective not only rationalizes the relationship between objects within a picture, but also establishes a relationship between the viewer and the represented images." [13] Anamorphosis, in which an image is amorphic except when viewed from a very specific point-of-view, is the most extreme example of this viewing process.

Perspective is a visual grammar developed historically and constituted by various interest factors of which it is *expressive;*

not 'inhabit' only 'the inner [person]', or more accurately there is no inner [person. Person is not] a source of intrinsic truth, but a subject destined to be in the world." [See *The Phenomenology of Merleau-Ponty* by Gary Brent Madison (Athens: Ohio University, 1981), p. 315, note 16.] Ong's fixation on the "presence" of the word forces him to arbitrarily limit his conception of the domain of writing to a highly rigidified, rule-governed practice, and in so doing to reject the unprecedented possibilities for aurality (albeit both *de-* and *re*vocalized) that post-Gutenberg writing and printing enables. Thus we see the spectacle of Ong valorizing telephone and television for foregrounding voice while banishing writing from the kingdom of the aural: "All reductions of the spoken word to nonauditory media, however necessary they may be, attenuate and debase it, as Plato so intensely felt" [p. 322]. I can only suggest that Ong rethink the meaning of, for instance, medieval kabbalistic practices in which alphabetic transformations of "base" words transport them—by a kind of alchemy—into just the "presence" he seems to be seeking.

13. Fred Leeman, *Hidden Images* (New York: Harry Abrams, 1976), p. 9.

much as is, for example, the verbal grammar employed in
Bacon's or Descartes' expository method. However, neither
of these grammars can be comprehended in isolation—as
purely verbal or purely visual—since they are symbiotically
synaesthetized through language.

Maurice Merleau-Ponty begins to touch on this:

> . . . classical perspective is not a law of perceptual
> behavior. It derives from the cultural order . . . not
> because the perceived world contradicts [its rules] and
> imposes others but rather because [spontaneous vision]
> belongs to another order than these rules. . . . The
> moon on the horizon is not "bigger" than the coin I
> hold. . . . [With] perspective, I must cease to look
> freely over the whole spectacle, close one eye, and
> circumscribe my vision. . . . But during this time the
> perceived world has disappeared. I cannot obtain the
> *common denominator* or the *common measure which allows
> projection on a single plane* except by renouncing the
> simultaneity of objects. While I was seeing the coin
> and the moon in one view, my look had to be fixed on
> one of them, so that the other appeared to be on the
> margin . . . *incommensurable* with the first and as
> though situated in a different universe. . . . I decide
> to make them *cohabit in the same plane* . . . by
> coagulating on paper a series of local and monocular
> views. . . . In spontaneous vision, things rivaled one
> another for my look. . . . In perspective, I renounce
> that ambiguity [for] an *immobile eye, fixed* on a certain
> "vanishing point" . . . chosen once and for all. . . .
> The whole scene is in the past, in the mode of
> completion and eternity. Everything [as in the correla-
> tive mode of writing!] adopts an air of propriety and

> discretion. Things no longer call upon me and I am
> not compromised by them. [14]

However, Merleau-Ponty is not without a bias for the
"things" of the world conceptualized in visualist terms,
which leads him toward suggesting a dual-level ontology of
cultural immanence for the visual (in which Being presents
itself as corporality, as the advent of the sensible, but also as
conceptless, silent) and cultural transcendence for the verbal
(which can, that is, *transcend itself* into some absolute
"thought without words".) But there is no thought without
words and no sight without concepts. This reasoning is
characteristic of the phenomenon of overvaluing/undervalu-
ing discussed above. "The first painting opens up a world,
but the first word opens up a universe. In short, language
speaks, and the voices of painting are the 'voices of silence'"
[p. 102]. By atomizing the sensorium in this way, Merleau-
Ponty remains under a spell of dualism from which he
decisively breaks in his late, and unfinished, writing.

   Don Byrd, in a letter, locates the issue in terms of "the
lens, and all the imagistic possibilities which derive from it
by analogy. . . . Lens technology always locates a necessary
point of view. In this sense, painting in perspective was
lens-technology, albeit sans lens. For example in Renaissance theatrical design, when stage sets were built to perspective, there was in fact only one seat in the house, and

---

14. Maurice Merleau-Ponty, *The Prose of the World*, ed. Claude Lefort,
trans. John O'Neill (Evanston: Northwestern University, 1973), pp. 51-53.
Italics added. The citation following is also from this text; on that point see
also Madison, *The Phenomenology of Merleau-Ponty*, pp. 102-7.

that was, of course, the King's. So the King sees the reality
and everyone else in reference to him."

Oscar Wilde observes in "The Decay of Lying" in *Intentions*
that life holds a mirror up to art: "Reality is art's only
pupil." Images shape the perception of the visual world; we
see in terms of pictures because we *look for* what we have
seen. From another point of view, this is not so different
from William Burroughs's "image is virus" (an insidious
and epidemic infection) in *Nova Express*. "Things are
because we see them, and what we see, and how we see it,
depends on the Arts that have influenced us. To look at a
thing is very different from seeing a thing" [Wilde].

Wilde laments the loss of lying and artifice in the arts, by
which he criticizes the plethora of naturalist artworks that
recreate the look or sound of everyday life. But such
naturalism may be the greatest artifice of all. In contrast,
Western painting over the past 100 years has been moving
toward materializing the gaze; that is, making explicit the
dynamics of seeing—a visibility of de- and reterritorializa-
tions rather than an idealized representation of things seen.
Painting, to a large extent, has moved toward acknowledging, or foregrounding, the qualities of the visual as discourse; it has been one of the most developed of the arts in
terms of its consciousness of its own language.

This is not to say that on individual terms *Tender Buttons* is
not fully comparable to *Les Demoiselles d'Avignon* or Wassily
Kandinsky's abstract compositions. But work such as Stein's
remained largely unknown in comparison to work such as
Picasso's or Kandinsky's. While a dominant practice in
painting eventually followed in directions related to the

work of these two painters, this is not as true for writing in
respect to the work of Stein. I can only speculate as to the
explanation for this.

For one thing, a painting can be seen if not "all at once"
at least than with a quicker *hit* than available in duration-
bound writing. For another, paintings, because they have
been sold for very high prices in the recent past, and because
they have reproducible images, have been able to cash in on
the glamour of being one-of-a-kind luxury commodities.
Paintings can be assimilated as decoration and style in a way
not obviously possible for writing. In addition, complex
investigation of the visual realm may have flowered because
it was no longer taken as undermining "meaning", which is
too often mistakenly conceived as primarily invested in the
verbal domain of "ideas". Manipulation and abstraction of
visual language, while certainly not without its detractors,
can often be accepted as pattern and decoration, if not as the
augmentation of such language that it is. In contrast,
manipulation and abstraction of verbal language is most
often perceived as undermining meaning. Nor can this
perception be easily transformed into an acceptance of such
work as decorative since words have an extra proscriptive
presumption of utility. All speakers, after all, have a vested
interest in the verbal, just as all perceivers have a vested
interest in the visual. But there may be a greater willingness
to separate "sight acts" from painting than there is to
separate "speech acts" from writing. Indeed, the tenacious
refusal to accept speech as distinct from writing defines the
general conservativeness of the modern literature of our
language.

Ironically, however, without writing there could be no

strict codification of speech for writing to conform to. Writing *creates* the possibility for an idealized speech syntax that can be imposed as "correct" on speakers, and by a vicious circle on writers, to curb the language's otherwise unstoppable drifts and mutations. So writing, which can be a means to escape the constriction of tribally *(community)* governed speech practices, becomes the mechanism for the equally tight but more far-reaching centralized reign of, in the extreme, an Académie française. The comparable vicious circle has been easier to break in the visual domain than in the verbal one—a state of affairs that seems a possible product of popular visual illiteracy combined with a high visual sophistication among many "visual" workers. This may not be as odd as it first appears if historical experience is any measure: compared with the graphic arts, alphabetic writing is a relatively recent, if psychologically middle-aged, phenomenon. Much more significantly, private (silent) *reading* as a popular form (which postdates the Gutenberg revolution) is only a few hundred years old, practically (if to say film is in its infancy) in its childhood.

At the same time as painting and related arts have been acknowledging their constituting practices, the most popular art form in the West, movies, is for the most part not involved in an investigation of the discourse of the visual realm but in the representation of it by means of totalization and idealization. Movies capitalize on a culturally supported underdevelopment (naiveté) which allows for a belief in such *trompe-l'oeil* even where a comparable verbal representation would not be as credible; by which I mean that more people go to the movie (or see it on TV) than read the book. (After the movie, visual imagination charged, sales of the book soar.) Underdevelopment of a working knowledge of the language of sight—the knowledge that perception is not a passive consumption of the already given but is involved in constituting what is seen, in response to desires, uses, and mentions—accounts for the raw power visual totalizations—pictures, moving or otherwise—are able to exert.

6. THE POETICS OF SIGHT

> Consciousness can never be anything else than conscious existence, and the existence of [human beings] is their actual life-process. If in all ideology, [people] and their circumstances appear upside down as in a camera obscura, this phenomenon arises just as much from their historical life-process as the inversion of objects on the retina does from their physical life-process. We begin with real, active [human beings], and from their real life-process show the ideological reflexes and echoes of this life-process. . . . The phantoms of the human brain also are necessary sublimates of . . . material life-process, which can be empirically established and which is bound to material conditions. —KARL MARX, *The German Ideology*

The eye is not a passive mechanism for intercepting the image of objects. It is necessary to look, to discern, in order to visualize. Seeing is as involved with differentiation as reception; as with all language, its primary means of constitution is by establishing differences. [15]

15. See, for example, the account of "ordinary seeing" in Ulric Neisser, *Cognition and Reality* (San Francisco: W.H. Freeman, 1976), chapter 3. According to George A. Miller and Philip N. Johnson-Laird, in *Language and Perception* (Cambridge: Harvard University, 1976), it is the "individu-

No isolated visual image exists as primary—e.g., William Carlos Williams's "Red Wheelbarrow"—any more than any isolated word exists as primary. Any picture, isolated and framed, presupposes an entire visual language; any word exists only in the context of a complete verbal language.

The stop-frame can never, appearances to the contrary, be removed from duration: it is an interval neither timeless nor total: "the false horizon", as Craig Watson puts it, of the "false horizon". "Appearances /remain suspended /in transmission", are not so much perceived as apprehended, handled; the one affecting, infecting, the next. After the first image there is no other undaunted by its precursors, training the eye to see what the ear hears: "creation is continual mouth"."And then, without/asking any question,/we wake up waiting." So expectation controls our days, and release from expectation our nights. "I stood on middle ground, / Ghosted by the sighs of objects." "The trees stand in front of /our desire to be among them." 16

"Anytime we think of an artist coming into focus, we must see," writes Don Byrd, in terms of a perspective directed towards the king's point of view. "It doesn't solve the problem, as Browning tries in *The Ring and the Book*, for example, to multiply perspectives. That only recreates—as

ating function" that is conceptual. "The mechanism involved in separating an object from its surrounds are not well understood" [p. 40]. As in Marr and Piaget, the authors go on to say that no account can be given of perceiving objects without presupposing the concept of object as a 3-D entity in time and space and applying this concept to a perception. In sum, 3-D object representation is the most abstract and conceptual aspect of seeing.

16. Quotations in this paragraph are from Craig Watson, *0.10* (Windsor, VT: Awede, in press).

that poem magnificently shows—numerous irreconcilable points of view, which are inevitably mediated." But how can we stop thinking in terms of lenses, sights, views, perspective? Much of the most formally imaginative American poetry of this century flirts, oddly, with a poetics of sight, in search of the elusive material particular, while as often as not, at other times, throwing it out the window. For instance, Louis Zukofsky's "(Optics)—The lens bringing the rays from an object to a focus. That which is aimed at" [*Prep*, p. 12], [17] or Charles Olson's statement of the equality of each person's view, "Polis is eyes", [18] or Williams's ever more dematerializing wheelbarrow: the conspicuousness and obtrusiveness of objects.

By "sight" I mean something more limited than that word might otherwise permit; I'm referring to the object-focussed, extratemporal, singled perspective that is, in actuality, a static idealization of the experience of looking. A better name might be the poetics of optics. [19] Say, Williams's "The Lily": "The branching head of tiger-lilies / through the window / . . . It's raining— / water caught / among the curled-back petals / Caught and held." Caught and held—

17. Louis Zukofsky, *Prepositions* (Berkeley: University of California, 1981), p. 12. Hereafter cited in the text as *Prep*.

18. Charles Olson, "Letter 6", *The Maximus Poems* (New York: Jargon/ Corinth, 1960), p. 26. "There are no hierarchies, no infinite, no such many as mass, there are only /eyes in all heads, /to be looked out of" [p. 29]. Polis is ears, alas; propaganda. Polis is tears.

19. For a relevant discussion of the problems of a poetics centered on a static "overfocussing" see Alan Davies and Nick Piombino, "The Indeterminate Interval: From History to Blur" in *L=A=N=G=U=A=G=E* Vol. 4 (New York: 1981).

the perception of the tangible visible object, without interference: "miraculously fixed in my /arresting eyes." [20]

> We keep coming back and coming back
> To the real: to the hotel instead of the hymns
> That fall upon it out of the wind. We seek
>
> The poem of pure reality, untouched
> By trope or deviation, straight to the word
> Straight to the transfixing object, to the object
>
> At the exactest point at which it is itself
> Transfixing by being purely what is,
> A view of New Haven, say, through a certain eye,
>
> The eye made clear of uncertainty, with the sight
> Of simple seeing, without reflection. We seek
> Nothing beyond reality. . . .
>
> [Wallace Stevens] [21]

As history, there's Pound's and Aldington's and H.D.'s
somewhat ambiguous "direct treatment of the 'thing'"
along with the admonition "to use absolutely no word that
does not contribute" to this direct treatment (perception?).
Pound adds later, in brushing off Symbolism, that the
"proper and perfect symbol is the natural object." [22] Robert

20. William Carlos Williams, "The Lily", in *Selected Poems* (New York:
New Directions, 1969), p. 53 and "Bird" in *Pictures from Breughel* (New
York: New Directions, 1962), p. 41. My reading of "The Lily" is that the
poem catches and holds the flower like the flower catches and holds the
water.
21. "An Ordinary Evening in New Haven", in *The Collected Poems of
Wallace Stevens* (New York: Knopf, 1954), p. 471. Hereafter cited in the text
as Stevens.
22. Ezra Pound, "A Retrospect", in *The Poetics of the New American Poetry*,
ed. Donald Allen and Warren Tallman (New York: Grove, 1973), p. 42.

Duncan explains: "The discipline of the eye, clarity. . . . A Poet who cant [sic] . . . see is now obviously deficient (tho they exist & thrive all about us, and greatest poets, like Milton and Joyce, have 'lost sight' of the target)." [23] (Though Pound did speak of "an intellectual and emotional *complex*", which suggests a duration more than a snapshot; but probably wouldn't allow for the blur of the unfocussed eye in time.)

Correlative to "sight" is "insight"; as the one assumes a world of constituted objects, the other assumes a constituted self (bringing again to mind Piaget's observation that perception of an object in a unitary space and the perception of a subject as a unitary self are constructed simultaneously); the poetics of insight, then—confessionalism, "persona"ism.

Beyond the poetics of sight, there is the poetics of vision. Beyond the poetics of insight, there is the poetics of reflection. Vision and reflection are an escape from the repetition of sight and insight.

7. VISION

By vision I mean an engagement of all the senses, and of thought, beyond the readily visible, the statically apparent. "The point of vision and desire are the same. /. . . It is desire, set deep in the eye, / Beyond all actual seeing" [Stevens, pp. 466-67]. Olson's "USE USE USE the process at all points, in any given poem always, always one perception must must MOVE, INSTANTER, ON AN-

23. Robert Duncan, "Notes on Poetics Regarding Olson's *Maximus*", in ibid., p. 189.

OTHER!" [24] Even more, Olson's "Proprioception"—with "the body itself . . . the cavity of the body . . . the data of depth sensibility" recalling Piaget's description of archaic childhood experiences—"heterogenous space all centered on the child's own body—buccal, tactile, visual, auditory . . . but without objective coordination."

> Richard Foreman:
>
> . . . a kind of erotics of thought . . . using thought to manipulate the imagination, which is a body. Fill that space . . . not by being at the center (center: the placing (there) of a "subject") [the lens! perspective! the singled space!] but rather by a twist administered to the imagination-body: an un-natural extension of some sort, generating a new periphery, a difference. . . . So the Utopia—there, before your eyes—is unseen by most people. . . . To catch it, to make it hold still, you have to kill it . . . so I have to talk about OTHER things. . . . *Real perception is resistance to perception.* . . . THINKING treated as a *sensing*, as the sixth sense. . . . See the . . . (object) dissolve into a kind of web-of-association awareness. [25]

24. Charles Olson, "Projective Verse", ibid., p. 149. Olson's motto is comparable to Lazlo Moholy-Nagy's program in *Vision in Motion* (Chicago: Paul Theobald, 1969), which is a "textbook" par excellance for visual literacy, grounded in an aesthetics of the antistatic that incorporates a compelling discussion of literature as an intrinsic part of the curriculum. Among a number of recent realizations of "writing in motion" is the dynamic syntax of Bernadette Mayer's aptly titled *Moving* (New York: Angel Hair, 1971) and the vertiginous speed of parataxis in Bruce Andrews's *I Don't Have Any Paper So Shut Up (or, Social Romanticism)* (MS, 1983).

25. Richard Foreman, "The Carrot and the Stick", *October* No. 1 (New York: 1976), pp. 22-30. Italics added.

While "sight" presupposes a singled perspective, one sight for all to see, "vision" holds open the possibility for multiple, not necessarily reconcilable, perspectives: not sight of a world already totalized or complete but vision as a process of constituting and reconstituting the world. Ron Silliman, in "Blue", [26] allows the various competing discourses of sight to speak for themselves, each framed by the others, forming a seriality of possible sights and so a structured investigation of the materialities of seeing. Each sentence conjures up a different type of picture, as in the opening sequence: a titled person (well dressed?) leaving a house, the color of the sky, the "jewelled expanse" of a street, politics as a perspective, an unlikely zoo, trees, a car, sex from a distance, playing badminton, streaks in the road, genitals, a truck. . . . Silliman's exploration of the various components of traditional fiction ends up being an exploration of the various kinds of visual descriptions: an eye a sentence. "The number of objects is limited", however, because fiction can only be finite. Overall, "Blue" proposes not the absence of totalization but rather the materialized totalizations of living in the world—not a sight consumed but a series of partialities inhabited. Like the indeterminancy of the title, "Blue", there are numerous possible meanings, which means not that meaning is impossible but that it cannot be isolated from context, from structure, and from duration. In contrast, the penultimate sentence in the poem points to that other kind of totalization; it pictures the warmth of the family hearthfire—sight as comfort.

26. Ron Silliman, *ABC* (Berkeley: Tuumba, 1983).

Vision is eyes hearing, hands smelling:

It is dark . . .
the floor is ice . . .

Ah invisible . . .
constellations of duration . . .

green syllables of scenery in spring

[Susan Howe] [27]

8. CASE STUDY: BLAKE'S VISION, ZUKOFSKY'S SIGHT

Blake's "visionary physics" is an all-out attack on "sight", conceived as a Newtonian optics of rationalized, continuous space filled with uniformly measurable permanent objects. "The Eye of Man with little narrow orb closd up & dark" [*Mil* 1:5:21; E, p. 98]. [28] "But we see only as if it were the hem of their garments / When with our vegetable eyes we view these wondr'ous Visions" [*Mil* 1:26:11-12; E, p. 122].

Blake envisions a world not schooled by the logico-mathematical conceptual constructions documented by Piaget. For Blake, permanent objects are an abstraction— "Mental Things are alone Real" [E, p. 555]. His vision is of a multiplicity of nonhomogenizable specifics, with none of these particulars deducible from any higher-order principle. Blake's space is a non-Euclidian expanse of simultaneous and logically incompatible perspectives. It implies a rejection of static coherence and identity of space and time, of a con-

---

27. Susan Howe, *Pythagorean Silence* (New York: Montemora, 1982).
28. *The Poetry and Prose of William Blake*, ed. David V. Erdman (Garden City: Doubleday, 1970), p. 98. Hereafter cited in the text as E. (*Mil* is *Milton; Jer* is *Jerusalem.*)

tinuous connecting shape to the system as a whole. The aim is to "clear the doors of perception"—to clear them, that is, of sight, of Newtonian optics—"the Vegetated Mortal Eye's perverted & single vision" [*Jer* 3:53:11; E, p. 200].

Blake's vision is of the synchronicity rather than the causal sequentiality of events:

He views the City of Golgonooza . . .

[*Jer* 1:13:56; E, p. 156]

And all that existed in the space of six thousand years:
Permanent, & not lost not lost nor vanishd, & every little act,
Word, work, & wish, that has existed, all remaining still . . .

[*Jer* 1:13:59-61; E, p. 156]

For every thing exists & not one sigh nor smile nor tear,
One hair nor particle of dust, not one can pass away . . .

[*Jer* 1:13:66-14:1; E, p. 156]

I see the Past, Present & Future, existing all at once
Before me; O Divine Spirit sustain me on thy wings!
That I may awake Albion from his long & cold repose.

[*Jer* 1:15:8–10; E, p. 157]

The Sky is an immortal Tent built by the Sons of Los
And every Space that a Man views around his dwelling-place:
Standing . . . such space is his Universe;

[*Mil* 1:29:4-7; E, p. 126]

The Microscope knows not of this nor the Telescope, they alter
The ratio of the Spectators Organs but leave Objects untouchd
For every Space larger than a red Globule of Mans blood.
Is visionary.

[*Jer* 1:29:17–20; E, p. 126]

Donald Ault explains Blake's compositional strategy as confounding the normal scientific meaning of terms, turning them against expectations. As the sun glares in Blake's eyes, they do not narrow, as in ocular physiology, but "Expand /into regions of air /away from all Care" [E, p. 683]. Ault sees the discontinuous narrative and perspective, exactly what is most confusing about the prophetic works at the discursive level, as central to Blake's method:

> Blake . . . uses such fundamental mathematical [and spatial] terms as center and circumference in ways which would seem paradoxical to the typical eighteenth-century mathematician (and would perhaps be perplexing even to "occult" readers since Blake also inverts their expectations for the "mystical" use of center and circumference). Thus Blake's use of terms in such transformed ways is meant to be corrective in the most fundamental sense: it is to give the reader . . . a new and expanded view of the terms and doctrines they take for granted as fixed and univocal. . . . [R]ather than causing the reader to focus on a closed set of solvable problems which can be explained in terms of a closed set of images, Blake's poetry requires the reader to be constantly shifting . . . perspective and never to be willing to settle on a finite solution to a problem. [29]

The standard measure of time and the equality of measure in tranformations (conserving), perceptions Piaget links to the construction of logico-mathematical concepts, are modes of perception Blake finds reductive of the possibilities for human experience. His Eternals each have their own measure, their own vision, which is not comparable: "one

29. Donald Ault, *Visionary Physics: Blake's Response to Newton* (Chicago: University of Chicago Press, 1974), p. 51. Cited below as Ault.

law for the Lion and the Ox is Oppression" [E, p. 43]. Blake
also attacks the "bondage of Rhyming" and "Monotonous
Cadence": "I therefore have produced variety in every line,
both of breath and number of syllables. Every word and
every letter is studied and put into its fit place" [E, p. 144].

> The complexity of Blake's poetry to us arises out of his
> attempt to correct our confused perception which is
> constantly lured toward the forms of perception syn-
> thesized in Newton's system. Mainly [Newton's]
> technique tries to . . . rescue spatialized permanence
> from the flux of time. . . . [The] rationalized space
> and time . . . [of] Newton's system consolidates and
> makes believable the incredible state of abstraction our
> normal perceptions involve. As such, Newton's system
> becomes the focus for revealing the Satanic usurpations
> of Eternity in their most outrageous, yet most per-
> suasive form. [Ault, pp. 194-95]

Blake's most complex account of visionary rather than
optical space is the "Vortex" passage in *Milton* [1:15:21-35;
E, pp. 108-109]. It is no coincidence that this same word
would be picked up by Pound in his "Vorticist Manifesto" a
hundred years later. It is also the image Poe uses—midway
between Blake and Pound—in his "Descent into the
Maelstrom." [30] Blake's vortex is

> the eddy or whirlpool of eternal consciousness, whose
> center is the object eternal consciousness intends.
> Since the center and circumference are not separate in

30. For a discussion of the use of vortices in Arakawa's work, and its
Cartesian implications, see "Meaning the Meaning: Arakawa's Critique of
Space" in this collection. See section 4 of "Frames of Reference" for a
discussion of Poe's "Descent".

eternal vision [cf. Foreman, above], the perceiver is at
once at the apex of his [or her] vision, and yet able to
regard it from a distance. But when Milton . . . leaves
eternity for time [he] moves to the apex of his own
vision. He is thus *objectified*, and the eternal circumference of his vision rolls up behind him. The eddy of
perception is *solidified* into the global universe of
Newtonian observation. What survives of eternal
vision depends upon the temporal perceiver's imagination, for [she or] he can still encompass [her or] his
vortex and see the object world in its human dimension
as "one infinite plane." [31]

Zukofsky eschews the Blakean vision of "Mental Things
are alone Real", favoring "the clear physical eye against the
erring brain" [*Prep*, p. 167]. The "objectified" and "solidified" perception that Blake's vortex contemns are precisely
the terms of Zukofsky's praise in his own poetics. Zukofsky
makes his discomfort with Blake apparent in *Bottom: On
Shakespeare*. [32] He quotes Blake:

A Spirit and a Vision are not, as the modern philosophy supposes, a cloudy vapour, or a Nothing: they are
organized and minutely articulated beyond all that the
mortal and perishing nature can produce. He who
does not imagine in stronger and better lineaments,
and in stronger and better light than his perishing
mortal eye can see does not imagine at all. [33]

31. Commentary by Harold Bloom in Erdman, p. 829. Italics added.
32. Louis Zukofsky, *Bottom: On Shakespeare*, Vol. 1 (Austin, TX: Humanities Research Center, 1963). Hereafter cited in the text as *Bot*.
33. William Blake, "A Descriptive Catalog", p. 37; in Erdman, p. 532.
Quoted, with several variations from Erdman's text, in *Bot*, pp. 199-200.

And follows, somewhat later, with this rejoinder: "Blake's reasons are those of an old man of a second season . . . [who is] more philosophical than 'unphilosophical' . . . " [*Bot*, p. 201]. Earlier, Zukofsky pertinently observes that "some poetry has been involved in philosophy to the hurt of its own eyes" [*Bot*, p. 114]. Indeed, Zukofsky has little patience for Blake's distrust of the "vegetative eye"—"The tree which moves some to tears of joy is in the Eyes of others [this is clearly addressed to Blake] only a Green thing that stands in the way" [*Bot*, p. 200]. This quarrel extends to prosody as well; Zukofsky shows little sympathy for Blake's aversion to ratio-nalized metrics as "Monotonous" and "bondage" [*Bot*, p. 204].

Zukofsky opposes eye to the shortcomings of mind [*Bot*, p. 268], while Blake finds only ratio and logic in the eye. "That it is best to actually look with the eyes—otherwise reason is not happy love; that thoughts without the eyes' judgments are strays" [*Bot*, p. 267]. " . . . only clear eyes see" [*Bot*, p. 190]. "When reason judges with eyes love and mind are one" [*Bot*, p. 215]. "[W]hen the seen object that causes the song blacks out, the singing soon tends to stop—and then, only words without ground?" [*Bot*, p. 38]. And over and over again in *Bottom*, Shakespeare's "No tongue! all eyes! be silent!"

Othello would seem to be a story that belies the reliance on the eyes; Othello's tragedy is the demand he makes for "ocular proof". Zukofsky, however, remarks that "Othello with eyes too strong or too weak was moved to stare or pry into unreason" [*Bot*, p. 175], as if sight could ever be so chaste as not to pry or stare. Othello's problem is not a failure to see but, as Cavell argues, a failure to acknowledge the conditions of sight, that is, trust and love.

Othello plays out the insistence on lens-bound sight to its lethal end—to make a thing "hold still you have to kill it" as Foreman points out. He is doomed by virtue of demanding an objectified sight when love could be enough. "Weeping timely eyes that misinterpret", Zukofsky says [*Bot*, p. 309]: so all the more human eyes.

> Othello. Villain, be sure thou prove my love a whore,
>   Be sure of it; give me the ocular proof
>   Or by the worth of man's eternal soul
>   Thou hadst better been born a dog
>   Than answer my waked wrath!
>
> Iago.   Is't come to this.
>
> Othello. Make me see't; or, at least, so prove it.
>   That probation bear no hinge or loop
>   To hang a doubt on; or woe upon the life!
>
> [III.iii.359-367]

Zukofsky makes only oblique reference to this passage [*Bot*, p. 325] but quotes another about the "proof": "The object poisons sight; let it be hid" [V.ii.364], which despite the possible Blakean interpretation, Zukofsky takes as the "want to see with the good of eyes" [*Bot*, p. 309].

Othello's eyes make their object—Desdemona—into an "objectification" at "perfect rest", to use Zukofsky's terms for his poetics in "An Objective" [*Prep*, pp. 12-13]:

> Whiter skin of hers than snow
> And smooth, as monumental alabaster
>
> [V.ii.4-5]

Desdemona, cast into stone, is a *solid* sight to look at, not mutable flesh to respond to:

> A statue, a stone, is something whose existence is
> fundamentally open to ocular proof. A human being is
> not. The two bodies lying together . . . on their bridal
> bed and death sheets . . . form an emblem of this fact,
> the truth of skepticism. . . .[34]

What is lacking from Zukofsky's over 400 page valorization of "physical sight" is any biological, ideological, or
psychological material on the structures of sight. There are
many different types of seeing—perpectives, motives, exchanges, observations—not one "true" one, un"betrayed"
by mind [see *Bot*, pp. 336 and 304]. Despite his remark that
he had "done away with the theory of knowledge" [35] in
Bottom, his theory of sight is purely metaphysical and
naively neopositivist at that.

Zukofsky's *Bottom* is filled with a nostalgia for a primal
world of instant, unmediated perception, severing eyes from
erring mind and memory. His concept of this purified sight
is like a partial version of Freud's model of the perception-
consciousness apparatus in "A Note on the Mystic Writing
Pad". [36] The pad is a device made of a slab of dark brown
resin overlaid with a thin transparent sheet of celluloid.
Marks made by a pointed stylus become visible because the
depressions in the celluloid are pressed into the resin slab.
The marks are erased by pulling up the oversheet. Zukofsky
seems to trust only the immediate marks made visible on the
writing pad—"the system of Pcpt-Cs [which] forms no

34. Stanley Cavell, *The Claim of Reason* (New York: Oxford University,
1979), p. 476. Cavell's remarks on *Othello* begin on p. 463.
35. Interview with L. S. Dembo, *Contemporary Literature* 10:2, (Madison:
1969).
36. Sigmund Freud, *Collected Papers*, trans. Alix and James Strachey (New
York: Basic, 1959), XV:175.

permanent trace." Freud, however, points out that "a permanent trace of what was written is retained upon the wax slab itself and is legible in certain lights." He compares this to the unconscious, which is part of what Zukofsky calls the "erring brain that's no good" [*Prep*, p. 120].

While Zukofsky is attracted to the static world view of the early Wittgenstein (*Tractatus Logico-Philosophicus* is quoted extensively in *Bottom*), he seems unaware of Wittgenstein's total overthrow of this sort of atemporal antiepistemology in his later writings. As David Melnick writes:

> Zukofsky [shares with] Spinoza and the early Witt-
> genstein [who are] the coordinates of his argument,
> . . . as with Shakespeare, fears of chance and change,
> i.e. of Time itself. [Again: "weeping timely eyes that
> misinterpret"!] Like them, but unlike Shakespeare, he
> deals with Time by not dealing with it, by denying its
> reality, by making it into an unfortunate and self-
> deceptive quirk of mind. [37]

Still, it is hard to take *Bottom* at face value; its resonances, like Bottom's Dream, makes it bottomless. The title of the book both suggests that there is a bottom line—eyes—and that only an ass would "go about to expound" *that*, which is "past the wit of a man to say" [*Bot*, p. 9]. Like Shakespeare's Bottom, Zukofsky's *Bottom* would show a way to make reason and love friends again as a precondition for sight. The problem is that this sight, even if understood meta-phorically to include insight, is characterized as a kind of triumph over words. "Words merely show that it takes time

37. David Melnick, "The 'Ought' of Seeing—Zukofsky's *Bottom*", in *Maps* No. 5 (Shippensburg, PA: 1973), p. 58.

for human eyes to grow into an Eye not always I (apparently), but that all metaphysics falls back on the human source whose assurance is only I" [*Bot*, p. 215]. Rather, words *significantly* show that ears everywhere inform eyes always I's, in the plural, *us*. Zukofsky's argument is all the more striking when the source for his eye = I formulation is understood as a reference to the "non-psychological I" in the *Tractatus*, which immediately precedes Wittgenstein's famous equation of positivism and solipsism: "5.64: Here we see that solipsism strictly carried out coincides with pure realism. The I in solipsism shrinks to an extensionless point and there remains the reality co-ordinated with it" [*Bot*, p. 52].

If one didn't know Zukofsky's poetry, and had read only *Bottom*, it might seem that he would be involved with the direct treatment of the objects of perception, such as in the two Williams poems quoted above. Yet nothing could be further from the case. Despite his tenaciously "objectivist" poetics, his works present some of the most realized alternatives to the poetry of sight in modern American writing. (Indeed, *Bottom* may be read more profitably as an exemplary poetics than as an antiepistemological tract; in this sense, it can be seen as a companion text to *"A"*, illustrating at a grosser level of collage the technique of finely milled textual citations that is central to Zukofsky's other work.)

Zukofsky never confused words with physical eyes, indeed the disassociation of language and sight is the theme of *Bottom*. The experience of sight, as Piaget points out, is to imagine grasping the object "all at once". *"No tongue! all eyes! be silent!* But no artist in words dares act the six words of this command, unless he desires not to exist" [*Bot*, p. 77].

Writing, inevitably durational, can achieve a state of "rested totality" (all-at-onceness) only in terms of overall form: "objectification—the apprehension satisfied completely as to the appearance of the art form as an object. . . . [An] arrangement, into one apprehended unit. . . . [I]n other words, the resolving of words and their ideation into structure" [*Prep*, p. 13]. In other words, we have a displacement of rationalized and totalized space—what Piaget calls the construction of "objectified and spatialized causality"— onto form: Zukofsky's "totality of perfect rest".

"Desire for what is objectively perfect" [*Prep*, p. 12]: some way out of the flux of instability—two world wars, the Russian Revolution and its Stalinist subversion, etc. So there's Zukofsky's hierarchy: gas's the worst (which is thinking: intellectual things!) (though it too can have its beauty); liquid's next (which is music); and solid's best. And the most solid thing for poetry, the most like the obtruding objects of sight's contents, is objectification, "intending a *solid object*"—the primacy of the single image of the poem as structure ["About the Gas Age", *Prep*].

But the transformation of object-ive sight to objective form doesn't dissolve the problem of rationalized uniformity: monocular vision becomes monoplanar surface, atemporal space becomes idealized form. Both the objectively perfect and rested totality seem less Utopian than machinic, anti-historical rather than materialist. Or perhaps it's that "a solid object" values the monolithic and the austere while forgetting that fragility and mutability have their own perfections.

> Like an evening evoking the spectrum of violet
> A philosopher practicing scales on his piano
> A woman writing a note and tearing it up

> It is not the premise that reality
> Is a solid. It may be a shade that traverses
> A dust, a force that traverses a shade.
>
> [Stevens, pp. 488-89]

But perhaps, after all, Zukofsky's "sight" is visionary, even Messianic, as Walter Benjamin's timeless time of history dissolving; perhaps Paradise is the utopian moment of Bottom's dream—"The eye of man hath not heard, the ear of man hath not seen, man's hand is not able to taste, his tongue to conceive, nor his heart to report . . ." [*Bot*, p. 9]. As Zukofsky quotes the early Wittgenstein, "There is indeed the inexpressible. This *shows* itself; it is the mystical" [*Bot*, p. 84]. Radically limited by being in time and of time, words by song become solid, solace for the loss of sight of the world. So that poetry's vision is word's music, that liquid, frozen—jellied—into solid form.

9. REFLECTION

I've contrasted vision with sight, reflection with insight. By reflection I mean Laura (Riding) Jackson's "visibility of blindedness—these thoughts",[38] so much like Stevens' "visibility of thought / In which hundreds of eyes, in one mind, see at once" [p. 488]; I mean language turning upon itself; I mean the dissolving of appearance into thought and of thought into energy and of energy into matter. Or else, "the absence of imagination . . . itself to be imagined" [Stevens, p. 503].

Reflection, however, has not always been an easy course for its American practitioners. Emblematic of this unease or

38. Laura (Riding) Jackson, "By a Crude Rotation," in *The Poems of Laura Riding* (New York: Persea, 1980), p. 107.

ambivolence (Steve McCaffery's word for *wanting* two things) is Zukofsky's quest for the "solid object" and his associated distrust of thought and mind. "Thinking's the lowest rung / No one'll believe I feel this" (though he adds, "I can't help thinking") [*Prep*, p. 169]. His perception of his time as "the gas age" suggests the loss of an immutable reality, a solid ground, that poetry must try, as best it can, to regain.

> For the thought as thought, in so far as it is the remotest phase of sense and imagining is Something that is literally much ado about Nothing. The actual thought (distinguished from expressed concept) cannot, for the sake of demonstration, be said even 'to graze,' since it affects not to touch and never shows to, the eyes. . . . Words merely show that it takes time for human eyes to grow into an Eye. . . ." [*Bot*, p. 215]

It is not apparent how the "inner thought" is to be distinguished from the outer—"expressed"—"concept"; we get here the dualism exorcised repeatedly by Wittgenstein in *Philosophical Investigations*. Thought is not removed from "sense and imagining" but inextricably interpenetrates them.

It is a measure of how deep the roots of anti-intellectualism go in American writing that a self-identified intellectual poet such as Zukofsky should have formulated such a position. It certainly attests to a commitment to a (make-shift) materialism, justifiably fueled by the idealist obfuscations of the dominant political and philosophical thought of the period. In this context, Zukofsky's injunction "that it is best to look with the eyes" is a sharp rebuke to the rhetorical vagaries of a poetry lost in the staleness of its own etiquettes, a call to break with literariness and see—and hear!—anew. That is, Zukofsky's ambivalence was no doubt a necessary response to the vapid intellectualization of the academic verse of the period: Eliot's influence (the "great disaster for our letters" as Williams called it) and the rise of the New Criticism. There was an understandable desire to break through the constraints of tradition-bound forms and decorous ideas so as to empower and revivify the language of poetry.

"The nature of Eliot's influence was to emphasize the materials of literature and literary tradition rather than the materials of everyday life. Williams was reacting against poems being removed from life and pushed back into the classroom" [Ray DiPalma, in conversation]. The American academy, generally reductivist in its ideologies, has been one of the major adversaries of thought and reason. Ratio-nality, as Blake points out, is the suppression of the mind. Those displaced from the university for "making it new"[39] may well have encouraged the false equation of the failure of the academy with the failure of mind. The desire for greater *tangibility* of language or image was a powerful response to the dominant anemic verse of the time, whose practitioners declared their audience as the culturally and intellectually elite, so disenfranchising other languages and audiences. The alternative, as defined by Robert Kelly, was

> a poem that means something because it is no longer *about* something, but *is* something; but, and this is all-important, a poem that, as a thing, does not come to

39. See Michael Davidson's account of ideological discrimination in university creative writing programs, "Notes on Writing and Production", *Paper Air* 3:1 (Blue Bell, PA: 1982).

> exist aesthetically and in remoteness, as a thing would
> in a museum, unthinged, but as a thing would exist,
> and possess meaning, in a world of living [people]. As a
> chair possesses meaning. Not as furniture, but as a
> place to sit down. [40]

Nonetheless, the straitjacket of received forms, or the intellectualization of neat literary irony or elusive high tone or coy historical reference or discursive mannerism represent not the hallmarks of thought but its effacement. Blake, for instance, never considered his attack on Newton to be an attack on "intellectual things". And his critique of optical sight was against its inherent abstraction and aimed toward greater tangibility and particularity. "For a Tear is an Intellectual Thing" [E, p. 48].

Reflection may also be associated with insecurity, uncertainty, and frailty—"negative capability"—in comparison with "objectivist" concerns for the solid object and the thing seen. Discomfort with vulnerability and mutability is a commonly "male"-identified value. Unfortunately, the Pound-Williams [sic] tradition is not noted for its understanding of sexual politics. Thus, a poet working within that tradition and instinctively sensing its limitations might well be ambivolent about a number of theoretical and practical problems but be unable to articulate the nature of the ambivolence. Such articulations are possible in response to the development and publication of the feminist criticism of the past 20 years. It is noteworthy, however, that the poetics of vision and reflection as practiced by Stein or (Riding)

---

40. Robert Kelly, "Postscript II", *A Controversy of Poets*, ed. Paris Leary and Robert Kelly (Garden City: Doubleday, 1965), p. 564.

Jackson or H.D. did not involve the ambivolence under consideration here.

Perhaps, again, it was the intellectual difficulty presented by Zukofsky's work that led him, as a defensive stand, to adopt a poetics oddly in tune with American "show me" pragmatism. Too often, American writers have boxed themselves into a middle ground between "effete" reflection and "schizoid" vision. The "ratio-nalist" manifestations of this fear of thought are the comfortably furnished landscapes and confessed selves often found in such venues as *The New Yorker*. The "antirationalist" manifestation takes "thought" as "prohibiting emotion", as if they were two discrete objects trying to occupy the same space. But the *heroics* of personality, or the *everydayness* of everyday voice or thought, only disguises the intellectuality of the medium through which these things are expressed. It is this disguising, and not the expression, that is the problem.

A writer who seems singularly unambivolent about the intangibility of the poetics of reflection is William Bronk: "We are made afraid not to believe the fraud / of this world: believe or be lost" [p. 129].[41] "Landscape is metaphor / and only metaphor. But oh, I have loved it so" [p. 142]. Bronk's radical skepticism—the real world is beyond what we can say or know [p. 145]—is only one possibility for a reflective poetry. Bronk also holds out the possibility that the material of our not knowing may itself have something to say. ". . . the unbelievable, which nothing believes, / says something. Listen. Says itself" [p. 129].

41. William Bronk, *Life Supports* (San Francisco: North Point, 1981). Page citations in this paragraph are from this text.

10. SHADOW

"I am writing in shadows" is one of Silliman's last pictures
in "Blue", a self-portrait not of himself but of his text.
Shadows are the space between sentences, a reminder that
the text does not represent a single atemporal sight but
enacts a duration of meanings. "It is not the premise that
reality is a solid. It may be a shade that traverses a dust, a
force that traverses a shade."

Shadows are the reflection of thought into the world; the
sign not of the optical image but of imagination. Shadows
suggest an indefinite and intangible visual world—an
obscuring of borders, of edges of objects.

>The eye "roves"
>back and forth, as
>indictment catches up?
>
>If shadows tatoo
>the bare shelf,
>they enter by comparison? . . .
>
>Think in order
>to recall
>what the striking thing
>
>resembles.
>(So impotently
>loved the world

[Rae Armantrout] [42]

Despite Armantrout's Bronk-like skepticism here ("impo-
tently") the indeterminacy (*viz.* the question marks) is the
first stage of "admission" (the poem's title). The eye has a

42. Rae Armantrout, "Admission", *Precedence* (Providence: Burning
Deck, 1985), p. 20.

limited orbit, hardly "roams" at all. The world's in shadows, comparison, thought, and memory; only out of those can a "thing / resemble".

"Only the imagination is real!" says Williams in the coda to "Asphodel", as if to set the record straight toward the end: no things but in time. [43] ". . . and there came to me / just now / the knowledge of / the tyranny of the image / and how / men / in their designs / have learned / to shatter it / whatever it may be, / that the trouble / in their minds / shall be quieted. . . . " [44] This movement in Williams, decisively away from the static, ahistorical "thing seen" is the theme of "Shadows". [45] "The hollows of the eye"—that is merely physical eyes, unschooled by language, by memory, by duration—"are unpeopled. . . . Memory / is liver than sight. / A man / looking out, / seeing the shadows." Shadows—an underworld of imagination in which the muted differentiation of figure and ground is source *(stuff)*— beyond uncertainty and its attendant fear—for freedom from the contortion of language to conjure discrete objects.

Apollinaire, fifty years earlier, had also written a poem called "Shadow" ["Ombre", *Calligrammes*]. In this poem, the inscription of language is the negation of light: the world of objects is mediated by our inscriptions, that by means of shade differentiation rescues that world from the blinding whiteness—the memorylessness—of light.

> Shadow ink of the sun
> Text of my light
> Caisson of regret
> A god who humiliates himself

43. Williams, *Pictures from Brueghel*, p. 179.
44. "Tribute to the Painters", ibid., p. 137.
45. Ibid., pp. 150-52.

As in a creation myth in the *Upanishads*, the world comes to be multiple by the self-rending of a one. In this moment, language and shadow share their birth.

11. PICTURELESS WORDS

I began this text with silence, the power of pictures without words: how pictures show. I'll end with blankness or blindedness—pictureless words. Not that any of the senses can ever be split-off from the others: that is the myth of a languageless world to which Wittgenstein refers in saying: "A *picture* held us captive. And we could not get outside of it, for it lay in our language and language seemed to repeat it to us inexorably."[46] In*hear*ing in a poetics of vision or relection (as if to counter a visualist frame of reference in these terms) is a poetics of sound. Words returned to a sonorousness that does not require the validation of fixed images, of sight and insight, nor deny its common roots with visibility.

In the shadows, in the acknowledgement of the impermanence of objects, that sight in time is blurred, is to be found an end to the deafening repetition of either/or. Blake's "mental things" have never excluded the "solid objects" of the physical world. The intangibility of reflection is the doorway to the tangibility of language. "From above, things are materializing in the ears" [Ted Greenwald]. [47] "Delicate

46. Ludwig Wittgenstein, *Philosophical Investigations*, trans. G. E. M. Anscombe (New York: Macmillan, 1958), §115.
47. Ted Greenwald, "Fab You Luss Queens (Gaping)", *Poetry Project Newsletter*, December 1982 (New York), p. 8.

and unperturbed / a slithering iridescence / that would be inscrutable / were it not fact" [DiPalma].[48]

It is night in which day grows. "I'd had / A chance to tell rock from shadow, from this darker thing // And make a shadow that was alive and was aware / Of what it's doing, dodging / A reflection of light, it touches / A deeper shelter . . ." [Peter Seaton].[49] "A wooden syntax of shadow forms a pillar of its own. A highly syntax confusing both image and word and detail and notation. A shape which is rounded off so that the corners fall away. Blank and another ordering attention paying off. Blank intensity stares" [Diane Ward].[50]

Or that with poetry we / try other than to / set down or / sound the way / of the world / we see / and still are / in.

48. Ray DiPalma, "The Bed", *Two Poems* (Windsor, VT: Awede Press, 1982).
49. Peter Seaton, "Need from a Wound Would Do It", *Paris Review* No. 86 (New York: Winter, 1982).
50. Diane Ward, "Approximately", in *Never Without One* (New York: Roof, 1984), p. 4.

Three / Reading, Person, Philosophy

THE OBJECTS OF MEANING: READING CAVELL READING WITTGENSTEIN

Now I know I have a heart because it's broken.

In the opening pages of *The Claim of Reason*, Stanley Cavell points to the splitting of the philosophical tradition of the West into a British and American mode and a Continental mode as somehow analogous to the split within our own (one) culture between philosophy and literature. That these schisms everywhere inform Cavell's work signals an appreciation that for him they are emblematic of even deeper recurring schisms in the fabric of human life and our conceptions of it, of feeling (or being) split off from a world which we are wholly inside of. Cavell's work, it seems to me, is largely absorbed with giving an accounting of these

The Claim of Reason: Wittgenstein, Skepticism, Morality, and Tragedy by Stanley Cavell (New York: Oxford University, 1979)—cited in the text as *Claim. Senses of Walden* by Stanley Cavell (New York: Viking, 1972)—cited in the text as *Senses. Anti-Oedipus: Capitalism and Schizophrenia* by Gilles Deleuze and Félix Guattari, trans. Robert Hurley, Mark Seem, and Helen R. Lane (New York: Viking, 1977)—cited in the text as *Anti-Oedipus.*

165

schisms; his sense of what constitutes an account is, for me, the place where he is able to occupy a ground held in common by both philosophy and literature.

Much of Cavell's work (it is an affinity with Barthes) consists of giving accountings of—reading—texts (i.e., written accounts). (Some exceptions to this would be the conceptual remarks in *The World Viewed* whose subject is how to read films as texts and those in *Must We Mean What We Say?* justifying reading "ordinary language" as texts.) It is not incidental to the importance this practice has for him that the skeptical problems that are central to his writing largely turn on how to read the world as a kind of text, and more significantly, how to *read* (and how to account for) each other. In a sense, his view is that text precedes the world, or anyway any one of our arrivals into it, that one's view of the world is bound up inextricably with a particular language ("textuality") that we live within. His sense of schism between philosophy and literature, it seems to me, is partly played out by the practice of reading texts as a way of generating them; his work is a sort of accounting of accounts.

Cavell's use of texts relates to the use of collage and juxtaposition in more strictly literary writing, especially to the use of prior texts, of pervasively citational language, in Pound, Zukofsky and Olson, up to the present. (Cavell himself points out that his quotes from Wittgenstein in the last section of *The Claim of Reason* are not interpretive but citational [p. xiii].) In this respect, Cavell has at hand the full dimensions of what David Antin has described as "the hyperspace of modernist composition". While it would be extremely misleading to say that Cavell is creating poetic texts by collage—it would mistake both his genre and his style—it is to the point that his compositional method is one of ordering and arrangement more than exposition, that he is aware that the creation of the world, as much as writing, is a matter of *succession*, of conjunction and disjunction, of production, more than approximation and reflection [see *Senses of Walden*, p. 110]. His style, accordingly, is not really deductive and expository—although it is filled with arguments—as much as *invocative*. Whatever answer, what authority, he provides comes not from argument but from sounding the words to see what they tell, to make their resonances tangible, and, specifically, with the realization that we literally make the world come into being by giving voice to it, by our (re)calls. (*words, words / as if all / worlds were there*—Robert Creeley, "A Token".)

I also do not mean to suggest that Cavell has created works of literature rather than works of philosophy. Insofar as there is a conflict, Cavell will certainly have to be seen as writing philosophy—the paths are that separate, the choice does get made. In *Walden*, Thoreau writes, not, I think, ironically, "There are nowadays professors of philosophy, but not philosophers. Yet it is admirable to profess because it was once admirable to live." Cavell's work plays out some of the depth of this remark in terms of each of our, and so our culture's, self-division. I think Cavell proposes that *Walden* and *Philosophical Investigations* are two texts in which this division, as well as the one between philosophy and literature, finally do not take hold. But our lives are not whole, and we have, so to say, philosophical and poetic responsibilities; one will not necessarily acquit the other.

Cavell does not put forward assertions. The truth of what he says is finally left to whether it holds for you ("to check its sentences against our convictions" [*Senses*, p. 62]). This is the significance of the fact that his work, especially *The Claim of Reason*, is riddled with questions. It is ourselves, our ways of making sense, that are being interrogated. His conception of philosophy shares with poetry the project of increasing an awareness of conditions—of where we are agreed, of what we have convened on; of the structures and grammars we live in; of how the syntaxes and grammars we create in turn create the world. To tell how it is with us, to reveal our attuning (which is often hidden). Cavell wishes to bring philosophy back from the self-conception of being "Recording Angel, outside the world, neither affecting it nor affected by it, taking stock" [*Claim*, p. 204]. His literary power is to bring forward the predicaments that certain kinds of reasoning lead to with all their nuances and all their conviction—what gets criticized, by the profession, as his "literariness"; as if philosophy had to be removed from the forms and textures of life—our embeddedness in it—before it could claim to be philosophy. Rather than "argument" out of context, Cavell makes the case for immersion inside moods, fears, hopes—not to make philosophy literature but to call philosophy back to its sources of judgment. For philosophy cannot be literature as long as our minds do not sit comfortably in our bodies—that is one mark of our condition. Or, perhaps: that the natural condition of philosophy is to aspire to ("reunification" with) literature and that of literature to aspire to the power of philosophy to speak to and of our lives.

Reading Cavell can seem like a game of tag through intellectual history, citations coming with dizzying speed and aphoristic brevity. Actually, Cavell cites less than two dozen authors over and again throughout his writing: those who for him constitute an alive part of the accepted British and American tradition—Plato, Descartes, Hume, Mill, Wittgenstein, and J. L. Austin; a major part of the Continental tradition—Kant, Hegel, Rousseau, Luther, Kierkegaard, Marx, Nietzsche, Freud and Heidegger (it is worth noting that Cavell has so far made no mention of recent French thought or of the Frankfurt School, despite the affinity with his own work I suggest here); a claimed American tradition—Thoreau and Emerson; Blake and Wordsworth; Beckett, here by virtue of the long essay on *Endgame*; and Shakespeare, especially *King Lear* and *Othello*, tragedies which for Cavell play out essential features of the philosophical problems most on his mind. (The absence of women from this list is a measure of the failure of these traditions and an indication of what we cannot rely on them for.) The assumption is that the history of our writing and thought, fully as much as any other kind of history, must be claimed if it is not to be lost, and that the only way to make that claim is to actively put that history to use. If as a culture, as a society, we find no consensus on a single tradition that marks our heritage and discloses our alignments and misalignments, then it is up to each of us—*bricoleurs*—to make our own; not, however, in our own name but in the name of whatever socious for which we wish to stand. "The claim of reason": a claim *on* us, hence responsibility, as much as the stake reason declares to be its rightful territory.

Reading *The Claim of Reason* is not as difficult as some of Cavell's other works in respect to name references, since the fugue of citations starts more slowly and the terms for which they stand are more readily graspable; it is a good place to learn the tunes for which each reference stands, to begin an education in these texts. But even given that, reading Cavell can be irritating: it can seem a bit like going through a catalogue of the great issues of modern civilization, after a while (or at first before you get used to it) the style can feel ponderous, given Cavell's weighty, almost Talmudic, sense of responsibility toward these issues—as if the meticulousness of self-consciousness and the thoroughness in acknowledging all aspects that come to consciousness constitute a pact with himself for good faith. (Or is this unease an unease with the demands of the project itself?) You might call this an occupational hazard.

The Claim of Reason begins with a full-scale account of Wittgenstein's view of language, knowledge, and skepticism in *Philosophical Investigations*. Cavell sees Wittgenstein neither as a behaviorist who imagines that all we have to go on in making a claim to know something—the recurring example is that another person is in pain—is the outward (public) manifestations—"criteria"—the "pain behavior"; nor as a proponent of the private language argument, imagining that the pain is forever hidden within each person, a private sensation unknowable to others; nor, finally, as suggesting that the "outer criteria" indicate the presence of an "inner process" (i.e., the existence of the pain—pain being imagined to "accompany" pain behavior). Rather, Cavell suggests that all these pictures are, according to Wittgenstein, a distortion of the activity of knowing, which has its meaning only in use in the context of a language; that, in these three pictures, the limitations of the human activity of knowing are transformed into an intellectual puzzle. In one of the accounts, the pain behavior is

thought to *accompany* the pain, while Wittgenstein insists
rather that one is seen via the other, that criteria do not
indicate the existence of anything but are rather what we
"go on", our grounds. They are not signifiers referring us to
some projected objects (signifieds); not "behavior" being
"observed" but action being understood. In another of the
three accounts, Wittgenstein is misunderstood to be a
behaviorist rejecting "inner process" (the signified) as a
mirage, believing that only behavior is knowable. But what
Wittgenstein is rejecting is rather the false picture of
"outer" and "inner" ("signifier" and "signified") that is at
the root of seeing behavior as a surrogate for the sensation.
Behaviorism goes wrong in accepting the "outer/inner"
picture and merely rejecting the "inner", leaving only an
empty shell of behavior, isolated criteria that are no more
than trappings. The third account, the private language
argument, is the flip side of behaviorism, simply taking it in
reverse: I can only get as far as the other person's behavioral
manifestations, her sensations are forever hidden from me.
"If I speak of a fiction," Wittgenstein writes, "then it is of a
grammatical fiction" [*Investigations*, §307]; for knowledge
does not tell us of the existence of anything. "Inner" and
"outer" are directions of relativity, like "above" and
"below": I feel my pain from the inside out, you see it from
the outside in. I know another is in pain by responding to it,
or, as Cavell repeatedly puts it, by acknowledging it. *(From
outside, it must have seemed / a wonder that it was / the inside* he
as me *saw / in the dark there*—Creeley, "Somewhere".)

The distortion is to imagine that knowledge has an
"object" outside of the "language games" of which it is a
part—that words refer to "transcendental signifieds", to use

an expression from another tradition, rather than being part
of a language which itself produces meaning in terms of its
grammar, its conventions, its "agreements in judgement".
Learning a language is not learning the names of things
outside language, as if it were simply a matter of matching
up signifiers with signifieds, as if signifieds already existed
and we were just learning new names for them (which seems
to be Augustine's picture in the opening quote of *Investigations*). Rather, we are initiated by language into a socious,
which is for us the world. So that the foundations of
knowledge are not so much based on a preexisting empirical
world as on shared conventions and mutual attunement. It is
this understanding of Wittgenstein's view of language that
leads Cavell to say that our conventions (grammar, codes,
territorialities, myths, rules, standards, criteria) are our
nature, that there is no gap between nature and culture,
between fact and convention. "This explicitly makes our
agreement in judgments, our attunement expressed through
criteria, agreement in valuing. So that what can be communicated, say a fact, depends on agreement in valuing"
[*Claim*, p. 91]. In this context, to speak of absolutes is to
speak outside language games, to construct a grammatical
fiction—it is to deny the human limitations of knowledge
(for example, in the pursuit of certainty or universality).
Wittgenstein's relation of grammar to "forms of life"
emphasizes that "human convention is not arbitrary but
constitutive of significant speech and activity...[that] mutual
understanding, and hence language, depends on nothing
more and nothing less than shared forms of life, call it our
mutual attunement or agreement in our criteria" [*Claim*,
p. 162].

Cavell argues against seeing Wittgenstein as refuting skepticism—all he "refutes" is the "transcendental illusion" [*Claim*, p. 231]. Indeed, the truth of skepticism is that there is meaning only "inside" our conventions, that it makes no sense to speak of meaning outside these contexts. That words have meaning not by virtue of universals, of underlying structures or rules, but in *use*, in—to use the expression of Gilles Deleuze and Félix Guattari—*desiring production*. ("...desire produces reality, or stated another way, desiring production is one and the same as social production" [*Anti-Oedipus*, p. 30].) For Cavell, skepticism is false insofar as it invalidates the claim to knowledge of "other minds" or "objects of the world"; wrong, that is, to take "metaphysical finitude as a failure of knowledge" [*Claim*, p. 473]; insofar, that is, as it takes certainty, or prediction and control, to be the sole basis for the claim to knowledge. (Jürgen Habermas, in *Knowledge and Human Interest*, usefully contrasts two forms of knowledge—the dialogic or hermeneutic and the monologic or scientific. He differentiates the two modes by their interest component, pointing to prediction and control as the knowledge-constitutive interest of the scientific mode.) Cavell also does not think that Wittgenstein is making an "ordinary language" refutation of skepticism. The ordinary language philosopher is as wrong to say, flatly, that we "just do" *know* the existence of the world (that this is what it "means" to know) as the traditional epistemologist is wrong to say we don't know. Both misunderstand the precarious conventionality of knowledge because they imagine knowledge always in terms of (knowing or not being able to know) "thing-in-themselves"; they fail to see that if that is what "knowing" is, our relation to the world-as-a-whole is

not one of knowing but of being in, of *acting* in (here is
where Cavell sees Heidegger and Wittgenstein as closest).
That, as Kant puts it, the limitations of knowledge are not
failures of it [*Claim*, p. 233 and *Senses*, p. 104]. (*It is as if we
want a sense of wetness apart from water itself* —Creeley, *A
Quick Graph.*)

At the basis of the human socious is the ceding of
skepticism so that society can take place. And the retreat
from the monsterousness of society is the abrogation of this
ceding. "The essential message of the idea of a social
contract is that political institutions require justification,
that they are absolutely without sanctity, that power over us
is held on trust from us, that institutions have no authority
other than we lend them, that we are their architects..."
[*Senses*, p. 81]. Such an abrogation can acknowledge these
basic conditions of human community and convention by
revolution (a reconvening, a reattunement) or by self-ban-
ishment (to live apart from ordinary human life, "without
appeal, without protest" [*Claim*, p. 459]). The refusal of this
acknowledgment is the refusal of reason itself, and so a form
of insanity. —It is with insanity, the other side of reason,
that Guattari and Deleuze wish us to be in touch so that we
do not misunderstand the bases of our social contracts. For
them, the schizophrenic is a process in which bands of
intensity flow through one like waves of energy, sheer
impulses, the self as it were collapsing into the world, at one
with it. These flows "disinvest the social field" by decoding,
deterritorializing, deconventionalizing. The "subject itself
is not at the center, which is occupied by the machine [by
desiring production], but on the periphery, with no fixed
identity, forever decentered, *defined* by the states through

which it passes" [*Anti-Oedipus*, p. 20]. This last compares interestingly with Cavell's account of "being next to " in Thoreau [*Senses*, pp. 103-106]—that we are in the world unselfconsciously as pure production and flow—existence— and that at the same time we front ourselves as spectators of our existence. "To suggest that one may stand there, stay there in a sane sense, is to suggest that the [being beside oneself] of which ecstasy speaks is my experience of my existence, my knowledge 'of myself as a human entity'...." This notion of doubleness, Cavell suggests, announces another truth of skepticism—that our relation to the externality of the world, of *"a world apart from me in which* objects are met", is not one of knowing but besideness.

The Claim of Reason, in the course of its reading of *Investigations*, also makes a full-scale case in opposition to the assumptions of the predominant tendency in professional philosophy in England and North America, that is, analytic philosophy. On this account, it may seem to those already sympathetic to Cavell's position that he spends an inordinate amount of time refuting what is obviously wrong from the first. I suspect Cavell, in part, may share that view, and it may partly explain why this work, a large section of which was written almost twenty years ago, has taken so long to come out. Cavell notes in his preface that he would not now attempt what I assume to be this aspect of the project, and others of his books, *The World Viewed* and *Senses of Walden*, are in no way directly concerned with this sort of critique, a fact also true of most of *Must We Mean What We Say?*. Of course from the point of view of the profession ("professional lives, frightening matters" [*Claim*, p. 5]) he cannot be said to be beating a dead horse, but then, as Mary Mothersill's

sympathetic but uncomprehending response shows [*The
Journal of Philosophy*, January 30, 1975], the profession has
not really taken Cavell to be one of its own. In any case, I
think one can take delight in seeing demons of our culture
exorcised; the importance of the project will depend on how
deep you think the particular demons of analytic philosophy
go.

In its parochialization and technologicization, professional
philosophy in America and Britain has in this century
increasingly removed itself from the broad social and cultural
involvement that characterizes much Continental philosophy
as well as prespecialization practices in its own tradition.
Wittgenstein may be the only person to emerge out of
analytic philosophy as a major cultural figure. But certainly
his work remains—as an aspect of Cavell's work—esoteric,
or at least with an eye to a particular brand of "professional
philosophic" esoteria. (One might wonder what the choice
is: Is the profession of art or literature any less limited and
specific, any less marginalized?) In *The Claim of Reason*,
Cavell has chosen to speak to the profession: to make it more
aware of itself. And he has tried to bring out the forms of
madness that centrally underly its project—what he calls
"soul-blindness"—"to reclaim the human self from its denial
and neglect by modern philosophy" [*Claim*, p. 149].

Scientism is the demon that haunts analytic philosophy—
the belief of science that its empirical method of prediction
and control of phenomena provides the only legitimate
claim to knowledge and certainty: the cult of technology
(occultism is also a cult). The problem arises over and
again—and not only in terms of the analysis of knowledge: it
is by now an all too familiar litany. Behaviorism is perhaps

just the most overt case, but then there is the reduction of motivation to Oedipus in orthodox psychoanalysis ("so that's what it was, so it's my father, my mother"), the statistics of "value free" sociology, the universalized binaryness of structuralist interpretation ("challenging all beliefs, rising above all images, and from the realm of mother and father retaining only functions" [*Anti-Oedipus*, p. 111]). The project is to be found in all attempts to give a symbolic order of representation in place of the real ("translation betrayal"), all attempts to invest meaning in a world pre-existing—separated from—the world that comes into being with the production of the language that we use.

Cavell's extensive puzzling over the problem of other minds leads always to the fact that analytic rationalism ends up posing as an intellectual problem a fundamental condition of human life—and denies the limitations of human knowledge as well as its location. (In the final section of *The Claim of Reason* Cavell sketches this out in terms of tragedy.) The gap between knowledge and the world (between nature and culture) gets created when we remove knowing from its *use* in *context*, from desiring production. "In Wittgenstein's view the gap between the mind and the world is closed, or the distortion between them straightened, in the appreciation and acceptance of particular forms of human life, human 'convention'. This implies that the *sense* of gap originates in an attempt, or wish, to escape (to remain a 'stranger' to, 'alienated' from) those shared forms of life, to give up the responsibility of their maintenance" [*Claim*, p. 105]. The demons go as deep as Oedipus; as deep as the perverted desires of rationality; as deep as the desiring impulses in rationality for certainty, for a world of representation beyond

178 The Objects of Meaning

the world. They are in ourselves and we put them into the world. The world is inextricable from ourselves.

"It is not the slumber of reason that engenders monsters, but vigilant, insomniac rationality" [*Anti-Oedipus*, p. 112]. A rationality that starts with the idea of representation ("universal" "underlying") and constantly translates the world back into this shadow world: just the picture Wittgenstein wishes to exorcise by starting *Investigations* with a quote from Augustine in which he imagines learning a language as a child to be like learning a second language, translating from the old already-given names, as if he came into the world with an already full-blown language. The erection of the Theater of Representation in the place of production. "The unconscious is an orphan and produces itself within the identity of nature and man.... [It] poses no problem of meaning, simply problems of use. The question put by desire is not 'what does it mean' but *'how does it work?'''* [*Anti-Oedipus*, pp. 49 and 109]. "The human body is the best picture of the human soul—not...because it represents the soul but because it expresses it" [*Claim*, p. 344].

Cavell argues that we must "live out our skepticism", that to avoid its truths may be to drive oneself crazy or, in any case, to remove oneself from human community. It is interesting, in this respect, to compare Deleuze's and Guattari's vision of the madness of capitalism with Cavell's account of the madness to which philosophy can be brought that is at the center of Cavell's devastating portrait of Charles Stevenson's positivist moral theory. Stevenson argues to the effect that all moral views are mere attitudes and persuasion, that no valid basis exists for choosing among them, thereby, Cavell points out, overthrowing morality fully as much as those (he cites Marx and Nietzsche and Freud) who have found our moral codes wanting as a way of regulating our lives. "When [the] others have undertaken this task [of subverting the concept of morality itself], they have recognized the enormity of their claim; and in accepting personal responsibility they have gone mad, or to prison, or into various forms of exile [or, I would add, on to form new societies]. It is a relatively new idea that the claim itself is a relatively neutral one, taken in the service of advanced ideas of logic and scientific method, the dictates of reason" [*Claim*, p. 279]. For Guattari and Deleuze, the madness of the deterritorializing and deconventionalizing processes of capitalism mocks the madness of these processes in the "schizo"; in the latter case these processes are activated with full force, releasing flows of desiring production (Nietzsche and Marx are again exemplary), while in the case of capitalism they are immediately, to use Cavell's word, *neutralized*, or as Guattari and Deleuze have it, *axiomatized*, as it were reterritorialized without the new territory having any location, recodified without any culture (form of life) of which the coding is a part—making us, that is, impotent in the face of action, groundless, rootless, stripped of our senses and judgments, in Cavell's phrase, "sealed off from the world".

As to the positive possibilities that Deleuze and Guattari hold out on the model of "schizo"—Cavell is as much at pains as they to distinguish these two forms of madness, the one in the quest to free the human as fully as possible to itself, the other the "denial of the human", or anyway human society or morality, in the avoidance of "metaphysical finitude". (Deleuze and Guattari call the latter paranoia—being beside oneself in an insane way—and distinguish it from the schizophrenic process—they are not talking about "clinical entities"—seeing paranoia as an experience of distance and separation, of being next to your experiences but not being able to feel them happening, occurring.) "For, of course," Cavell says, "there are those for whom the denial of the human *is* the human.... It would be why Nietzsche undertook to identify the task of overcoming the human with the task of overcoming the denial of the human; which implies overcoming the human not through mortification but through joy, say ecstasy" [*Claim*, p. 474]. This, indeed, promises a grounding for the project of *Anti-Oedipus*, in its search for "nonhuman" "machinic" drives and in its crude terminology of "desiring machines" and "bodies without organs". Cavell locates this impulse as "the affirmation of the body" [*Claim*, p. 474]. If the project is to be criticized, in its manifestation in *Anti-Oedipus*, I think it would be along the lines that Guattari and Deleuze do not sufficiently acknowledge how deep our conventions go. What makes Wittgenstein unique is that his work has so fully investigated how conventions (grammars, rules, codes) allow for meaning rather than focussing primarily on endpoints of their inscription. If Wittgenstein and Cavell seem more cautionary and conservative than Deleuze and Guattari, it is because they locate value totally within the context of use and production in the language/socious while Deleuze and Guattari locate value totally within the deconventionalizing, deterritorializing flows of desiring production itself. In this way, they are more willing to see the "human" continuously overthrown by a regime of desiring production, while Cavell might say that there can only be value insofar as these flows are concretized into a world, territorialized. In addition,

Cavell shares with Wittgenstein a general silence on the specific nature of the interests—on a political and economic level—of many of our conventions, in sharp contrast to Guattari and Deleuze, whose analysis is filled with such vital specifics and who make a far sharper appeal for the necessity of change.

I want, finally, to briefly compare Wittgenstein's views (in Cavell's reading) with those of the Jacques Derrida of *Of Grammatology*. For whatever similiarities there may be— specifically in respect to getting rid of the idea that words refer to metaphysical absolutes, to universals, to "transcendental signifieds" rather than being part of a grammar of shared conventions, a grammatology—the two seem fundamentally irreconcilable. What Derrida ends up transforming to houses of cards—shimmering traces of life insubstantial as elusive—Wittgenstein locates as *meaning*, with the full range of intention, responsibility, coherence, and possibility for revolt against or madness without. In Wittgenstein's accounting, one is not left sealed off from the world with only "markings" to "decipher" but rather *located* in a world with meanings to *respond to*. It is no wonder that Derrida is unable to come to terms with Marx. His is the philosophy of paranoia in the sense I point to above. Indeed, Derrida ends up in a situation comparable to the traditional epistemologist in *The Claim of Reason* who misunderstands the implications of the discovery that the experience of knowing things in terms of their presence to us does not mean these things are "transcendentally" present and so imagines there is something wrong with presence itself, that it is illegitimate or failed, as if presence could only be of this kind. (There is *something* wrong and the loss can be felt. "The object of faith

hides itself from him. Not that he has given it up, and the
hope for it; he is on the track [cp.: *trace*]. He knows where it
is to be found, in the true acceptance of loss, the refusal of
any substitute for true recovery" [*Senses*, p. 50]. The lesson of
metaphysical finitude is not that the world is just codes and
as a result presence is to be ruled out as anything more than
nostalgia, but that we can have presence, insofar as we are
able, only *through* a shared grammar. That our losses are not
based on the conceptual impossibility of presence in the face
of the "objects" of presence not being "transcendentally"
locked into place, but rather on grounds that each person
must take responsibility for—the failure to make ourselves
present to each other, to respond or act when the occasion
demands. "The place you will come to may be black,
something you would disown; but if you have found yourself
there, that is so far home; you will either domesticate that,
naturalize yourself there, or you will recover nothing"
[*Senses*, p. 52]. But for Derrida, as for the positivistic moralist
in *The Claim of Reason*, the overthrow of our conventions,
our shared truths, entails no revolution, no exile—it is
neutralized into the axioms of a textual practice, a new
criticism (perhaps awaiting its Gnostic destruction, or is it
that all is maya?). One might say, against Derrida, that
desiring production is the "primary signified", if that is
understood as production of a form of life, where words have
truth where they have meaning, in *use*. "We crave only
reality, but we cannot stomach it; we do not believe in our
lives, so we trade them for stories; their real history is more
interesting than we know" [*Senses*, p. 80].

If we are to live with the "truths of skepticism", one of
them is the mystery that the world exists at all [*Claim*,

p. 234]. It is to this truth that literature can speak—of the wonder of the world being at all, and its being "so", as is.

> These decibels
> Are a kind of flagellation, an entity of sound
> Into which being enters, and is apart.

Though we may recoil from the world, its facts and its responsibilities, and the world itself may seem to retreat from us, the presence of the world, still, as by magic, awaits.

> The answer is that it is novelty
> That guides these swift blades o'er the ice....
> Colors slip away and chide us. The human mind
> Cannot retain anything except perhaps the dismal
>   two-note theme
> Of some sodden "dump" or lament.
>
> But the water surface ripples, the whole light changes.
>   [John Ashbery, "The Skaters"]

MEANING THE MEANING: ARAKAWA'S CRITIQUE OF SPACE

COAUTHOR: SUSAN BEE

Arakawa's paintings have as their subject matter the nature of meaning. They are investigative and constructive, although the construction that is the work is necessarily the manifestation of the investigation. That investigation is into the visual field and takes as its primary tools basic visual structuring modalities such as perspective, figuration, color, and plane and solid geometry. Arakawa deals with the visual field as discourse, modal systems that constitute the world rather than being constituted by it. In this sense, his work is neither a reconstruction of a given visual reality or an ontologically autonomous, "pure", formalism. Rather, it is a project of inquiry, in which the dialogic and inquisitive become an architecture of visual thinking.

Arakawa's procedure is a philosophical one, but this is not to say that he incorporates philosophical issues into his work in a literary manner. This work involves a systematic rethinking of the philosophical project, specifically in dealing with philosophical problems not as verbal entities but as visual ones. For Arakawa, the act or experience of seeing is an act or experience of language. Language, in this view, cannot be thought of only as a verbal, word-bound system but is equally involved with the construction and mediation of visual seeing and of space. While he is interested in relating some of the results of this work to the verbal/conceptual mapping of traditional philosophy, for example in some of the texts interfused into the paintings, his primary mode of investigation is into the nature of the visual perception/constitution of objects and of space, and the types of associations these processes bring about under various atmospheres or textures.

In Arakawa's work the consistent use of superimposed written texts becomes a system for determining (constructing) visual space, at the same time defining a textual space (literally inside the paintings) and commenting on and critiquing the other spaces within the painting. The placement of writing, which forms internal captions, suggests that the canvas is to be seen as a page and, indeed, that all marks on these canvases are to be seen as inscriptions. Whereas artists generally separate out linguistic meaning from their visual work in the form of titles or captions, allowing these alone to bear the verbal weight, Arakawa combines comments, philosophical references, imperatives, mottos, and morals into his pieces. This presence of words cannot be explained only by a desire for establishing correlations to more standard philosophical discourse but also by a deeper conviction that neither the verbal or visual realms are self-sufficient, and that this schism or dualism is an underlying problem within Western thought and art. As a result, a verbal equivalent or explication of the visual component is always included and, in fact, the viewer is never allowed to be alone with the purely visual elements of the work.

In the early canvases (1963-72), the words are frontally placed. However, in the more recent paintings, such as "Or Air" (1973-74), words are used more actively as a counterpoint to linear and coloristic elements and as an increasingly complex layering device within the structure of the painting. As the lexical units become more difficult to decipher, their qualities as lettrist elements, that is, as visual forms, is foregrounded, so that the more functionless the language the more force it has as a recurring artifact. This geometry of gesture formed by the use of words becomes a motif integrated into the painting along with other recurrent elements such as fans, drips, splotches, dots, arrows, spins, tubes, arcs/circles, and crystalline dodecahedrons.

In the 1967 painting "Landscape", a rainbow-colored line runs horizontally across the upper portion of the canvas, with the phrase (which also occurs in some of the other paintings) "A LINE IS A CRACK" written directly above it: the line is an horizon in the way language itself is an horizon, containing the field of possible meanings from which any given of the world emerges. "A line is a crack": a crack in the sense of allowing a glimpse of something through it—a crack of light, a crack in the door—but also a fissure, a break of an expanse or field, a cut. A line not only dividing the visual field but also in this process containing spatial areas, making figures, inscribing the recurrent tubes ("moral volumes" of a projected interior/subjective space as in "Tubes, 1965" and the 1979 "Study for 'I' "). A bounding by dividing that is always the genesis of meaning in language, allowing for demarcation, the creation of territories, objects, values—played out by Arakawa in the visual dimension. But also, the inscription of language onto the visual field as literal fact of seeing through words. So, for example, a line of poetry breaking at measured pace the totality of the text; therefore, using Arakawa's equation, the crack as measure.

Arakawa's lines do not simply contain; his tubes rapidly swirl into "self-contradicting spins" that open up and rebind in spiralling motion, making outside of inside, or visibly confounding, refuting, this separation. For Arakawa, figuration is not a static given but rather always an activity, a motion; his lines do not so much contain or describe as potentiate ("hypostatization", a recurrent word in Arakawa's vocabulary, means the act of construing a conceptual entity as actually existing). This investigation of the bounding potential of lines is partly involved with the nature of the person, of individualized space, and as such is a critique of the metaphysical idea of the separateness of "moral volumes" as an inherent fallacy within the Cartesian grid system of rationalized space. It is simultaneously an analogous inquiry into the nature of individuation itself—whether of objects, categories, or persons. That the critique is conducted here in spatial terms illustrates how this philosophical inquiry is primarily a visual one and not simply an appropriation of verbal conceptions into the visual realm.

The inscription of bounded space, a pervasive issue in the work, dates back to the early "floor plan" paintings which diagram the interior spaces of houses. The images in "Tubes, 1965" are particularly central in this respect and versions of them recur in other paintings. The painting consists of three labeled figures—"tube" (a diagrammatic cylinder), "twisted tube" (the paradigm for the later "spins"), and "broken tube" (opening up into the blankness of space). The painting is a parable on the nature of ego conceived as a spatial ontology. The twist, by turning "inner" space "out", involves a play with the materiality of spatial depths— inside/out, the dynamic focus of energy and movement, elaborated on in the many vortex-like "spins" in the paintings. As Arakawa puts it, "Angular spin: generating a sense of in (out) out (in): also (a sense of) depth."

The spins, defining an interior or subjective space, suggest that the self is less a metaphysical reality than a visual construction. They form a compelling image, seeming to construct a model of self as contained yet expanding. Often spins are shown that contain within a larger spin a smaller turning form. They map out possibilities, loci, of expansion— the linear determinates of a projection outward to the space of the canvas.

"The vortex is the maximum point of energy" as Pound defines it in one of his vorticist manifestos. Arakawa writes of spins, "sucking passage (omni-directional): a group of vortexes (high and low etc.)", "as if broken tubes: passage-ways: tunneling volumes of degrees", "dome within tun-nel". Vortices are also a central notion in Cartesian physics, "the innumerable circular motions of (roughly) whirlpools in the continuous fluid of the universe", as Bernard Williams defines them. Indeed, given that Arakawa's work represents a fundamental rethinking of Descartes, it is worth noting this point shared in the two systems.

Descartes laid down the foundations of analytic geometry

believing further that physics could be explained in purely geometric terms. The Cartesian geometric system, with its coordinate/grid system with two or three axes, attempted to rationalize space into extensions of length, breadth, and depth. As such, it became the normative view of space and is largely reflected in traditional theories of perspective and volume.

In this respect, it is interesting to note the banishing of space as an active issue in philosophy since Descartes' rationalization of it in his analytic geometry and its subsequent takeover by the technical sciences. (Space: unbounded extension in all directions, or any portion or limit of extension; position, placement/displacement, site, field, territory, horizon, region, landscape, situation, room; originally a verb for roaming, wandering about, moving.) This banishment of space left philosophy primarily concerned with time and its extension history, where not simply concerned with the timeless and spaceless issues of the mathematical-cum-analytic realm. Indeed, it is the Idealist critique of Cartesian analysis that gave rise to a concept of history that completely annexed language and meaning, in this way emptying language of its spatial dimensions and leaving space as a neutral or passive territory—prehistorical, natural—on which history and language act. This devaluation of space is most recently evident in semiotic/structural theory, and accounts for its inability to deal with the concreteness of particulars, instead dematerializing them into a realm of deep structure underlying all historical manifestations. The "arbitrariness" of the sign is a view predicated on the exclusion of the body as an object *in* space as well as time. But, as Arakawa demonstrates, the logic of space, as much as time, is not an analytic logic but a material one and its critique is fully as central to epistemology. One can also think, in this regard, of Braudel's geographic studies, or recent architectural research into inner spaces by Peter Eisenman, or the work of many land and site/environmental artists.

The tradition of modernist painting has, of course, been concerned with space, with the Cubist critique of illusionist space a central example, even though an aspect of this tradition has been the effacing of any illusion of spatial depth in the flat, pure opticality of many formalist paintings. Arakawa's work has involved going back to Cubism and extending its critique of space into quite different areas, including both an analytic and synthetic component. This extension can be seen in his insistence that his work is a "mapping", a word that emphasizes a geographic dimension to a spatial preoccupation, although this mapping is more a production of space (as meaning) than a recording of it. Arakawa's more recent tendency to talk of the work as preparatory to a "model of mind", an eventual larger-scale construction in three (or more) dimensions, to be collaborated on with Madeleine Gins and others, suggests that the mind is a geographic entity chartable through the mapping of the mechanisms of meaning.

Arakawa's critique of the Cartesian system of space involves the use of different, seemingly competing, systems of visual organization within the same work. While Cartesian geometry proposed a single, monologic approach in its rationalization of space, Arakawa exhibits a polylogic approach linking contradictory visual structuring mechanisms. Each of these systems sets up the expectation that it will govern the overall composition, but dominance of a single visual system of organization is far from Arakawa's method. He does not, however, simply juxtapose systems. Rather, he has realized a simultaneity involving the synthesis of these partialities into a total viewing experience that cannot be parsed into its parts—a work whose procedure involves analyses into competing systems that are shown to exist in chordal relations to one another.

This synthesis is achieved in two different ways. In *The Mechanism of Meaning*, a book collaborated on with Gins, the individual panels are swatches of discrete design and the simultaneity takes place at the level of the book as a whole, that is, serially. This serial simultaneity is also relevant to the paintings before 1972, each of which is concerned with a particular modality or genre of visual ideology or organization. Thus we are presented with examples, artifactualized specimens, of the different atmospheres or "scales" or "textures" of meaning that suggest the range of possible modes—swatches of perspective, grids, cubist analytic and synthetic space, diagrammed optical illusions, maps and charts, constructive hypostasizing, geometric abstraction, modified abstract expressionist elements (all over fields, linear layered surfaces, erasure, bleeding, drips), conceptual ideations, the variety of decorative surfaces. In this multi-discourse art, any style, any technique, can seemingly be included into the investigative cataloguing.

After 1972, Arakawa subsumes these different modes of visual discourse into each one of his large-scale paintings. These paintings convey the sense of a panorama unfolding, unfurling. The scale is so immense that the eye cannot behold the entire work from one vantage point, and the

viewer is overcome by a sensation of vista; these paintings
have become the horizons that Arakawa earlier spoke of.
Embodying overlapping and undercutting patterns, systems,
and spins, as well as vectors of intersection and curtailment,
the canvas becomes a giant vortex, inducing the vertigo of
not being able to find a regular centric footing. Yet this
feeling is counterposed by the remarkable stillness and
containment in the crystalline accuracy of composition, so
that, in painting terms, the slowness and pointedness of the
gestural turnings from one system to another suggest the
ancient rhythm of Noh drama. "There is only one atmos-
phere" is Arakawa's statement of the unitary vision behind
the diversity of his techniques.

"Within a moment of distance there will be two or three
centers" Arakawa writes in one of the 1980 drawings,
"Study for Blank". "These shifting centers (up, down,
back, forth, from side to side) turn from one to the other.
Also turn from one into the other." "Blank" is the inability
to see the overall in the absence of a single organizing
principle. (This blank corresponds to the blank of the
vanishing point in the monologic system of perspective, and
of a blind spot in optics.) Arakawa's zen-like jokes in the
paintings are also relevant to the concept of blank since their
humor often turns on the blank response elicited from a
command or question that it is impossible to carry out or
answer within the system of discourse in which it is made.
Blank is not so much a process of elimination as a confounding by multiplication. Short-term memory experiments
show that as few as seven different elements presented
simultaneously prevent the image track from taking hold;
Arakawa's overdetermination of visual systems produce

blank in a similar way. However, for Arakawa, blank is not just a momentary response but rather is an underlying ground or condition against which any meaning figures. By bringing blankness itself into greater visibility, he makes manifest or palpable a quality which is normally transparent.

Arakawa seeks to captivate the viewer on more than one plane, to create a world of objects adrift in space, casting nets over space and forming avenues of passage among them, to and from different layerings of meaning. The results are singular, complexly coordinated paintings in which "linear burps", as Arakawa calls the jumps from system to system, are in a sense the material of the painting, orchestrated with virtuosity. As Stein wrote of Duchamp: "To interlace a story with glass and with rope with color and roam."

The relentless schematization of Arakawa's drawings of thought recall the notebooks of Da Vinci with his sketches of turbulence and interference in the natural world in the form of vertexes, vortices, spins, and torques. Arakawa brings the intellectual tactility of the artist's notebook into the realm of painting. His diagrammatic constructions have a weblike delicacy, with the lacy interweavings forming the parameters of what is made visible.

The pervasive use of a neutral ground in the paintings enables the linear elements to function without background interference. Space (ground, canvas) is frequently left partially empty, allowing for a carefully considered breathing area. Despite its more obvious dissimilarity, Arakawa's work bears some relation, in this respect, to traditional Oriental (Chinese and Japanese) paintings with their extensive use of neutral ground, emphasis on the linear, and the delicacy, precision, and classicism of the placement of lines and color

washes. As in such work, the same themes, often captioned
by texts, are explored over and over again with changing
emphasis on quality of gesture and composition.

Arakawa uses color, in his early work, as an embroidery
on black and white, always with a sense of its power and a
sparing irony in its application. Color becomes a self-
conscious player in these dramas, an example of his precision
in articulating the purely visual aspects of the work. In the
later paintings, such as "Gasp of Continuity" (1975), washes
of neutral, transparent color expand to fill large areas of the
canvas, segmenting regions as distinct spatial areas. However, Arakawa generally avoids any solid areas of bright
color. In this context, it is interesting to note his frequent
coloring of diagrammatic lines, which are set off against a
neutral ground.

Arakawa's work shows a technical control, an attention to
nuance and intellect, particularly linguistic, that separates it
from much of the art of this time. The work is not violently
emotional, not purely painterly, not modishly garish. His
years of work unroll like a scroll, showing a continuity of
evolution and development, of style and presence—a consistency that forms a statement of individuality, intelligence,
and discernment.

These paintings do not present themselves to the viewer
with a meaning or image that can be immediately apprehended: they demand to be read, in the sense of puzzled
over, thought about, sifted through. His multidiscourse
approach, combining interrogative, witty, and self-reflective
texts, brings the viewer into dialogue with each work. As
Gins writes, "The viewer should be accustomed to knowing
in this case that the painting he is looking at was intended to

be something which would one day look at him. No longer only a viewer or spectator, not even a correspondent or witness only, once the activity of regarding has been enjoined, the viewer will become a collaborator and as such either a mediator or an experimenter or both."

In Brecht's definition of epic style, he writes of the spectator not being caught up or emotionally engaged in the action of the play but rather looking at the events critically, assessing the meaning of history as it passes before her or his gaze. This distancing effect is very much at the heart of Arakawa's project. "This distance which is a texture" is the literalizing Brechtian caption of the recent tube painting discussed earlier ("Study for the 'I' ", 1979). In this specific sense, it would not be inappropriate to think of Arakawa's work as epic painting. "Gradually," Gins notes, "the collaborator will realize when spending time with this giant stretched mass, yes, my thinking field is at least this large."

THE STADIUM OF EXPLANATION

Baudrillard has written a master critique of positivist tendencies in Marxism and, as such, of the universalizing epistemology of the modern scientistic/objective theory of analysis. As a result, the book's critique applies not only to Marxian thought but also to bourgeois economics and social science, and to psychological, linguistic, and anthropological structuralism.

Baudrillard calls into question the Marxian projection of the primacy of labor as value, which creates a valorization of production as the "meaning" of human being. Marxism, according to this argument, gives privileged status to the economic realm, misinterpreting all past and present societies under this model. Baudrillard goes so far as to suggest that the proletariat is given, wrongly, "objective" and privileged status by this account—a rationalization of a projected concept of "class" that neatly and inevitably plays into the Communist State rationalization for a vanguard/centrist party and a bureaucracy to carry out its will [p. 158].

A change in the control of production that does not call

The Mirror of Production by Jean Baudrillard, trans. Mark Poster (St. Louis: Telos, 1975).

the value of production itself into question is of no benefit since the real tyranny, or "terrorism", is the concept of Product as Value. *Revolt*, in contrast, is always in the present and consists of what Baudrillard calls "symbolic", i.e., non-instrumental, nonfinalized exchanges. Orthodox Marxian revolution plays into a teleological historicity—sacrificing the present for a future utopia, the means for the end. "For utopia is never written for the future; it is always already present" [p. 163]. The book ends on this note of utopian immanentism—a questionable exchange of a rejection of "economic" logos for a logos of nonfinality, discharge, uncoded/unsignalling "speech". "The cursed poet, non-official art, and utopian writing in general, by giving content to [human] liberation, should be the very speech of communism, its direct prophecy" [p. 164].

This is reminiscent (and probably an influence on) the concept of "desire" in *Anti-Oedipus;* though of course here not desiring *production* but the "actualization of desire" in the symbolic realm, where "symbolic" means nonuniversalized, nondialectical, and not rationalized in the mirror of an imaginary objective history. (Poster, in his introduction, remarks on the possible similarity this may have to Habermas's ideal speech situation.)

Baudrillard criticizes Marx's unreflected acceptance of the prevailing "code" (political economy) in a typically grinding, if sometimes impassioned, exposition of these issues. Baudrillard's style of writing can be critiqued on the same grounds as his attack on Marx for not breaking with "rational discursiveness" and the "logic of representation—of the duplication of its object" [p. 50]. The real oppression, says Baudrillard, is "less the monopoly of the means of production (which is never total) than *the monopoly of the code*" [p. 127], with its "Euclidian geometry" of history and its Renaissance perspectivism "allow[ing] the spatial imposition of an arbitrary, unitary whole" [p. 114]. Baudrillard's writing practice, however, mirrors the very code he wishes to be set loose from, without self-reflection on this fact. His style is more like a "mirror of production" than a "symbolic exchange" (between reader and writer). Like Moses, Baudrillard seems only able to point to the promised (premised) land without entering in. Nonetheless, *The Mirror of Production* is buoyant and inspiring writing in the tradition of neo-Luddite, utopian, and anarchist works. Along with the new Situationist anthology, the book may be the quintessential theoretical document of the best of the spirit of Paris '68.

ON THEATRICALITY

My thinking on theater always circles back to Rousseau's remarks in his letters to D'Alembert in which he urges that the theater be banned because it brings a public together to reinforce the prevailing mores rather than to exercise its constituency as constitutors of both our forms of life and principles of government. For when the public is convened it should be to exercise its will not consume its manners.

The theater makes a spectacle out of presentness, its drama enacts the fantasy of the world as a shell, before us only as gesture. The more earnest, believable, the cry of an actor the more the coherence of our interpretation of the meaning of others' actions is defamed. One of the reasons the conditions of film as a medium are so much more intrinsically satisfying is that they effectively defeat this theatricalization of presence by the machinic otherness of the projected world; watching a movie, I remain outside the time and place of what I see; and what I see is always *framed*, a mediation/conditioning intrinsic to the medium itself.

One problem with so much performance of Beckett's work (such as Mabou Mines's *The Lost Ones* with David Warrilow a few years ago or Jack McGowran's a few years before that) is the theatricalizing of voice and its presence as a speaker to us in the audience. Beckett's work, so presented, loses the denser, shifting polyvalences of the text itself; his work is of an elsewhere that is always now, while such theatricality performs the obverse. On the other hand, Joseph Chaiken's very recent reading of excerpts from *Texts for Nothing* and *How It Is* successfully defeated this theatricalizing of voice, making it the most satisfying performance of Beckett I have ever heard. Chaiken's reading situates the address of the text not to a listener but to itself, as reverie, the self—or more properly the writing—talking to itself, proceeding, stopping, questioning, circling back: a textual practice organized by internal compositional necessities and not by the sound of a speaking voice. By performing a text as a musician might play a score, rather than enacting a persona, Chaiken was able to realize the textual dimension of Beckett's work.

A related issue has to do with the value of poetry readings, since just this problem of the voice or person as organizing mode of the reading often works against the qualities of the writing. But how to read without this sense of voiced presence being foregrounded? Certainly a sharp break is needed both from the shamanistic incantation of neoritualistic sound poetry and from the presentation of personality as a projected cohering force. Perhaps some clue is to be found in the idea of *song*, where the compression of meaning is scored on the basis of music rather than voice, creating an overall self-containment that defeats presentness with its intricate autonomy. Some of these conditions can be realized in a poetry reading by an attention to the artifactual features of the text itself—line breaks, punctuation, visual organization—insofar as these veer from "scored speech", and by an attempt to create rhythms in reading that are based on the compositional possibilities of the text and not simply appropriated from speech or rhetoric.

In the textual theater of Richard Foreman, building on Brecht's own model for defeating the presentness of theater, some of the conditions of film and song (and of opera) are achieved on stage by an intensely architectural design and choreography and the use of such mechanical devices as voice-over tape recording and buzzers. One of the reasons why this work is so compelling and so significant is that there is no illusion of presentness to the audience, only the diachronic and diatropic envisioning of a duration estranged from us so that we can see it.

*

[I raised some of these issues at a Co-Accident workshop at the August Moon Arts Festival in Catskill, New York, with Cris Cheek, an English performance artist and writer, and Kirby Malone and Marshall Reese of Co-Accident/Desire Productions. I preceded my comments by looking at Kirby while saying with maximum conviction "I am Here. You are there. We are both together in this space and I am looking at your eyes. I feel you here with me" etc.]

BERNSTEIN: . . . What we'd like to do is to break away from that, not to have that sense of simulated presence, simulated honesty, simulated thereness, so that the person in the audience is somehow supposed to forget about the fact that there is acting, and at the same time is made to feel that her or his presence in the audience is a crucial part of creating an event. Rather than acknowledging in some ways the fact that every person is separate from another and that the way to communicate is not always by trying to dissolve the absence that we feel from each other and that the audience might feel from the stage. But I wonder what it is that is your sense. Do you feel you're creating representations, re-presentations?

CHEEK: I don't think you can call it a presentation, actually. It has ways of teaching both the performer and the audience that isn't part of the perception of time and the perception of action and intensity and that kind of intensity is the only tangible feature.

BERNSTEIN: Do you try to alter the sense of time?

CHEEK: Well, performance does alter the sense of time, there's no doubt about that, because it is totally different from the kind of sense of time that you experience like sitting here, in a sense that you try and get a lot more done. You act more determinately to explore the possibilities of the environment and what you've set up in terms of reaction to the change of light, reaction to the sound and moving in bands of light. You can tell me I'm not making sense in a minute cause it would be quite true. . . . Or talking through cliché to try to get a response to a given set of sexual forms with one person doing this, that, and the other and the other person desperately trying to relate to it. I think that's definitely what we're not doing. We're not trying to relate, not trying a single narrative or simple representational level. So that things become much more abstract. Abstraction is a concrete space within a performance, which is why you do get that difference between the performer and the audience.

BERNSTEIN: So you get a sense of distance, in what you're saying, that's very clearly acknowledged. A lot of theater, whether it's called traditional, or a certain sort of earnest new theater, such as the Iowa Theater Lab's "White Night" last night, doesn't give you that clearly defined architectural space that the performers are in. When you said time . . . it's true that theatrical time is not real time, there is no such thing as real time, I mean there is no such thing as real time, I mean this isn't real time. But there is a sense of simulation of real time that you get that tries to make you forget that there's time going on, that any performance is a manipulation, or anyway, creation or production of time. Production rather than representation. When you perform it seems to me you have a very clear sense, I might call it, in the sense when I was talking over in the corner, you know, a distortion or a bizarre rending apart of normal senses of time, but what it actually is I think, if it's working well, is a production of time, that you can see the time being produced.

CHEEK: That's why I say it's not a presentation because a presentation is far too fixed. A presentation also implies we have a very clear idea of how each piece is going to work together before we start, which definitely isn't the way it is appreciable.

BERNSTEIN: Well, hm, I'm not sure I think that improvisation, per se, or not being planned is the key to . . .

CHEEK: Well, in a sense through working together you script . . .

BERNSTEIN: It's not saying that you have to be unplanned or

spontaneous. That technique, if it allows for the greatest articulation, probably requires the most considerable skill. But it is part of just the perceptual experience that one has doing it and watching it that one feels like the time/space of the performance is different from your own and so you see how time itself gets produced.

CHEEK: There's a difference in calculation. It's not calculated . . . to produce a specific effect to be presented, or to show specific images, so that the calculation is far more deeply engrained in a total living process rather than just that one art action.

BERNSTEIN: One thing I thought was that this type of work is experienced more like a text. You have to read it. It becomes an active process rather than a consumptive process. The model of the theater of representation is the theater that you consume with a kind of starry gaze, that you just are there for it, so it tries to eliminate a self-consciousness about itself as artifice while usually upping my self-consciousness as a spectator. In contrast, performance art of a certain sort has been interested in just that self-consciousness about the artifice, which sometimes can be overindulged or not, but in any case forces you to read the piece, the text, as something separate, to interpret it and to decide for yourself. I think that that very much is at the root of Brecht's sense of what he wanted you to look at—history unfolding. And I think that we might, as well, want to look at history itself, not just to talk about the theatrical situation, but when you look at events in the street, when going to the supermarket, when you look at people that you're relating to. It's not simply something to consume, it's something to read and to try to figure out what the formulations are at the same time as you experience them. This isn't an attempt to distance you from your feelings so much as to make you aware that feelings exist within a social context. What I find the violence of the stripped down theater of presence, like the Iowa performance, is that it wrenches emotions and experiences out of context and just gives them to you almost as pure being, so-called. And it becomes very totalitarian. This kind of theatrical technique is not only used by the traditional Broadway theater of dished-up sentiment or by the theater of emotion, or encounter group theater, or psychodrama theater, but also by lots of the spiritualist groups. Things like Ram Dass saying "Be here now with me" in that deep slow voice of religiosity, that kind of manipulation of time so that you feel that there is some 'here' is the same kind of manipulation that I'm talking about and as I was trying to demonstrate with Kirby—"Here . . . I am . . . feel it . . . you are there. . . ." You know, I mean you could go on, you actually do create a space that tries to defeat or make invisible the production of the space that you are creating. And to me that's simulation of feeling that's not real feelings. Whether a person thinks that she or he is feeling something or not. It's necessarily simulation to me. And in that sense I think most people simulate most of the time, when they go into the Jamesway and they buy their . . . I think all that is in a certain sense simulation, theatricalization. That's what the commodification of products is.

Still, I'm not convinced by much of the performance art of the "amateur and proud" variety either. For instance, the desultory casualness of a "spontaneous" and minimally prepared performance method is too weak to escape from the undercurrent of simulation and monotony that envelops not only more conventional theatrical practice but everyday life as well. This type of performance work is deeply rooted in an art world chic that values a simplified, cooled-out posturing often spiced by a foregrounded and unambiguous irony that suggests a) everyone is forever posturing but some are more stylish because they are aware of it, or b) *they* posture and *we* know it. In my unsympathetic way, the only theater I can imagine valuing is one that defeats its theatricality by total immersion in its production of space and time without acknowledging the "real-time" response of the audience. This involves a total arrangement and consolidation of the language, movement, setting, costuming, etc. such that all of these are inscribed into the performance space. No aspect can be left unattended, untransformed into the composed tempos of the construction. Such autonomy needs to be especially intensive since everything about the performance context will tend to induce a schism between making an impression (a *hit*) and making a meaning. No art form (the combination of hyperbole and truism is an illustration of theatricality) is as pulled toward its own trivialization as is performance art, for this trivialization—of gestures, of time, of communication—is inherent in the medium. The presence of an audience to the artist is like the song of the Sirens to the sailor: its attendance not only distracts but destroys. This is not to suggest, simplistically, that the audient (the reader) is not to be considered but that consideration is, literally, compromised by the 'liveness' of such presence. In this sense, theatricalization pervades our relation to the world of things, ideas, and people not only in simulating but also in sensationalizing: works become events, speaking overshadows talking, look overlooks vision, interpreting dreams replaces dreaming. A theater that resists theatricality is, in any age, necessarily rare; it is not of this world but for it.

***

Coda for Co-Accident

They want, for instance, for // THE SOUND THAT // *often plunges backward, wholeways* // is lost // *could force it back* // boisterousness melting into media // *enthusiasm of a time who* // renders sometimes // harmonics, harmonies // *strains* // EAR HID // delicacy crushes . . .

G—/

the earphone jack instead of the microphone jack   so
im talking to myself the last ten minutes   and uh i
enter this conversation by tape   midstream   i
was saying   let me see   questioning the idea of
what a person is   in the context of my being depressed
personally   in what sense   does it does it
        does that concept of personhood have   i write
a poem   and i say well its my poem   if its a good
poem that means im writing well if its a bad poem that
means im not   writing well   what does that
mean   well somehow ive managed to
express   get out   some kind of   thing
in the world   some kind of   thing that is a real
thing   that if people look at   stare at   work
at   will really mean something   like   a
person has an intention has something they can make out
as being real   but if im succeeding in that in what
sense is it mine   and i was thinking about   poe
and all of poes nightmares   uh fantasies   stories
in what sense are they his   poes   edgar allen poes
a person   lets take for example   the pit and the

208

pendulum or   the room that closes in   crushes
people   i mean in what sense are they poes   poe
came upon them but arent they just as much mine   or
yours   arent they part somehow of   of our sense
of the world our nightmare sense of the world our fantasy
of the world   in what sense is the waste lands t s
eliots   he got it   he expressed it yes   and
acknowledgement is due   but in what sense is it
his   or pounds and his   and i think that sense of
whats mine   is a   is a large part   of the
problem   the problem of a certain kind of of problem
that we face in terms of relationships with other
people   and for me in terms of my own perception of
myself   the things that block me   in a
way   from other people   that debilitate
me   i had this liberating thought the other night
imagine that nothing that i write or thought
was good   it was all crummy   and the fact of its
crumminess would somehow free me up from this burden
that i feel to speak to express   to say something
meaningful   because i couldnt   and i an i started
to laugh   it just seemed a joyous   kind
of   concept   and then this thinking lead me i
mean sometimes i feel depressed i feel a little bit that way
this morning   about obscurity and what is it to be
obscure   i mean   i have friends   who
listen   and yet especially in new york   which is
like the scene of scenes   the place   one feels
enormously anonymous because one is unknown to almost
everyone   one looks on the street one goes through
the subways one sees people who would have no possible

interest in what one is writing or doing quite rightly
i cant imagine ever of them coming upon
interest and one wants somehow i want   my work to
be   to some degree   to be published   and
yet   what does it mean to   to publish work
to get it read   just having 400 copies
printed which is what   the average number of copies
of a book of poetry say   and what does that
mean   but in any case   and and why is it that i
am or am not one of the people whose getting 400 copies
published and someone else is or is not   that kind of
self consciousness so i should get into that im as good as
they are im as good as they are im as good as they are im
im im i am i   i am as good as they are i am as good as
they are   okay   so you are as good as they are
but   in what sense   in what sense   that
i   thats where ive begun to question the whole
concept of person   its its   a sense that when im
really being there i dissolve   in that sense of
person   that its only when somehow im being aware
of myself in that sense of me doing things that im
not   for instance   susan sort of
criticized   me   for overly performing
the night when i was playing with the
microphone   breathing and so forth   and i was
really   enjoying that   but it was as if   i was
asserting myself too much   in that self consciousness
that maybe i was performing too much   maybe i was
being obnoxious   thats the sense of person i think is a
mistaken sense   in some way   its a miracle said
someone that we dont   just   vanish down the

drain that we dont go down with the bath water   i
feel um like im not being clear   its not your
night   okay   some notes   some notes on uh
your discussion of the law   okay   the family is
the only one you can trust   specifically the wife the
married wife   or husband not   just somebody
youre living with   that seemed very true i mean
obviously it is true   and that is one of the things that
reinforces the whole family structure   the nuclear
family structure   you can only trust your
wife   shes the only person you can really
trust   or the husband   now what does that mean
to me   well i think about it in terms of a in social
terms its just apparent transparent in the ways that youre
talking that we are limited to trusting other people
          relationships say outside of the relationship
with ones spouse and ones family are objectified to some
degree are   held back   we hold ourselves
back   we're afraid to express ourselves   that
makes us vulnerable   um when we   i   talk
to other people   because only a wife is allowed not to
incriminate us   testify against us   so that
they   or the husband   are the only one we can
confess to   and who else well a priest you can confess
to a priest   if youre a catholic   and that image of
the priest seems to me   its one of the great you know
coups of the catholic church   that one can confess to a
priest someone outside oneself who one doesnt know gives
one a sense immediately of community   that some one
could hear ones confession   and tell one what one
could do to repent   who is not a part of the

family   gives one a sense that there is something
beyond myself   and and that sense of
person   there beyond me as a person   but then
lets think about what the need for people to testify is
okay say we're in a community which we believe in
and someone   um   steals   someone elses
um   dope   someone elses writing someone
elses   food   we want to know who that person
is   whose stealing   but what do we want to do
with them we dont want to put them in jail   the
whole concept of jail is really kind of
anachronistic   that we put people away in
prison   and thats whats fucked   in the end we
put people behind bars who offend us   we put
schizophrenics in institutions who offend us we re so easily
offended   but there is still a sense in which one wants
to confront to deal with those people who are hurting other
people being cruel to other people   i mean i dont want
my friends to be killed   and if someone in my
community is killing my friends i want to stop them
and if if you know who is killing my friends i want
you to tell me who that person is   not so i can put
them behind bars   but so i can find out whats
happening with them with us   every murder is a is a
failure of community   so thats where the need for
people to testify is   but in our society everything is
askew   and the way it comes out   to conspire is
to breathe together with someone else   like expire is
to breathe out   co breather   to breathe
together   is to conspire   i conspire with you by

making this tape   for you   freedom of
speech   freedom not to express to be silent   i was
thinking that to testify   to testify   is like
a   christian   fundamentalist concept to testify to
confess   is a   confessing is an enormous
release   to talk about ones most personal fears and
release them   onto the community   if i talk to
you about uh   my sexual frustrations   my desire
for sexual relations with other people and yet my fear of
that sometimes   my fear uh   it will affect those
relationships i have established   by releasing   by
releasing that   information about myself   its no
longer a part of me   its when i hold it in that its a part
of my person   its hard to confess on tape its so public i
feel   that what i say could be broadcast so i am
somewhat cagey   a little bit   not very much
                    in person is where confession takes place not on
tape   i dont want my intimate things to be on tape
somehow   i mean i feel that violation   and yet
my most intimate things are   always coming
out   i was thinking in respect to your freedom not to
express   some stuff that goffman talks about in his
book on asylums   lets see now   oh here a social
entity he says is an ideology a nation a trade a family a
conversation   any interaction between people becomes
a social entity   and has two components a
commitment   an agreement to do specific things
and an attachment   a sense of belongingness
so theres both an explicit commitment   an
external behavior   and an inner
attachment a sense of belongingness   and

the limits on commitment are often made explicit in a
contract but they are also implicit   the sort of thing
one expects of a person if one hires him for a job one
doesnt sign a contract but one expects him to be there the
times that are specified and not just to leave for any erratic
reason but to make an attempt   to stay on the job
so that one has really the conception in any social
action of the type of person who is involved   and even
in a friendship one has a conception   of the type of
person who might be a friend   that they be there
when you want them to be there   that they somehow
help you out   that they respond   to
you   and then   then thats a commitment   a
commitment   and theres also an attachment   a
sense of belongingness   an individual can hold
himself or herself off   from these
implications   allowing for a sense of some
disaffection   even while fulfilling the major
obligation   and thats the situation that most of us are
in   that we fulfill our obligations in various social
situations   including conversations but
especially   nationhood we pay our
taxes   but   we uh   hold ourselves back
from it   from the inner attachment   but what is
it to cooperate and just simply cooperation lends validity to
the sense of self that the institution puts down for you
now   specifically   freedom of
speech   the freedom not to express   the freedom
not to express is simply to refuse in the commitment to the
institution   not to do that which is expected   but
those refusals i mean what is it to express in our society to

give consent to the law   this is a problem that POWs
have   for instance   everything they do
including   uh   the most conscientious of them
taking exercise   eating   all of that underwrites
the legitimacy of the jailers position and the legitimacy of
his conception of oneself   and the question arises in a
very severe way in a POW camp   as to what you can
express what you can do actively if it goes along with what
the jailers expectations of what you should do
are   that that lends legitimacy to his concept
of you   and your self   so how can you be staunch
and true and refuse what does one have to refuse one can
refuse   everything one must   one has to refuse to
speak   but not only refuse to speak refuse to work and
so forth   i mean its tremendous the implications that
every act   say paying for a five and dime at
woolworths   instead of stealing   paying for a
notebook instead of stealing it   has implications that
you accept that youre the kind of person who pays for
something instead of not paying for it   i mean
whenever you have the choice you could shoplift or you
couldnt   youre making a choice about your self
conception that others have of you   and once again
you can get into that concept of person which i think is
tremendously misguided   okay   if we re really to
understand what a group is and what a trusting group is i
mean i think thats ultimately the the what i took to be the
subtext of your argument   to trust what a group
is   its a very   you know   related to the law
and whats expected of us and and how we use our concept
of person to isolate ourselves from each other   and

what you said about watergate was very much to the point
in that respect   that is wasnt   the law compelling
people   to tell   but it was their coming of their
own spirit of their own accord to confess   but justice
isnt just   freedom of expression   or silence

WRITING AND METHOD

1. THE LIMITS OF STYLE/THE POSSIBILITIES OF PHENOMENA

An inquiry into the differences between philosophical and literary writing practices is of value insofar as it can shed light on both the nature of philosophy and poetry and, more importantly, on the development and implications of such genre or professional distinctions within writing and thinking. For what makes poetry poetry and philosophy philosophy is largely a tradition of thinking and writing, a social matrix of publications, professional associations, audience; more, indeed, facts of history and social convention than intrinsic necessities of the "medium" or "idea" of either one. So such an inquiry will end up being into the social meaning of specific modes of discourse, a topic that is both a stylistic resource for the writing of poetry and a content for philosophy.

Philosophy has traditionally been concerned with the nature of the world and the possibilities of human knowledge of it; in a large sense, the nature of perception, phenomenon, objects, mind, person, meaning, and action. Richard Kuhns, in his book about the affinities of philosophy and literature,

Structures of Experience, writes, "Philosophy asks 'What makes experience possible?' and 'What makes *this* kind of experience possible?' Literature establishes the realities for which philosophy must seek explanations." Kuhns bases the distinction between philosophy and literature on the appeal each makes, the address of the text. Philosophy is involved with an appeal to validity and argument (i.e., to impersonal, suprapersonal, "objective" abstractions, to logic) and poetry with an appeal to memory and synaesthesia (i.e., to the reader's own experience). Kuhns, then, is suggesting two different, though interrelated, modes of discourse. "Philosophy" requires "logical" argument and noncontradiction as basic textual modes of discourse; "poetry" seems to reject argument as essential, though of course it may "incorporate" argument. —Even were I to accept Kuhns's traditional distinctions, which I do not, I would add that poetry can focus attention on the structure of meaning by the exemplification of structures of discourse—how the *kind* of discourse effects what can be said within it.

Another traditional distinction between philosophy and poetry now sounds anachronistic: that philosophy is involved with system building and consistency and poetry with the beauty of the language and emotion. Apart from the grotesque dualism of this distinction (as if consistency and the quest for certainty were not emotional!), this view imagines poetry and philosophy to be defined by the product of their activity, consistent texts in the one case, beautiful texts in the other. Rather, philosophy and poetry are at least equally definable not as the product of philosophizing and poetic thinking but, indeed, as the process (the activity) of philosophizing or poetic thinking.

Jean-Paul Sartre, in his "Self-Portrait at 70" (in *Life/ Situations*) argues that while literature *should* be ambiguous, "in philosophy, every sentence should have only one meaning"; he even reproaches himself for the "too literary" language of *Being and Nothingness*, "whose language should have been strictly technical. It is the accumulation of technical phrases which creates the total meaning, a meaning which", at this overall level, "has more than one level." Literature, on the other hand, is a matter of style, style that requires greater effort in writing and pervasive revision. "Stylistic work does not consist of sculpting a sentence, but of permanently keeping in mind the totality of the scene, the chapter . . . the entire book" as each sentence is being composed. So, a superimposition of many meanings in each sentence. —Sartre's remarks are interesting in this context because he so clearly exemplifies the poetry/philosophy split, being equally known for his fiction and nonfiction. Yet for me, *Being and Nothingness* is a more poetic work than *The Age of Reason* in the sense that I find it more a structural investigation of perception and experience—"being"— whose call is to "memory and synaesthesia", while the novels often seem to exemplify various "problems" using a rationalistic appeal to argument and validity.

Indeed, if one takes it to be a primary philosophical problem—many philosophers of course do not—that the description (ontology) of events, persons, experiences, objects, etc., is at issue, and it is not just a question of *axiomatizing* types of these things, then forms of art not only "define the structure of human experience" as Kuhns has it but *investigate* the terms of human experience and their implications. Then poetry and philosophy share *the project of investigating the possibilities (nature) and structures of pheno-mena.* The motto for this might come from Wittgenstein in *Philosophical Investigations*: "We feel as if we had to *penetrate* phenomena: our investigation, however, is directed not toward phenomena but, as one might say, the 'possibilities' of phenomena."

As a result, the genre or style of a writing practice becomes centrally a question of method, rather than a transparent given of form. It is this understanding of philosophy that lead Heidegger in his later work to reject philosophy and instead call for instruction in "true think-ing" (in *What Is Called Thinking*), or has lead Stanley Cavell, recently writing on Emerson, to talk of the relation of mood to philosophic inquiry. Or what has lead so many poets to feel the need to reject philosophy outright as a ground for poetry, as Craig Watson recently commented, saying that it sentimentalized a picture of perception. The answer to that is that of course people do get attached to their systems: but this should not subvert seeing the possibilities for method itself, for system, for ways of looking at perception. In *Walden*, Thoreau writes, "There are nowadays professors of philosophy, but not philosophers. Yet it is admirable to profess because it was once admirable to live. To be a philosopher is not merely to have subtle thoughts, nor even to found a school, but so to love wisdom as to live according to its dictates. . . . It is to solve some of the problems of life, not only theoretically, but practically. The success of great scholars and thinkers is commonly a courtier-like suc-cess. . . . They make shift to live merely by conformity, practically as their fathers did, and are in no sense the progenitors of a nobler race of men. . . . The philosopher is in advance of his age even in the outward form of his life. He is not fed, sheltered, clothed, warmed, like his contemporaries. How can a man be a philosopher and not maintain his vital heat by better methods than other men?" Which I cite partly for that last sentence—the centrality of method.

If philosophy is to be characterized as a form consisting of clearly exposited arguments whose appeal is to the logic of validity, then it would systematically be limited by the limits of expository practice. I don't think it makes sense to restrict philosophy to this particular mode of discourse both because it would rule out some of the best work in philosophy and because it suggests that reason's most "clear" expression is exposition. Rather it seems to me that, as a mode, contemporary expository writing edges close to being merely a *style* of decorous thinking, rigidified and formalized to a point severed from its historical relation to method in Descartes and Bacon. It is no longer an enactment of thinking or reasoning but a representation (and simplification) of an eighteenth-century ideal of reasoning. And yet the hegemony of its practice is rarely questioned outside certain poetic and philosophic contexts. On this level, I would characterize as sharing a political project both a philosophic practice and a poetic practice that refuse to adopt expository principles as their basic claim to validity.

For both poetry and philosophy, the order of the elements of a discourse is value constituting and indeed experience engendering, and therefore always at issue, never assumable.

In some sense these are just issues of style; a style is chosen and it is not to the point simply to be evaluative about which is best intrinsically. But to acknowledge that there are philosophical assumptions that underlie given stylistic practices—assumptions about the nature of reason, objects, the world, persons, morality, justice. At a certain historical moment certain paths were chosen as to the style that would express a quasiscientific voice of reason and authority—even though, as Thomas Kuhn points out in *The Structure of Scientific Revolution*, this "normal" science language cannot account for the paradigm shifts central to scientific progress—a voice that was patriarchal, monologic, authoritative, impersonal. The predominance of this authoritative plain style (taught in such guides as Strunk and White) and its valorization as a picture of clarity and reason is a relatively recent phenomenon and its social meaning will no doubt be clarified by a careful tracing of its origins that would be a central project for the historian of social forms. Morris Croll has elucidated an earlier stage of these developments in his account of the rise of the anti-Ciceronian prose style in the late sixteenth century, a development in some ways paralleling such current critiques as this one of contemporary expository forms, in its rejection of a static predetermined formality and its attempt "to portray not a thought, but a mind thinking". Montaigne most clearly exemplifies this movement, especially in terms of his methodological awareness of the implications of style: "I stray from the path, but it is rather by licence than oversight. My ideas follow each other, but sometimes it is at a distance, and they look toward each other, but with an oblique gaze. . . . It is the lazy reader who loses sight of the subject, not I. . . . I keep changing without constraint or order. My style and my mind both go a-vagabonding. . . . I mean that my matter should distinguish itself. It shows sufficiently where it changes, where it ends, where begins, where resumes, without interlacing of words, of conjunctions, or connectives introduced for weak or negligent ears, and without glossing myself."

No doubt the history of our contemporary plain styles, with their emphasis on connectives, a tight rein on digression, and a continuing self-glossing, a history that could be traced to the last 100 years, would need to account for the effect of industrialization and mass literacy in order to explain the particular tendency toward greater and greater standardization. But the crucial mechanism to keep in mind is not the rules of current preferred forms versus possible alternatives but *the mechanism of distinction and discrimination itself* that allows for certain language practices to be legitimized (as correct, clear, coherent) and other language practices to be discredited (as wrong, vague, nonsensical, antisocial, ambiguous, irrational, illogical, crude, dumb . . .). This "mechanism of exclusion" is described by Michel Foucault in relation to the designation both of the "criminal" and the "insane", with the comment that it is the mechanism itself and its techniques and procedures which were found useful in creating and preserving the predominating hierarchical power relations of the nineteenth-century bourgeoisie (as well, it should be added, the twentieth-century Soviet state). It is not, then, the intrinsic meaning of the particular distinction that is crucial, not, that is, the particular standard but standardization itself. "What in fact happened", Foucault writes in "Two Lectures" in *Power/Knowledge*, "was that the mechanisms of exclusion . . . began from a particular point in time . . . to reveal their political usefulness and to lend themselves to economic profit, and that as a natural consequence, all of a sudden,

they came to be colonized and maintained by global mechanisms and the entire State system. It is only if we grasp
these techniques of power and demonstrate the economic
advantages or political utility that derives from them . . .
that we can understand how these mechanisms come to be
effectively incorporated into the social whole." Part of the
task of a history of social forms would be to bring into
visibility as chosen instruments of power what is taken as
neutral or given. Part of the task of an active poetry or
philosophy is to explore these instruments by a critique of
their partiality and to develop alternatives to them that can
serve as models of truth and meaning not dependent for
their power on the dominating structures.

The contemporary expository mode was adopted because
it effectively did the business of the society's vested interests,
by its very mode quelling the sound of oppositional language
by equating coherence with mannered and refined speaking.
In this context, Sartre tells the story of *La Cause du peuple*, a
Paris newspaper that the government actively seized, ar-
resting its editors, in the seventies because, unlike the leftist
Les Temps moderne, Sartre's own paper, it did not speak in the
language of bourgeois discourse but had accounts by workers, in their own sharper language, of rebellions and atroci-
ties throughout France. I think the outrage against accepting black English diction in a school context is a similar
instance of a threat to the legitimizing function served by
standardization.

The question is always: what is the meaning of this
language practice; what values does it propagate; to what
degree does it encourage an understanding, a visibility, of its
own values or to what degree does it repress that awareness?

To what degree is it in dialogue with the reader and to what
degree does it command or hypnotize the reader? Is its social
function liberating or repressive? Such questions of course
open up into much larger issues than ones of aesthetics, open
the door by which aesthetics and ethics are unified. And so
they pertain to not only the art situation but more generally
the language of the job, of the state, of the family, and of the
street. And my understanding of these issues comes as much
from working as a commercial writer as from reading and
writing poetry. Indeed, the fact that the overwhelming
majority of steady paid employment for writing involves
using the authoritative plain styles, if it is not explicitly
advertising; involves writing, that is, filled with preclusions,
is a measure of why this is not simply a matter of stylistic
choice but of social governance: we are not free to choose the
language of the workplace or of the family we are born into,
though we are free, within limits, to rebel against it. Nor am
I therefore advocating that expository writing should not be
taught; I can think of few more valuable survival skills. "But
if one learns to dress as the white man dresses one does not
have to think the white man dresses best." And again the
danger is that writing is taught in so formal and objectified a
way that most people are forever alienated from it as Other.
It needs, to use Alan Davies's terms, to be taught as the
presentation of *a* tool, not mystified as a value-free product,
in which the value-creating process that led to it is repressed
into a norm and the mode itself is *imperialized*. Coherence
cannot be reduced to the product of any given set of tools.
This will not necessarily entail that all writing be revolutionary in respect to style or even formally self-conscious
about it—though that is a valuable course—but rather that

styles and modes have social meaning that cannot be escaped and that can and should be understood.

This understanding should lead to a very acute sense of the depletion of styles and tones in the public realm of factual discourse, including in professional philosophy and the academy in general, but also newspapers, magazines, radio, and TV. Even within the predominant styles of contemporary philosophy, few of the tones and moods that potentially exist within the chosen style are utilized to any great extent. Indeed, the only significant alternative to the neutral-toned plain style of most philosophical writing of the present time is the weightier tone of judiciousness; but rarely whimsical tones or angry, or befuddled or lethargic or ironic, as if these tones were moods that have been banished, realms of human experience thus systematically untouchable. Not only is the question of method suppressed, but even the possibilities of tone within the style are reduced!

All writing is a demonstration of method; it can assume a method or investigate it. In this sense, style and mode are always at issue, for all styles are socially mediated conventions open to reconvening at any time.

Yet, along with the depletion of styles and tones of writing is a repression of these categories as chosen elements. Appropriating a similar division by Barrett Watten, one might speak of concentric circles of technique, style, mode or genre, and method, each of these terms encompassing a sequentially larger circle that informs the possibilities for the categories within it. That is, a technique exists within the context of a style toward which it is employed, a style can be seen as an instance of a more general genre or mode, and a mode is informed by a still more general method that gives rise to it. Different works will show vastly different indications of these domains. A row of suburban houses, for example, may mask the uniformity of their style by slight alterations (personalizations) made by the individual owners. Art or movie reviewing, for instance, will usually focus on the style or technique and leave unexamined the prevailing assumptions of mode and method, either out of blindness to these aspects or out of a conviction that such issues are contentless or imponderable. Indeed much "normal" philosophy and poetry simply adopts a style and works on techniques within it, without considering either the implications of the larger modality or its methodological assumptions. In contrast, a "constructive" mode would suggest that the mode itself is explored as content, its possibilities of meaning are investigated and presented, and that this process is itself recognized as a method.

One vision of a constructive writing practice I have, and it can be approached in both poetry and philosophy, is of a multidiscourse text, a work that would involve many different types and styles and modes of language in the same "hyperspace". Such a textual practice would have a dialogic or polylogic rather than monologic method. The loss of dialogue in philosophy has been a central problem since Plato; Cavell, applying this to his own work, and that of Thoreau, talks about the dialogue of a "text answerable to itself". Certainly, *Philosophical Investigations* is the primary instance of such a text in this century, and also a primary instance of taking this practice as method. I can easily imagine more extreme forms of this: where contrasting moods and modes of argument, shifting styles and perspectives, would surface the individual modes and their

meaning in illuminating ways and perhaps further Heidegger's call for an investigation into "true thinking".
(Thinking is also a construction.) Indeed, I can imagine a
writing that would provoke philosophic insight but keep
essentially a fabric of dance—logopoeia—whose appeal would
not be to the validity of argument but to the ontological
truthfulness of its meanings.

Another alternative type of discursive work is suggested
by the later writing of Laura (Riding) Jackson. (Riding)
Jackson's work has consistently investigated the limits of
meaning and the limits of our forms of trying to mean. After
twenty years of active poetic practice, she renounced poetry
in 1938 as "blocking truth's ultimate verbal harmonies".
Had she been a philosopher she might have made a similar
renunciation, as, in a sense, Wittgenstein did of the kind of
discourse he and Russell had produced in the early part of
the century, or as Heidegger did make in his later writing
where he characterized philosophy as at odds with "true
thinking". (Riding) Jackson's renunciation cuts through
distinctions of philosophy and poetry, suggesting that it is
the professionalization of—the craft of—each that is the
mistake. I've suggested here that if philosophy is reduced
simply to a mode of employing argument then the attention
shifts from what (Riding) Jackson might call "telling the
truth of us all" to the technical perfecting of the mode itself,
the kind of tinkering with the mechanics of given arguments, refining their formal elegance, that is apparent on
any page of *Mind*. Yet this professionalization, (Riding)
Jackson points out, is a danger in poetry too, as the craft of
fine expressiveness she feels necessarily supplants "the telling" that was poetry's initial motivation for the poet. A view

that is useful to consider if overly scriptural in its imagination of what this telling is. (Riding) Jackson's appeal in *The Telling* is not to the internal validity of her argument, or to the beauty or virtuosity of her performance or expression, but to the truthfulness of what she is saying in respect to our own, as readers, experiences and memories. We refer back to "ourselves", in that sense are made aware, conscious, of ourselves as readers; by addressing the reader, this work refuses to let its words disappear.

In his "Preface" to *Lyrical Ballads*, Wordsworth writes: "Aristotle, I have been told, has said that Poetry is the most philosophic of all writing: it is so: its object is truth, not individual and local, but general and operative; not standing upon external testimony, but carried alive into the heart by passion; truth which is its own testimony, which gives competence and confidence to the tribunal to which it appeals, and receives them from the same tribunal. Poetry in the image of [humanity] and nature."

2. SELF AS THE PROBLEM OF OTHER MINDS
Poetry, like philosophy, may be involved with the investigation of phenomena (events, objects, selves) and human knowledge of them; not just in giving examples but in developing methodological approaches. This implies not that the two traditions are indistinct but that aspects of each tradition, especially in respect to the basicness of method, may have more in common with aspects of the other tradition than with aspects of its own tradition; that the distinction between these two practices may be less a matter of intrinsic usefulness than of professionalization and segmentation of audience and so of the address of texts.

Twentieth-century writing has had as one of its most philosophically interesting projects the mapping of consciousness, an investigation implicitly involved with the nature of "mind" and "self" and indeed with the interrelation of these two conceptual constructions. The banners of this work are numerous—stream-of-consciousness, psychic automatism, surrealism, memory, free-association, impressionism, expressionism—and represent much of the most interesting writing of the first half of the century, continuing, indeed, into the present in various forms including chronicling of the life in persona, confessional, and autobiographical modes. A value of this writing for epistemological inquiry was the alternative model of mind it provided to the rationalistic constructions of neoclassical and quasiscientific discursiveness, since the organization of words and phrases, and so picture of the mind, is based on the perceiving and experiencing and remembering subject rather than on the more expositorily developmental lines of the "objective" and impersonal styles that picture the mind (and self) as a neutral observer of a given world. More importantly, this writing encouraged a different kind of reading, a reading that could be extended much beyond the specific writing practice itself. Indeed, all writing becomes open for interpretation as the trace of a self.

Yet, while certainly offering a different picture of mind by foregrounding the role of the self, this conception of reading/writing shares with more impersonal forms a projection of the text as sealed-off from the reader. Conventional reading/writing styles project this by the monologic character of their presentation. Both events and characters are assumed as being preconstituted and the discourse is pre-

sumed to be restricted to naming instances of these, to
commenting on them (the writing becoming the so-called
"transparent window on the world"). Just this picture of
reality is what, traditionally, has allowed the skeptical
argument its strongest foothold. (How do I know that these
things I see are not just an hallucination I am having, that
the external world, that other minds, exist independently of
me?) For this picture—"holding us captive", a "bewitch-
ment" of language itself, in Wittgenstein's phrases—cedes
from the first my role in the world as a partner in constituting
its meanings, picturing instead my passive consumption of
meanings already determined. Which becomes a paradigm
for both reading a text and reading the world, and for a style
of exposition—the neutral observer looking out—that itself
projects this subject/object subject/subject split. What we
are presented with is a picture of a person as tourist in a
world he or she does not fundamentally affect; but we
cannot see the world without at the same time touching it,
changing it.

The mapping of consciousness in writing does undercut
one sense of the sealed-offness from other minds by charting
the role of the self in mediating human knowledge of the
world. The peculiarities that form the trace of consciousness
and make it specific or individual demonstrate the *partialness*
of any construction of mind or reality, in sharp contrast to
the universality of claim in the tone of many conventional
writing modes. This acknowledging and charting of partialness does in fact break the monologic spell of writing seen as
a transparent medium to the world beyond it, but it does so
only by making a projection of self central to its methodology. In the end, this practice leaves the reader as sealed-off

from the self enacted within it as conventional writing does from the world pictured within it; while the trace may frame the reader, it also exteriorizes him/her; while it critiques the suprapersonal transcendental projection, it creates its own metaphysical fiction of the person. The experience is of a self bound off from me in its autonomy, enclosed in its self-sufficiency. The power of this besideness is that it (re)creates the conditions of nature itself, and so is a model of the human experience of it, human relations to it. But I feel not only simultaneously outside nature and constituted by nature, but also that I am constituting it! "Self" writing demonstrates this last condition in terms of its own construction of reality within the text, but the *reading* of this construction as the trace of consciousness structurally neutralizes this demonstration by presenting the reader with the self itself assumed. While reading/writing in an objective mode grotesques and theatricalizes my separation from the world, as if presenting only the hollow building fronts of a de Chirico painting, reading/writing in a subjective mode reinforces that separateness with its uncanny mimicry of my own experience of otherness. To be beside, to be next to (para/noid) is at least a significant break from a practice which places me outside, out of (ec/noid—out-of-one's-mind); it is the position of being in history, conditioned by time and place and body; and it is true that my relation to "things-in-themselves" is more accurately described by this account of experience of a self than by one that simply presumes such experience as impartial.

There is another conceptualization for writing and reading that presents a rather different idea of a map than that of mapping consciousness. The text is again seen as a map, but in the sense of a model, or outline, or legend and not trace. Rather than work which is the product of the "author's" projection/memory/associative process, it is work for the reader's (viewer's) projection/construction. The text calls upon the reader to be actively involved in the process of constituting its meaning, the reader becoming a neutral observer neither to a described exteriority nor to an enacted interiority. The text formally involves the process of response/interpretation and in so doing makes the reader aware of herself or himself as producer as well as consumer of meaning. It calls the reader to action, questioning, self-examination: to a reconsideration and remaking of the habits, automatisms, conventions, beliefs through which, and only through which, we see and interpret the world. It insists that there is, in any case, no seeing without interpretation and chooses to incorporate this interpretive process actively by bringing it into view rather than to exploit it passively by deleting its tracks.

The skeptical argument founders on its assumption that knowledge is a thing that can be possessed rather than a relation that can only be enacted; its argument holds sway only in a discourse that seeks one univocal definition of knowledge for all situations rather than one that has the capacity to acknowledge specific situations in which things get known. A writing that incorporates the issue of interpretation and interaction—use—insists on knowing as a response rather than a neutralized perception. By banishing the stasis of the monologic picture of a world sealed off in its preconstitution, the "picture" that "holds us captive" is dissolved and we are given in its place a world with which we must interact to understand: in which I know you not by a consumption of your persona, or by gazing intently at the trace of your body or mind, but by my response to you in a specific situation, my call of your name.

The individual is the product of a discourse, and so of a power relation in society, not an entity acted upon by all discourse. Writing (or reading) that uses the self as its organizing principle, either through a persona or through the more open field of consciousness mapping, appeals to as artificial, as socially constructed, an entity as expository writing's appeal to logic. As such, "self" writing or "self" reading has no intrinsic claim to universality, or to the primacy of its picture of partiality; its methodological assumptions both invest it with a domain of descriptive and explanatory power and also set its limits. While this reading/ writing practice may have strategic significance as opposi- tional to the hegemony of scientistic modes of discourse, those of us who support this opposition need not maintain that any mode, per se, is the most direct path to truth; rather, the struggle is to bring to conscious scrutiny the social function different modes of reading/writing play and how they function in legitimizing or constituting or undermining the hierarchical power relations within the socious.

Writing as a map for the reader to read into, to interpolate from the space of the page out onto a projected field of "thinking" ("thinking" as a sixth sense, to borrow Richard Foreman's concept, a perceiving/interpreting dimension or function more like tasting and smelling than seeing, or more like the kind of seeing that goes on if you imagine seeing as a kind of thinking, as Arakawa suggests, in his work where "verbal language becomes a proposition of the visual world", or in the sense John Berger discusses in *Ways of Seeing*). So that the meaning of the text is constituted only in collaboration with the reader's active construction of this hypertext. This construction by the reader transforms the text in a way analogous to a stereopticon's transformation of two photoslides, except that the final construction is not uniform with each reader/viewer. Indeed, this conceptualization could allow for indeterminate possibilities for the final construction of meaning, as theorized by Robert Morris in respect to his minimal sculpture of the late sixties; or to a more contained degree, as allowed for in the chance-derived compositions of John Cage and Jackson Mac Low, in which the possibilities are narrowed by the greater specificity of content. By map or model, however, I mean a much greater degree of design, detail and intention in which variations of final constructed meaning would have close "family resemblances" to each other and where, in fact, the kind of differences among them would be part of the intentional (instructive?) strategy of the text.

(I am not suggesting, of course, a work which is more coercive than ever of the reader, which, by its scale and indeterminacy subliminally induces the viewer's projections and so effects an investment of authority in the work or what stands behind it. This type of coercion and control is predicated on a very specific kind of projection controlled by the context in which it is viewed, by minimalizing what is projected onto, and by a suppression of the fact that projection is being induced. In antithesis, what I am discussing brings to consciousness the fact of projection as part of the content. Indeed, all forms, all modes, all methods are coercive in that they have a relation to power. What is being suggested is that this be brought into view, a critiquing which has potentially liberating effect.)

The conception of a text as a map or model whose final constitution requires the reader's active response is a theory of reading. This concept of reading extends beyond the text into the world, into the realm of reading human culture, furthering the activity of critique in Marx and interpretation in Freud. In such writing, the autonomy of a text is not broached, nor is the relation between reader and writer gesturalized or theatricalized. In contrast to the predetermined interpretations of a text based on the primacy of the self or of logic, it is the formal autonomy of the text as model that elicits a response, an interpolation. Its presence demands that I measure my relation to it, compute its scale. It is never incomplete or sealed off. Its completeness consists of its inclusiveness not exclusiveness. Its autonomy is not of the self or logic but of nature, the world. Its truth is not assumed but made.

Four/ Conspiracies

INTRODUCTION
["LANGUAGE SAMPLER", PARIS REVIEW]

What we have here is an insistence to communicate. Not, perhaps, where communication is schematized as a two-way wire with the message shuttling back and forth in blissful ignorance of the (its) transom (read: ideology). There are no terminal points (me→you) in a sounding of language from the inside, in which the dwelling is already/always given.

Hints, then, of a writing that takes as its medium, or domain of intention, every articulable aspect of language. It's as if a new scanning of consciousness were possible by introduction of the music of its constituting. And by this means to make audible the thinking field: to get access to the lens (the mixed metaphor is again ideology) through which the world's meanings are formed into audibilities.

The work collected here can be characterized in the negative as writing that does not privilege any single mode, including the expository logic and speech-derived syntax that dominate contemporary writing practice. Distinctions between essays and lyrics, prose and poetry are often not observed. For instance, some of this hybrid work (I like to think of it as amphibious) engages critical forms of discourse in a prosodic scrupulousness of intention that relies for its coherence more on internal necessities of the poetic process of meaning than on external constraints of rationalistic argument.

Issues of poetics, when not explicitly determining the genre of the work, often permeate its mode of address—a tendency that can pull the poem out of the realm of purely personal reference and into a consideration of the interaction among the seemingly competing spheres of politics, autobiography, fiction, philosophy, common sense, song, etc., as in Lyn Hejinian's relevantly titled "Province" or Diane Ward's asymptotic construction of simultaneous statements, "Approximately". There is a willingness to use, within the space of a text, a multiplicity of such different modes, which counts more on a recognition of the plastic qualities of traditional genres and styles than on their banishment.

At the same time, however (often mixed in with, or the overall compositional product of, this multimodal process), there is a claim being made to a syntax—to put it indefensibly—of pure music, of absolute attention to the ordering of sound's syllables, for instance in Ken Irby's "Etudes" or Peter Seaton's more densely scaled "Need from a Wound Would Do It". Not that this is "lyric" poetry, insofar as that term may assume a musical, or metric, *accompaniment* to the words: the music rather is built into the sequence of the words' tones, totally saturating the text's sound. "Indefensibly", that is, because there really is no pure music any more than there is pure language since any material practice becomes itself a mode. Striking, in this regard, is Alan Davies's sublime diction in "Lies", in which he invokes a Blakean Poetic Truth at the same time that he laments its structural impossibility.

These considerations suggest less a common stylistic center to the work collected here (despite the giddy infatuation with rubrics that spurs talk of schools) than a common point of departure in divergence from—questioning—conventional practices in the recognition of the intrinsic "modeness" of any writing.

Identifying "conventional practices" is a major preoccupation for many of these writers since such practices exist primarily as blind spots in our thinking field, or as "Blank" in the term of Arakawa and Madeline Gins. Gesturalized divergence, for instance, is as much a conventional practice as uninflected conformity; both can provide inexhaustible material for poetic scrutiny. Such scrutiny will not necessarily dispense with conventional practices when they are identified. Rather the forms being critiqued will often be mimicked, which is to say, cited. Two examples are Bruce Andrews's bracketing of gesturalized divergence in "Confidence Trick" ("Dragooned dork bird" "Embalming fluid fuchsia") and Ron Silliman's bracketing of uninflected conformity in the first sentence of "Blue" (which quotes Valéry's wry epitomization of the conventions of the novel: "The Marchioness went out at five o'clock"). Michael Gottlieb's pointedly titled "Social Realism" is nothing but citation, yet the inverse effect of its weaving is an elegantly poignant melody of inner life.

The process of identification and critique has no end; no process, including its own, can be exempted from it. This may allow for some value in the otherwise shopworn notion of "the new": for contemporary writing does have the opportunity to deal with the particular material at hand in this time. While the process itself may not be "new", the particular constellation of materials always is.

I am sufficiently skeptical of the presumption of "advance" in "avant-garde" to equally distrust formulations that appear to pit "the new" against tradition. What is presented here exemplifies a continuing dialogue with the past(s)—surely not, though, just a narrowed line of hallowed English verse!—and the future(s). Yet because it is a dialogue, it does not only involve repetition of old forms but also a response to them.

My discussion of modal properties and critiques of conventions does not, I hope, obscure the powerful and sometimes pessimistic social comment in much of the work collected here. Indeed, it is my contention that having all modes available for use increases the capacity of writing for expression. The tone of anger, for example in Bob Perelman's "Third and Townsand", or of quieter distress, say in Susan Howe's "war / obdurate as oceans", is not, of course, a formal dimension but a reaction, in part, to the events of the current period, including a barbaric U.S. military and social policy.

Throughout this collection there is a feeling of investigation as a way for both self- and social discovery, and for music. An opening of the field . . . that is already inhabited. The trouble with the conduit theory of communication (me→you) is that it presupposes individuals to exist as separate entities outside language and to be communicated *at* by language. "As/far/as/I/can/see/you/are/there", as Ted Greenwald has it: the other shares the same language space as I do. Correlatively, I take his "all/over/the/body/finishing/touches" to be a literal acknowledgement that it is touch that completes the body, that there is no individual, i.e., untouched, body. It is the touch of others that is the givenness of language. So writing could be such "finishing touches", not telling another what she or he does not know but a resonating (articulating) of the space in which both are enwrapped (enraptured).

The resonating of the wordness of language is manifested by the multiplicity of structures and of syntaxes in the small sampling here and in the work of other equally relevant poets. For Tina Darragh the "pun as ambiguous figure" becomes the focal point of inquiry; her text is composed of "fragments of dictionary pages transcribed in form of an Ames Distorted Room—a model constructed to seem like a usual rectangular room, but when objects are added they seem oddly sized". I think the measure of these poems, indeed, sizes us up. And soon the oddness of the sizing process gives way to the physical beauty of hearing syllables dance to things heard—by being made—anew.

THE ACADEMY IN PERIL:
WILLIAM CARLOS WILLIAMS
MEETS THE MLA

The occasion of Williams's 100th birthday celebration at the professional conference of American literary scholars is an appropriate one in which to evaluate the inroads that Williams's poetry and poetics have made in the official literary culture of the United States.

Williams, more than almost any other American poet of his time, took an activist position in respect to the place of poetry—his work is an intervention within the culture against static forms of knowledge, against schooled conceptions and traditional formulation. Williams vociferously rejected the predominant academic forms of writing he confronted: verse fiction masquerading as poetry and logocentrism claiming the rights of "philosophy and science". *The only real in writing is writing itself. . . . To transcribe the real creates, by the same act, an unreality, something besides the real which is its transcription, since the writing is one thing, what*

Italicized passages are from *The Embodiment of Knowledge* by William Carlos Williams (New York: New Directions, 1974).

244

it transcribes another, the writing a fiction, necessarily and always so [p. 13]. Taking Stein and Joyce's *Finnegan's Wake* as cases in point, Williams insists *writing to be of value to the intelligence is not made up of ideas, emotions, data, but of words in configurations fresh to our senses* [p. 17].

What characterizes the officially sanctioned verse of our time, no less than Williams's, is a restricted vocabulary, neutral and univocal tone in the guise of voice or persona, grammar-book syntax, received conceits, static and unitary form. In Williams's terms, writing like this is *used* to convey emotions or ideas rather than allowed to enact them. This is the kind of writing Richard Tillinghast recently extolled in *The New York Times* (5/1/83): "Mr. Halperin is expert at appealing to the senses in order to create convincing illusions of reality. . . . all is comfort and contentment—a mood that predominates in this very readable book. . . . Good wine and well-prepared food are frequently at hand. . . . This is pleasingly done." Tillinghast, who surprisingly enough is listed as teaching English literature at Harvard (I thought he must be with Club Med's continuing education division), goes on, in an aside, to condescend to John Ashbery, rebuking him for too much "verbal sleight of hand, be-dazzlement for its own sake", concluding his review with some stock sentences that Williams found tiresome a half-century ago—"in jettisoning the attempt to accomplish what is commonly known as 'making sense', also cut their ties to any traditional notion of form, thereby obviating a satisfying resolution." Says Williams, *all* traditional notions of form, unless they can be "de-formed", are not "*used* but copied". They preclude "invention" by *anchor[ing] beyond the will . . . not liberat[ing] the intelligence but stultify[ing] it—and by . . .*

cleverness, apt use stultifies it the more by making pleasurable that which should be removed [p. 17].

The divisions in our literary culture threaten to continue to make inaudible the bulk of Williams's work, and that of his contemporaries and those who continue in his spirit. As Williams passes through the narrow and well-guarded gates of official verse culture, it likely will be at the expense of so decontextualizing and neutralizing his work that it will be unrecognizable on his own terms. I say this because official verse culture is no more hospitable to Williams's literary politics now than it was fifty years ago, though the name William Carlos Williams—signifying in some cases only a few of the man's tamest poems—is no longer being ignored since to continue such a visibly adversarial practice jeopardizes the authority of official verse culture itself. Faced with an author who writes that poetry's function *is to re-enkindle language, to break it away from its enforcements, its prostitutions under all other categories. . . . Thus Jefferson said, Liberty to be preserved requires a revolution every twenty years* [p. 20], the response has been to ignore the "rhetoric" and "draw the line" at Williams, continuing to bypass the many relatedly heterogeneous currents in American writing and in Williams's own writing. In the end, Williams may be a token inclusion in a canon that excludes what he stands for.

This schism in American literary culture cannot be adequately explained by allowing official verse culture the mantle of the academic or the traditional—mantles I think Williams was too quick to cede in his tendency to identify the dominating strains of "philosophy and science" with these subjects as such. Of course, official verse culture is

housed and boarded by the academy and drapes itself in the
veils of traditionalism. But as is evident from Tillinghast's
review—and analyzed in Eliot Weinberger's amusing account of Frederick Seidel in *Sulfur* No. 1—official verse
culture is more a celebration of middle-class, middle-brow
lifestyle than a continuation of those literary and humanist
traditions that have something more at stake. For instance,
Williams has done more to further the prosodic tradition
than any of his so-called more traditional contemporaries by
not replicating received forms and *not* voiding an audible
acoustic dimension from his poetry. Meanwhile, the self-
proclaimed defenders of the tradition have abandoned it by
repetition: love requires not miming but response, continuation, new acts inspired not beholding to the old. *It is to
divorce words from the enslavement of the prevalent clichés that
all the violent torsions (Stein, Joyce) have occurred; violent in
direct relation to the gravity and success of their enslavements.
Language, bearing this relation to the understanding, is the care of
[persons] of letters. . . . Does it not occur to someone to stress the
reality of the word—as distinguished from the things which the
word engages and which kill it finally?* [p. 143-4].

Let me be specific as to what I mean by "official verse
culture"—I am referring to the poetry publishing and
reviewing practices of *The New York Times*, *The Nation*,
American Poetry Review, *The New York Review of Books*, *The
New Yorker*, *Poetry* (Chicago), *Antaeus*, *Parnassus*, Atheneum
Press, all the major trade publishers, the poetry series of
almost all of the major university presses (the University of
California Press being a significant exception at present).
Add to this the ideologically motivated selection of the vast

majority of poets teaching in university writing and literature programs and of poets taught in such programs as well as the interlocking accreditation of these selections through prizes and awards judged by these same individuals. Finally, there are the self-appointed keepers of the gate who actively put forward biased, narrowly focussed and frequently shrill and contentious accounts of American poetry, while claiming, like all disinformation propaganda, to be giving historical or nonpartisan views. In this category, the American Academy of Poetry and such books as *The Harvard Guide to Contemporary American Writing* stand out. (Any so-called guide to American poetry that amidst citations of about 170 poets in its poetry sections (commenting here only on the older poets in the book's purview—it is even more shameless in the breadth and blatancy of its omissions among subsequent generations) that doesn't even *mention* the writing of Stein, Reznikoff, Eigner, or Mac Low, that merely lists the names of Zukofsky, Oppen, Spicer, and that hurries over H.D., Loy, and (Riding) Jackson in the same half-paragraph, while going on to lavish page after page on the usual suspects, even while extolling Williams, doesn't have a clue about American literature or Williams.)

Official verse culture is not mainstream, nor is it monolithic, nor uniformly bad or good. Rather, like all literary culture, it is constituted by particular values that are as heterodox, within the broad context of multicultural American writing, as any other type of writing. What makes official verse culture official is that it denies the ideological nature of its practice while maintaining hegemony in terms of major media exposure and academic legitimation and funding. At any moment its resiliency is related to its ability to strategically incorporate tokens from competing poetry traditions and juggle them against one another while leaving for itself the main turf. These other traditions—which are usefully, if necessarily only partially, mapped in several of Jerome Rothenberg's anthologies—flourish outside official verse culture often by setting up institutions of their own. Within a context that would include Williams, a few are university-affiliated *(Sagetrieb, Credences, boundary 2)*, some (like Williams's publisher New Directions) are independently successful, most are poet-run and transient.

Williams has written persuasively about polarization within American literary culture within the context of his irascible opposition to conventional education and rationalistic scholarship. While these issues are conceptually separable, for Williams they share the common ground of the academy. This fact is particularly important for Williams scholars, who, finding the object of their studies believes "the more you learn the less you know" can choose to ignore the resulting dilemma only at the risk of losing their subject.

A solution might well be what Williams calls the "humanization" of knowledge—where abstraction would give way to "emplacement" as scholarship acknowledges its material base as writing. In contrast, deconstruction, which is quickly becoming a dominant critical style of academia, is not the answer. Indeed, Williams would have had little to learn from our American deconstructionists, for there is little that they have said that is not better said by Williams in *The Embodiment of Knowledge* and *Imaginations*, or for that matter by Thoreau or Dickinson, whose much more radical critique of logocentrism has led them not to theatricalize absence but rather to take that critique as a starting point of a project of building meaning, "embodying" it, in Williams's phrase, to make it our own, owned. *In writing there are depths to be sounded as deep as any sky—as material, as full of value* [p. 129]. The deconstructionists are flailing their hands at the starting line of a race they know shouldn't be run without quite realizing that this new drama provides the only interest this race has anymore, since the race track itself has long been abandoned by the descendants of its master-builders and only schoolchildren frequent the place as part of field excursions organized by their emeritus professors. The histrionic attempts to stop the race gather huge new crowds to the stadium because they remind the *nouveau* audience of a time when the stadium was full in its own name and they miss that and so come to see a reconstruction so that it can be demolished. No wonder deconstruction has found so little use for poetry not content to reject Origin and Voice, poetry, that is, which takes as its task finding and inhabiting origins and voices. Such work goes unnoticed because it fails to engage the nostalgia of the crowd.

What Williams insisted on was that no theory has any value except as enacted in a practical or particular context—for a writer, a text; that writing has its own exigencies that can be ignored only at the risk of saying what is not meant. Indeed, his insistence on no ideas but in things is not only a now-familiar critique of transcendental formulas removed from historical material circumstances but an attempt to formulate a practice of *embodying* a knowledge not grounded in the abstract universals of logocentric "science and philosophy" but in the language practices of living—i.e., *invented*—communities. *It is unescapable that on this, emplacement of the understanding, everything else rests, every action, thought, system* [p. 133]. Williams, at 100, is heard but not listened to.

JACKSON AT HOME

I feel like saying, "The Mac Lowian equation is never simple." Words get in the way.

For example, in the chance-generated poem: the text severed from its author-ity; language speaking for itself, restored to its autonomy. But these ideas are about styles of reading not writing.

So it may seem that if these systems are set up so, and these words are the result of such systemization, they are automatic deductions, the product of machinic activity, divorced from the immediate moment-by-moment decisiveness of conventional poetic intent. The Mac Lowian systematic poem refuses the normal process of identification of a 'self' (voice, persona, sensibility) *in* the text as expressed or revealed—of writing as confessional or personally expressive. Faced with the Mac Lowian structurally generated poem, and aware of its compositional procedures, one is hard put to 'read into' it to recognize a mapping of the author's consciousness or a narrative or pictorial image. The language is exteriorized, no longer a transparent transport to a given world depicted. This, however, is not an intrinsic quality of the writing; rather, assumptions about the nature of reading are sharply confronted and normal patterns of projection are initially brought into question or, at minimum, made self-conscious. It is difficult to read the chance-generated text as though it were the product of the free-associative or meaning-generating processes of the mind because it refuses both the discursive and expressive modes of textual interpretation each of which assume an underlying intentionality on the part of the author—that she or he is putting forward a view, describing a real or imaginary or other state, or revealing a stretch of consciousness. By forcing this issue of the identification process in reading—NOT HIM/HER, NOT HIS MIND AT WORK, NOT HIS SENSIBILITY—the Mac Lowian systematic poem foregrounds the sense of language speaking for itself, making its own sense rather than a sense imposed from outside. Words and their combinations are exhibited, just as 'sound' is exhibited in Cage, and allowed to find whatever sense ('music', 'poetry') they make in systems of organization decisively removed from standard syntactical and grammatical arrangements based on expository principles and/or speech scoring and/or consciousness mapping (in its infinite variety, unified by an assumption of eye or ear's perception, the body, the particulars of mind). In this writing, the things of the world (language seen as a thing of the world) are valued for themselves, without the intrusion of ego's desire for ordering, of its characterizing order. The work seems to demonstrate that any specimen of language is complete, stands by itself.

But not so simply. The circuit of intentionality is not so easily broken. Words get in the way. The writing gets read into anyway—and the expressive hand of the text's architect has devised fields for this reading into, appropriating the consciousness of the projective process into the texture of the reading. Not a projection of 'self' as centering the language experience but a discovery of its possibilities in an exteriorized, decentered experience of reading. (The writing of a reading.) I think the work is grounded in this dichotomy: that 'self' if it is to mean anything at all is to be found from the outside in, in the structures and materials that make up, in constantly changing ways, the world. World not an assumed prefixed form to be revealed but a series of possibilities to be realized.

Indeed, by seemingly machinic means the doors open up onto new domains, zoological gardens of at first exotic and soon strangely familiar sights—as if the products of microphotography were first being screened, or infraplanetary fifth dimensional time dissolve spectography. (Mac Low as science fiction writer.) As a result of his architectural imagination—planning a dazzling number of different structural, language-generating systems—Mac Low has produced a body of work that is a practical catalogue of what writing can do. In effect, his work has broadened the possibilities of the medium, and as a result deepened what can be done with it, by turning up syntactic patterns and textures that a less systematic and more traditionally expressive writing practice could not have. In the end, new terrains are made possible not just for structural and programmatic writing but for all writing and all reading.

I think this may help to explain why Mac Low's voluminous persistence is so crucial to his project, even in the face of a reader's exasperation at the 'unevenness' of the work, his refusal to 'edit' out the 'best'. Such an idea would presumably strike Mac Low as oddly as it would a natural historian criticized for gathering too many specimens. (Note, in this regard, Mac Low's meticulous insistence on documenting the system, conditions, and time of each work: a framing that suggests again what his sense of a poem is.) Indeed, Mac Low can be seen as a natural historian of language, investigating the qualities and properties of human being's most shared substance. Mac Low has put investigation and discovery above the aestheticization inherent in editing—that it is in the world that we may find ourselves and not the other way around. Which is also, perhaps, why he has suggested that his texts are scores whose primary realization comes in performance (an idea interestingly related to his notion of the text as documentation). Performance actualizing the possibilities inherent in the text by grounding it (embodying it) expressively and particularly in a sounding or voicing. So that the text only comes alive in an active reading of it (in a performance, or, silently, by a reader).

Reading Mac Low's systematic poems involves looking at the words and their groupings and seeing how they operate, noting their configurations, attending to the possibilities that the system being used has allowed for and has come up with. There is an exemplary quality to the language that has something in common with reading the proof of a theorem or looking at quotations of odd colloquialisms or puzzling over unfamiliar pictographic or hieroglyphic writing forms. To point to this 'citational' quality of the writing is also a way to point to how musical qualities are brought into the work, for Mac Low's work lets the reader hear the language by noticing the syntax, a quality that is often intentionally underplayed in conventional writing practices. That Mac Low wants us to both hear and look at wordness in ways that don't let the language dissolve into an experience just of its 'content' is evident in the strong visual dimension of much of his work. Pieces in which the words are handwritten on large sheets of paper in every possible direction are visual performances of texts that demand as much attention to the graphic look as to the verbal meaning. Again, his musical work involving words or letters—not to get into here his 'purely' musical works—foregrounds the sound, or more radically, notational interpretation of letters and letter groups.

In Mac Low's procedural and visual poems the spell of language is broken by the delineation of the parameters that generate it. The value of such predetermined structures is their ability to frame the constituting power of the form in such a way as to break the illusory invisibility such structures have in nonprogrammatic work. While the direction of much of the most interesting recent poetry has been to substitute new, sub-rosa structures that are embedded within the text in ways even more hidden than the relatively ascertainable patterns of standard rhetorical/descriptive practice—works sunk into the illusionary mysticism of expressive and romantic utopianism, creating a world but not necessarily showing how it's done (cf. my panegyric for this in "Semblance")—Mac Low has constructed an alternate model which has an important relation to such non-chance-generated, structural works as Ron Silliman's *Ketjak* and, to digress into film, Michael Snow's *La Région Centrale*, where we see the seams at the same time as experiencing their product: watch the spell being created without losing sight of the machinic principles through which it is engendered.

Mac Low's texts are often dryer, in themselves, than either of the two just mentioned works—he has generally been more interested in his written texts in building structures than in inhabiting them (leaving, that is, the inhabitation to performance—his or yours). Yet it is the consistency and relentlessness of this position that makes Mac Low's work so fundamental a contribution to the poetry of our language. His work is a great testament to the possibility for structures in and of themselves, and for the sufficiency of possibility. That it is architectures that shape the world, but *we* who must fill them up.

*

JACKSON MAC LOW
[Composed using the methods of *Stanzas for Iris Lezak*, with L=A=N=G=U=A=G=E No. 1 serving as source text. Each letter of Mac Low's name is given a numerical value according to its order in the alphabet. That number then determines the page in *L=* to turn to, taking the first word that begins with the key letter and continuing to end of sentence. The first letter of each sentence in each paragraph corresponds to the letters in each of Mac Low's three names.]

Julian Jaynes *Princeton U* Houghton GO BUY IT WHICH TALKS ABOUT ME IS WOULDN'T QUOTE IT. Anyway among some thousands or many of distinctive or distinguishable things (while according to your capacity some minutes, days or hours 2, 4, or 6 people, say, are company rather than crowds), & for instance you can try too hard or too little. Colored barrels we trip over inside. Kabalist traind in math (U Chicago) cld have proceded thus, poetry precedes language, *makes it*, & here is that sphere of light held high, dodecehedron. States can be immediately expressed. Occurrence. Nob Ave, Del Mar, CA.

Measured. And situation of scarcity, with material (things, words) more & more dense around you, closer at hand, easier and easier becomes invention, combustion, increasingly spontaneous. Closure.

Light, as from a projector in an otherwise dark room. Oculist Witnesses. Way for . . . for doing what? for solidifying random & heedless acts beyond comprehension to the everyday; since that everyday is confused too broadly even for chronicles or semblagist)): does this outshine parsimony?

MAINTAINING SPACE: CLARK COOLIDGE'S EARLY WORK

> . . . is one spoken by a mind that has penetrated into
> the inmost heart of a thing; detected the inmost
> mystery of it, namely, the melody that lies hidden in
> it; the inward harmony of coherence which is its soul,
> whereby it exists, and has a right to be, here in the
> world.   —CARLYLE

> It will be as much like granite as it can be.   —POUND

These words are inside things, and become, landscapes of
their internal relations.

The Chinese in Pound: everything as a process-in-the-
world. So no nouns or adjectives alone, but ideograms of
subject-verb-object, thing and action not formally separated.

The Maintains (San Francisco: This, 1975). "Oflengths", *Tottel's* No. 11
(San Francisco: 1973). *Space* (New York: Harper & Row, 1970). Italicized
passages are from an untitled prose work by Coolidge published in *This* No.
6 (San Francisco: 1975).

Language, then, not mere naming, and, specifically, not naming things. In these poems, objects nor actions described as objects are not the primary substance. Or perhaps: everything is objective.

So events, in the world, this, themselves.

Coolidge's "Oflengths": The preposition as significant as verb or noun, presenting a world of relation—of it, on it, in it, between or among—here landscapes of particular situations, precisely centered on how we are situated.

Denise Levertov's idea of organic form, as opposed to free verse, is a way to begin an aesthetics of modernist poetry. By free verse is meant a recording each line as thought or unit or entity. By organic form: the poem as a whole entity, a cross-section of time and place, a constellation that captures a particular experience, a particular-in-time. In Coolidge, the experience captured is the one set down, internal to the individual poem, to its compositional integrity, its limits. Internal to the poem is the experience it is about: the "inscape" of it. So not the recording of a reality outside the poem but the reality of the experience in it—or perhaps—during it. What this process reveals is that which is intended—chosen, arranged, judged, decided—aesthetical or ethical or moral or political—in other words, that which is human and which is particular of each human.

Which says nothing of the reference of any phrase or image or element. But the individual reference is surrendered to the overall composition.

At first, reading the poems in *Space*, a particular phrase sounds right, seems well placed, and I attend to a variety of elements—internal balance, word-to-word parataxis, pun & rhyme & allusion, assonance, dissonance, alliteration. But a nagging emerges: Is this all there is to it? A glistening surface? A dazzling facade? Are these only automatons, patterns, manipulations? Just intellectual designs? —I feel I need a meaning to accompany this surface of words, to reassure me that they are about something, mean something. I want a way of reading these words, a way of interpreting them, that yields a fact, story, statement to accompany this surface. —Here the meaning seems to lie in the surface. The (outer) surface has collapsed onto—become—the (inner) meaning: so that the meaning does not accompany the surface of words but is simultaneous with it.

Take a line. What is it about? What is it referring to? What picture can I think of to replace it?

> "is so
>   of
>   from"   *[Space]*

What is so? Of what is it? From whom?

It resists my pinning it down. Won't allow itself to be coralled or summed up in a sentence.

But why resist? Why insist on distance? On being enigmatic? Obscure? Alien? Unknowable?

It is as if it doesn't care about me but just stares. (He, She, ——.) (Trees, Rocks, Planets, Stars.) Still, I am inside it as much as under or across. I stare back at myself.

In Coolidge, a poetry of elimination: stripping away any thing that distances, a reducing to bare form, aesthetic, way of seeing, pure judgment (within the limits of time and place alone).

Because of the multiplicity of ways any of the poems can be interpreted, a critical reading gets bogged down into diversions and limitations. It is possible to point to directions or ways of meaning, as well as certain textual qualities, but the poems themselves seem to show these up as incompetent.

For instance, here are some textual remarks on "Calypso" —"is et clastic": existential assertion of the type of thing it (the poem, the experience in the poem, the experience of the poem) is, "clastic", its density plastic (words as shape) and classic (poetically classical in its use of assonance, alliteration, etc.). "bill & wide": its dimensions, as also "two wide" and "mixed matted". "Trad stone dumb": descriptive of what it is, as traditionally stone dumb, i.e., brute silent presence, dumbly speaking this thing, stoneness. "links": what it does. Single words filling a line I read as verbs, assertions about it—that which is, becomes, here, the subject—i.e., it links, it keel, it dimes, it ponds—files, reels, says—it ultimately language, which does all these things, it says and shows what saying is, a link, mixed, matted, keeling— making tropes that gab.

Throughout his work, Coolidge uses phrases—word clusters—that have a gooeyness and gumminess, a thickness of texture, hard, ungiving and indigestible—"clump — bends trill a jam" "mid punt egg zero" "copra stewage" "globule"—making the poems dense and heavy, filling their space with a high specific gravity that weighs them down to earth, keeps them resistant to easy assimilation, lets them hold their particular space through time.

These verbal clusters allow for the most extravagant and wonderful fantasy—words building entities wilder (and more hilarious) than our dreams. My favorites from "Calypso"— "hum over glow trout" and "cog world sigh blimp". One is, after all, left to one's own resources: one can only imagine what these things are.

Here, words are not used primarily to denote (to detonate!): the poems more shapely than ideational or descriptive. "That words hum" "in figurative sap" [*The Maintains*].

A poetry of hieroglyphics: an iconography peculiar to this writer, this poem, not symbolizing something outside the poem (as in Lawrence, Freud, etc.) but remaining an impenetrable embodiment, untranslatable into any single statement. Symbol as embodiment of its particularity-in-time, the material embodiment of form, an incarnation, hence the miracle of art, that it means. (The human form divine.)

Coolidge uses and reuses a group of words that make up a significant part of the texture of his work. Typical of the words he mines in *The Maintains*—time coal mine cog mink facer diurnal hum bop breather clap cup slim putter alp ace at a an of part word in granite looped dogbrick slate it fin pound pond nul grouper trope patter nutlet pull pug noun pit bivalent as globose bulbous slag part borax blimp dine dime borage actinic limestone: such a such, the very so— mingles means & maybes.

These words take on the texture, the complexion, the materiality, the physicality of it—of language: the embodiment of the spiritual in the material that is language. *(Time's massed at material bottoms.)* Coolidge's poetry is *part art part limestone* and the cave that recurs in his work, particularly in *The Maintains*, is the "word mine" of language—an excavation of word/language as granite, limestone, dogbrick, asbestos, slate, monozite, coal. *The hall we came to, one large asbestos like word . . . as stone as words*: "it a it". *The Maintains* a cave of language to be mined, resisting all attempts to possess it yet demanding possession. So that I come to feel it is mine—a mine—of me—as much a rocks, stars, and ranges.

Grammar a granite: As in Stein's investigation of grammar and syntax in "Arthur A. Grammar" *(How to Write)*, Coolidge's work is an investigation into the different forms, the varying patterns, poems can take. So each work (as each poem in *Space*) has a new structure, new conditions, in which patterns are generated by different programs. But throughout his work the words, the word mine, like the language itself, is relatively constant. So that language itself (and in particular that subset of words that Coolidge uses again and again) is used as a prior text for cut-ups, arrangements, constellations, repeatings. All the same played the parts of the so in program. So—it—the so—the such—this—happening— being repeated. Repeating particular words of a word mine like counting off the cities and towns of a landscape, a wordscape.

The most serious critique of this approach to poetry grants all the assumptions I have asserted, all the possibilities of language to mean concretely, and says, still, that in the grammatical sentence all that is happening alongside, if you know how to read it: All that is being done in this genre of poetry is the dramatization of the possibility of language to mean as sound, as texture, as physical presence, avoiding the double edge that lets words mean in the world (i.e., in a sentence) and beside it.

Poetry need not win a philosophical argument; it shows, in its purity, what it wants and what it cares about. We can ask of a person or a work of art, if we feel the authority, nothing more than a wholeness of intention in the willing of one thing—"the very so".

MAKING WORDS VISIBLE /
HANNAH WEINER

We all see words: signs of a language we live inside of. & yet these words seem exterior to us—we see them, projections of our desires, and act, often enough, out of a sense of their demands.

Hannah Weiner, in her various poetic works, and, most especially, in the long poem she calls "The Clairvoyant Journal" has taken this fact of living a life inside of language most literally. "I see words", by which Weiner insists that the letters that spell out the various words and phrases of her work appear in various sizes and colors on other people and objects, but also, more importantly, on her self. Her work, then, consists of taking the dictation of these seen ciphers— she calls them voices—and weaving them into a text.

To "see words" is to be inside language and looking out onto it. For Weiner, this has involved an actual seeing (clairvoyance), although at the level of the text it is present as a pervasive citationality (both in the sense of a sighting and a quoting).

The Clairvoyant Journal by Hannah Weiner (New York: Angel Hair, 1978) and (New York: New Wilderness Audiographics, 1978).

266

And yet, because Weiner's work is so rooted in the momentum of the act of writing,[1] the diaristic energy manages to totally submerge (immerse) the citational shards into its flow. She has herself said that she is interested in an electric energy that completely fills the page, transforming it into an impermeable field. It is this element that manages to fuse the eruptive fragments ("voices") into a continuity. So that the three voice simultaneity that makes up her text reads out as a linear syntax, while proposing an awareness of its paratactic method, its shard-like materials. Yet, finally, these different voices set up a syntax that is not linear or monologic (the continuous strip of the prose line) nor do they simply establish a discourse that is dialogic or reflective. Here, the mind is constantly interrupting—intruding upon, commenting on—its own processes with its caps THIS GIVES ME ORDERS and its italics *don't make so many generalizations stupid silly.* ("How can I describe anything when all these interruptions keep *arriving* and then tell me I didn't describe it well WELL") But, more than this, the text makes one piece of *(with)* all this activity, continuously integrating "outside"[2] elements into its compositional field

1. Weiner's work stands as a remarkable extension of the diaristic tradition in literature. The sense of writing out a life, the enormous force that words have to come of their own, is graphicly portrayed in Truffaut's *Diary of Adele H*, where the writing is more overpowering for the writer than anything else, largely because it is never reflected on. This question of intention pervades the reading of all of Weiner's work, where the unsettling fact that the words may be in control is dislocating and alarming. Bresson, in *Diary of a Country Priest*, also focusses on the keeping of a journal; here the paper absorbs the ink of each word penned as if it were life soaking up so much blood.

2. "The poetry . . . begins . . . when that composing factor—the

without compromising their vertical disruption of the uniplanar surface. ("Each page a state of consciousness.")

The sections of her Journal that Weiner has chosen to
publish in the Angel Hair edition are characterized, even
more apparently than some previously published sections of
the work, by a recurrence of the most commonplace mental
static that is as much an example of obsessiveness as a
method of release from it. I can't think of a book which has
more insistently faced these materials—"BIG OK SIT
STILL RHYS COMES *PREGO* INstructions this
morning: BATH, SIT FOR AN HOUR *bathrobe* A LOT
OF RHYS thinking of going to Jerry's reading it's at

dictation, the unknown, or the outside—enters the work and . . . began to
construct a poetry that was not lyric but narrative. . . . It involves a
reversal of language into experience . . . a polarity and experienced
dialectic with something other than ourselves. . . . A *reopened language* lets
the unknown, or the Other, the outside in again as a voice in the language.
. . . Here is the insistence of . . . outside, an other than the reasonable is
said to enter the real. . . . The voice arguing the necessity of an outside
may strike the reader as odd since the outside, in whatever sense one takes,
is usually assumed. . . . Its placement here as a composing factor in the
poem disturbs our sense of a settled relation to language. It does . . . insist
that language is not simply relational, but rather a knowing. . . . It is
within language that the world speaks to us with a voice that is not our own.
This is, I believe a first and fundamental experience of dictation. . . . In
the reversal of language into experience [visibility and invisibility] fold into
one another and unfold, composing as voices in our language. . . . To
understand the 'outside,' that curiously naive-sounding insistence of this
work, it will not do to take off on those supernaturalisms which precondition and explain the experience. The dictation remains persistently of the
world. . . . The outside as it becomes technical to our experience re-poses a
tense discourse, which interrogates the humanism and anthropomorphism
of what is usually thought to be the poem's expression." —From "The
Practice of Outside" by Robin Blaser in *The Collected Books of Jack Spicer*,
(Santa Barbara: Black Sparrow, 1975).

2   saw 2 OCLOCK   Still depressed, dreamt I was being
married off to some fat Jewish boy   I had to wear this
shower cap *be careful* tonight *don't dream.* PUT SOME
CLOTHES ON   Is that Peggy, the same as GET DRESS
There's a lot of energy is this *30's* robe can see parts of me
light up *glowing*"—nor one that has looked out on this world
with a more pervasively whimsical refusal to take oneself—
& these facts of life—too seriously. That this book is largely
composed of debris may account for some of the anxiety in
reading it.

In her work, Weiner has explored—come upon—the
language that fills, and often enough, controls our lives
(every day, *common* place: she says "group mind"). That
these elements are *seen* in the work, hence physicalized,
palpable, gives us a view of what is given, what has been
handed down: & by seeing language operate, we can start to
free ourselves from a compulsive obedience to it. The darker
other side of the coin is equally evident in Weiner's work.
When we begin to see words we may find ourselves tyran-
nized by them if we cannot at the same time question their
authority. —Yet explorers run a high risk of falling prey to
their own discoveries. A hope is that others might yet learn
from these without falling prey themselves.

The citational: shards of language, ciphers to be examined
for evidence, yet which we are forever beholden to . . .
which holds our sight within its views. The purpose of
writing, Weiner says, is to "change consciousness". —This
work is, for me, heroic because of its radical reaffirmation of
a commitment to writing as a specific kind of object making,
an investigation rather than an aestheticization.

Weiner's writing is a chronicle of a mind coming to terms

with itself, quite literally: for the terms are, in fact, made visible. We all see words, but it is our usual practice to see *through* them. Weiner has focussed her gaze not through, not beyond, but onto.

THE ALPHABET OF STRIDE
[ON RAY DIPALMA]

The world is a text with several meanings & we pass
from one to another by a process of work. It must be
work in which the body constantly bears a part, as,
for example, when we learn the alphabet of a foreign
language. This alphabet has to enter into our hand by
dint of forming the letters. If this condition is not
fulfilled every change in our way of thinking is
illusory.   —SIMONE WEIL, *Gravity and Grace*

A unity suffering its inception.   —DIPALMA

Everything makes a move, is fixed, moves on—. *Between the Shapes:* an early "collection"—what is the sense of writing that inspires a person to craft these poems?—& yet already the (a) twist ("early in the turkey / the ground had a pedi-

Between the Shapes (East Lansing, MI: Zeitgeist, 1970). Night (MS: 1968). *Works in a Drawer* (Bowling Green, OH: Blue Chair, 1972). *Sgraffiti* (MS: 1973). *The Birthday Notations* (MS: 1977). *Planh* (New York: Casement, 1979).

gree") and a (the) sense of *words stacking*, breaking down the
syntax of pictorial representation into strata of words, *things*
("Above the tracks / a slight embank / ment. Limestone. /
Mud. Weeds. A / concrete wall . . ."). *Night:* & immediately
(from a more sprawling . . .) to a crystallization of form,
only what is necessary ("the condition was relative to a
measure"), stillness (fix of words); here the syntax opening
up by ellipses—one pinpointed detail next to another, concentric ripples not touching; items, words as objects existing
side-by-side; yet the movement of one unit to the next—a
progression of sightings . . . which gets very rapidly (*Works
in a Drawer* &c) to a subtle detail, refinement, that gives
weight to each syllable ("sooner or later the sun cracks
rebecca") & it's apparent that there is a constant attention to
order & balance (in the sense that a coordination of elements
is always at play, as is the recognition, though not necessarily
the recreation, of a specifically geometric arrangement). We
take this into the visual placement of words in the more than
100 pages of *Sgraffiti*, name derived from a graphics technique in which the surface layer is scratched into to reveal a
different colored ground. A complex play of cut-out, design,
procedure—always delineated, articulated—intelligence
dancing through the words & rearranging them. Or *The
Birthday Notations:* in which it's not the syntax that gets
broken up to bring out the plasticity, ping & pong, of word
against word—but a syntax—"After lunch I slept almost all
the rest of the day; another man would have made it his duty
to go and see the waterfalls"—that gets looked at with a gaze
that makes it plastic, so we see it as its mode of language at
the same time as enjoying its "content". Time having
moved us away from these syntaxes—the work composed

entirely of citations from seventeenth to early twentieth
century diaries, journals, and letters written on the same
month and day as DiPalma's birth date—but that distance
also allowing us to see them with an angle of gaze that
reveals their meaning with renewed intensity. Genre writing: well each way of proceeding establishes its own kind of
rhetoric but never assumes it, so the language work is always
active: "'You must talk with two tongues, if you do not wish
to cause confusion.'" More recently: the rubberstamp books,
which create a pictographic grammar, where repetition,
blurring, juxtaposition, and serial ordering page to page (of a
fixed 'vocabulary' of stamp images) give rise to a movement
of meanings realized solely by this specially made coding
("plane *falls on* horse, sheep *falls on* tractor, soap *falls on* boat,
chair *falls on* bear, cow *falls on* car, . . .")—but codes not for
sake of conveying some message by use of symbolic elements, but for the sheer joy of the cipher: their internal
movements & their transformations. — & next, what new
gaze ("Planh"), clumped with "rolling vision / from staring
eyes". —A sequence of illuminations, clouded, pulsed.
"When in the dark move faster, make your own light."
—Hats on.

COUNTING AND UNCOUNTING

We enter into the world and as it busies itself around us—he and she talking at, acting in front of, and motioning toward; a sense of its being outside begins to set in. In retrospect, our own actions become behavior, apparently given up to this outside world: They are the "disappearing works" of Barbara Einzig's long prose meditation. This poem takes us inside a life inhabited by recurring thoughts, fears, anxieties, and perceptions, weaving them into a sensual tapestry of desire, where desire is an activity in the world as much as the central fact of a consciousness and memory of it.

So much is lost at any point *(Having expelled herself from her native country. . . . Leaving her job her husband her child.)*, yet looking back on it the texture has a wholeness, an inclusiveness, that compensates beyond what any sense of absence could allow. *Beat a path. It was what exhausted her, and what sustained her, the tireless picking up after.* Sustaining a variety of psychic *coups*, at the time registered while passing over, now a topology to recall. *It was the same way*

Disappearing Work, a recounting by Barbara Einzig (Berkeley: The Figures, 1979). Italicized passages from this text.

with her children. They were doing things she was either ashamed of or could not understand, and so she just mentioned them living but gave no more information about them. This is the burden she bears. But here this cycle broken in the telling, a picking up after that releases the burden.

In *Disappearing Work*, Einzig focuses on the details of a familiar dailiness (memories of childhood, marriage break-up) which she so externalizes as to make strange, at a distance. Getting to a kind of ontology of the terror of the everyday—paralysis: the world swirling around you, touching it, pulling back your hand. Mother, father, children, husband, wife are the primary—though not only—characters of the "recounting", played out as "He" "Her" "Him" "I" "She". And there is a various and unannounced shifting of voice among these, as from section to section, sentence to sentence.

A domestic interior *(Here work is replete with domestic images. I imagine her mind on the contrary an array of fists, all clambering upward in confusion.)*—recalled, gone over, inspected, *wondered at.* So with an earthbound gravity of our own measure: *I was a small shaman so I had travelled low. I flew at a height of only eight or nine metres. The great shamans rode very high, they flew on the clouds.*

WRITING AGAINST THE BODY

DEATH IN THE AFTERNOON

She sighed in vain for the chaff and the wheat, not
knowing the one from the other.

Contradictory impulses characterize my approach to Ted
Berrigan's work. It seems easy to become caught up in the
circumstances and style of his life, to portray the man in
terms of his personality, his influence, his often extravagant
behavior. Such a perspective, however, whether the response
is positive or negative, not only deters attention from
Berrigan's writing but also tends to misconstrue the nature
of his significance. For Berrigan's work—less interrupted
than completed by his recent death at 48—can most usefully
be read not as a document of a life in writing but, inversely,
as an *appropriation* of a life *by* writing.

This inversion of conventional "confessional" style is a

Epigraph and extracts are from *So Going Around Cities: New & Selected Poems*
by Ted Berrigan (Berkeley: Blue Wind, 1981). The final quotation is
Berrigan's working of Rimbaud.

276

key to Berrigan's method. Inversion is both a formal and a
moral technique for Berrigan, which partly accounts for the
anxiety generated by his flips of self and text—text overwhelms self, self overwhelms text. Many of Berrigan's
admirers and detractors share a miconception that his work
is an extension of diaristic "self" writing, despite his decisive
break with such practices. What makes Berrigan's writing
difficult to understand—or deceptively simple—is that he
built his edifice on the wreck of the old—using its broken
shards to build a structure with altogether different architectural principles.

The Sonnets—with its permutational use of the same
phrases in different sequences and its inclusion of external or
found language—stands as an explicit rejection of the psychological "I" as the locus of the poem's meaning. This
rejection, however, is complicated by the enormous pull *The
Sonnets* exerts on readers to project onto the text a cohering
"self" even in the face of overtly incommensurable evidence.
(Transferance may be a more apt term for this than projection.) This is an enmeshment that not only the reader but
the author may fall under the sway of. Indeed, Berrigan has
(as in different ways much current poetry has) mined this
misprisioning for its considerable emotional power—tail-
spinning self-implosions and self-explosions with remarkable
dexterity on the principle that such power is too much to
give up, because, quite rightly, a writer can't afford to give
anything up.

                                             frequent
            Reification of my own experiences delivered to me
            Several new vocabularies

One of the risks of this enterprise is that the detritus of this project-in-writing—by which I mean "the lifestyle of the poet"—now as ever runs the risk of being taken as its flesh.

> The poem up on the page
> will not kneel   for everything comes to it
> gratuitously

The biographist fallacy substitutes the chaff for the wheat by renormalizing this *body of work* into a work of "self". In this way, the production of meaning is trivialized as personal gestures rather than *read* as inscription in a text.

> I'm only pronouns, & I'm all of them, & I didn't ask
> for this
>   You did.

So there is nothing *simple* about the biographicity of this work. For any self-celebration there is also self-destruction, in the sense that for Berrigan the morning—meaning dawning—of the self is also the mourning—meaning dissolution—of the self. The fusing of form and subject matter is evident: the "integrity" of the poem/body is "violated" by various literary or corporeal "abuses". Note that the body is an overt metaphor for a coherent, integral, individuated self—it gives a biologic legitimacy to the concept. Berrigan's work is, then, a sustained assault on the sanitized body of the "self" *(health)* and simultaneously on the sanitized body of conventional verse (especially the furnished souls of confessionalism). In this textual practice, health is both a grammatical and a psychic fallacy. Health suggests an "objective" criteria for a normalcy that, in Berrigan's terms, would be the death of the psyche, which is to say the death of the body. To write outside the sanctioned subjects and syntaxes of health is to be forced into a situation of desperation; to be able to continue that work may require the sacrifice of, at times, more than can be sanely or gracefully accommodated into a life. Berrigan's writing poses the startling fact of writing's lethal and consuming importance in requiring the yielding of body and mind to its inexorable priority. It's always hard to understand how writing can *cost* so much— because it seems after all just putting words on a page. Berrigan's power was to incorporate that cost—of the creation of a psychic space in which writing can occur—into his texts. Writing against the body he was able to realize an image of it.

> We are drawn to shit because we are imperfect in our uses of the good.
>
> I was charging others to love me, instead of doing so myself.
>
> You shout very loudly.
>
> break yr legs & break yr heart
>
> We ate lunch, remember?, and I paid the check
>
> The pills aren't working.

Such an urgent approach to writing needs to be situated not in a personalist interpretation of the man but rather in the context of the national and international sociopolitical climate of the early 1960s, during which Berrigan's formative work was written. That is, it is important to understand this work as originating in the period prior to the widespread and highly publicized political and cultural oppositions of the late 1960s and early 1970s. America in that slightly earlier moment was infected with an unspoken violence, a violence masked by anaesthetizing/neutralizing/nullifying forces marching under such banners as nuclear security, counterinsurgency, American will, falling dominoes, cold war conformism, preparedness, suburban comfort, self-reliance, and self-actualization, etc. This dizzying succession of rationalizations demanded more than the lip-service opposition of a writing that was otherwise content to go about business as usual. However, Berrigan's commitment to writing "over and against"—that the body might be destroyed in order for its truth to be told—did not preclude comedy. The humor in this work is related, in part, to a disequilibrium of scale—the (f)utility of individual rejectionism against the backdrop of Multinational Steel and Glass, circa 1961—as if meaning could be produced by sheer force of will, charging at windmills.

The problem is that this work has a wake often more visible than itself that blends with the historical—you might call it psychological—fact that such work does not come cheaply, can be no kept avocation, but must be torn from— *out of*—life.

Morning
        (ripped out of my mind again!)

The biographist fallacy misses the boat for the water by focussing on the tactics that have allowed for such writing. These tactics are no more than the exigencies of being able to go on with the work; though it bears saying that such tactics—desperate in the logic of their pragmatism—need less to be judged in the abstract and more to be understood in the context of the necessity of continuing without the luxury of second-guessing the means by which this is made possible. Though we all can and do second-guess others and ourselves daily with paralyzing monotony.

> I have had the courage to look backward
> it was like polio
> I shot my mouth off

It is a measure of Berrigan's times and not only of his life that such a project-for-writing took on these particular necessities. There are, of course, other quite different courses—but none less radical, none less serious about the production of writing—would seem to justify that journey.

> The only travelled sea
> that I still dream of
> is a cold, black pond, where once
> on a fragrant evening fraught with sadness
> I launched a boat frail as a butterfly

ROBIN BLASER INTRODUCTION
St. Mark's Poetry Project, 5/18/83

Robin Blaser's reading here tonight is a doubly special occasion. It is both his 58th birthday and his first reading in New York. It is odd that Blaser should never have read in New York until this time, since his work first became widely known in 1960 with Donald Allen's *The New American Poetry* and four years later with the publication of *The Moth Poem*. Although Blaser lived for several years in Boston in the late 50s, during which time he became friends with Olson, Weiners, Ashbery, and O'Hara, he has spent most of his life in the West. He grew up literally beside the train tracks of Idaho, moving to Berkeley in 1944, where he met Duncan and Spicer. His association with Spicer continued for 20 years, until Spicer's death in 1965. In 1975, Black Sparrow published *The Collected Books of Jack Spicer*, edited by Blaser, which included his long essay on Spicer, "The Practice of Outside", which is, as well, a remarkably resonant testament of his own poetics.

With Spicer, Blaser developed the idea and practice of the serial poem in which the energy—you might say movement—of the poems enact a sequence without imposition of "an imposed story line". They conceived the poem not as a short, lyric unit but as an interlacing fabric the whole of which is not only "more" but "other" than the sum of its parts.

I first met Robin ten years ago when I spent a year in the rainy woods of Ruskin, British Columbia, making a weekly trip to Simon Fraser University to take part in his seminar on Dickinson. Blaser's understanding of poetry as the mapping of a cosmology (the application to Dickinson is perfect) was a model for the integration (dance might be a better word) of the philosophical, mythopoetic, and personal into a text sometimes called "poem", sometimes "essay", sometimes "speaking". "All true language is thought and so reverses into experience. . . . Things and words are not separate." In his work, Blaser questions the authority of given forms and given voices, including his own, in a desire for something other, that is yet contained in language, at its "edge", a realization, as he quotes Lacan in his own "Stadium of the Mirror", that "I am *spoken* rather than speaking." "My hostility is directed to 'psychologism, sociologism, and anthropomorphism' of thought." In "Image Nation 12", his composition of citations, he gives credence to Benjamin's idea of a text composed entirely of quotations. What he says of that poem is perhaps as good an introduction as any to his work. He creates "not bits and pieces of a culture or scholarship but literal places of the heart".

HEJINIAN'S NOTES

In *My Life* Lyn Hejinian has written a quietly moving testament to the necessities and recurrences that constitute a life. *Words heard with the eyes.* The 37 sections of 37 sentences in this long prose-format poem repeat and re-contextualize a number of phrases, often lyrically aphoristic, that also serve as subheads to each section. *A yearning in motion, original impulse.* The book is composed of sentences in a serial order; each of these sentences contains its own inner contentment, standing by itself complete as distillate—*what the single word could hold as* content *as put into sentences,* she puts it elsewhere. *Pudding in a pattern.* Yet the overall quality of this work is that of the weave these sentences make together. *It is hard to turn away from moving water.* Hejinian's modulation of the jump-cutting between sentences, the gradualness with which she manages these transitions, provide a sense of spaciousness, of gentleness, without effacing the constructed quality of this movement, modu-

My Life by Lyn Hejinian (Providence: Burning Deck, 1980). Italicized passages are from this text.

lated, as it is, by the exemplary quality of each sentence, so as to make a pause implicit between each. *A pause, a rose, something on paper*. The work is both a demonstration of, and instruction in, the savoring of the things of a life. And yet this is a life with few dark or jarring moments: perhaps it's that *we have come a long way from what we actually felt;* this method seems to want to overthrow alienation by its sentient sentiment—a bouquet of flowers; it's genuineness is as palpable as its reassurance. *A canoe among ducks.* She gets to this: humming a nameless, a tuneless, tune—which is, perhaps, only the aspiration of poetry—not to reassure— while surviving, retrospectively, as song; or such seem to be the terms of this work. A life, the things of a life, put in order. *I* dwell in these things. *Fonder of the place we have found*—absolutely!—maker, *founder*, of the place we have domesticated, acultured, found with our lives.

I THINK I UNDERSTAND
ALAN DAVIES

Dear Alan,

I found *Abuttal* to be a stunning presentation, in both senses of the word. & enormously confounding. Such an assault on not only common sense but indeed the whole apparatus of Marxist/Freudian/Wittgensteinian thinking can't help but be salubrious—a jolt to habit that returns to one's senses. Your Principles, as radically Utopian, as severely Idealist, as electrifyingly Ahistorical as I have heard in a recent poetry context, set a useful paradigm for the autonomy of a language in writing removed from its origins in *use*. Imagining language not in the service of reality—'noninstrumental', 'idled', 'split-off'—is a central project for poetry insofar as this allows for writing as the production rather than reproduction or representation of reality. To write as if language were an autonomous realm indeed profits reality, since reality itself is a formulation of the language we as a people construct. This is why the issue of 'perception', which you do not confront, is so crucial, because perception is a language-mediated activity. While there is a sense that

Abuttal by Alan Davies (New York: Case, 1981).

286

language can be split-off from reality (from, that is, the world) in the *methodology* of a writing practice, there is no sense that 'reality' can be split off from language, which shapes all aspects of our perception of it. Indeed, you seem to posit a naive idea of what reality is while at the same time suggesting a very sophisticated, artful, view of language. It is as if reality is a given object transcendental to human inhabitation of it. But reality does not have this kind of independent, autonomous existence; it is as a critique of this type of physicalist empiricism that views about the social constitution of reality and the relation this has to poetry have been articulated, and which have presumably given rise to aspects of your 'abuttal'. Your view, in allowing for a dualistic reduction, disallows the deeper reality of the inter-penetrability and interdependence of all oppositions as appositions.

—But such a rebuttal would only hold if the content of your text was removed from the internal world of the text you create for it, precisely a *misrecognition* in which I adduce a set of contextless 'factual' propositions from your Swiftian proposal. All criticism, if it is to get beyond the quibbling positioning of most expository writing, must aspire to fiction. The only true arguments are the ones we cannot make, and, in making, create universes we cannot, or will not, envision. All of your 'critical' work is of this type: deadpan beyond measure, as, say, Keaton removing/not removing the covey of cats in Beckett's *Film*. 'Abuttal' suggests a reply outside the discourse of debate (point, counterpoint), a text abutting —to the side of—such discourse. The logics of desire, with their prophetic hyperbole and incontinent incorrigibility, are closer to the truth of which you speak than the logic of critical realism with its Proportion, Judiciousness, and Fact. The prose of fact is like a giant vacuum cleaner sucking up the world into its cannister. Your prose of desire *gives forth*.

WITH WORDS: AN ASSEMBLING OF VISUAL WORKS FROM NEW YORK

To a large extent, the people in this show are primarily either writers or visual artists whose work has, at least in part, drawn them into an area of intersection. But, I think in general, the works exhibited here are best understood in terms not of "visual poetry"—in any sense that would make that a distinct entity—but rather in terms more directly related to poetry writing or the fine arts. Both Jackson Mac Low and Bruce Andrews—in the work presented here—seem interested in breaking words out of the normalizing and officiating codification of the world, allowing words to collide and jam rather than simply represent a picture of a beyond-language-world taken as status quo. Mac Low's pieces, in addition, are specifically designed to serve as performance scores: a practice which subverts an internalized process of reading by necessitating that each element be read not as part of an accumulating, horizontal, movement —a syntax—but vertically interrupted (an outward movement from the page at each moment) as the elements are interpreted in a way similar to musical notation—a radically

referential sense of words and letters very much at odds with
Andrews's attempt to make the words exist as far as possible
for themselves and in relation to each other in the context of
the page itself. What's continuously remarkable about Mac
Low's work, however, is that these opposing readings of the
text in the end just add to its richness—they exist as
simultaneities. Mira Schor's interest in personalizing art
objects by placing them into some direct relation to autobiographical content has resulted in her making diaristic
writing the actual material of her constructions—here pieces
are constructed of a translucent parchment dusted with
colors and covered with handwriting. With a similar impulse, though quite a different practice, Nick Piombino, a
writer, has situated a collage made of various notebook pages
and printed texts so as to be photographed by Roland
Antonelli. The result is a series of works in which the
photographic frame and plane take the place of the page as
the medium on which the language appears, while the
selective coloration gives to the texts an atmospheric airiness
with shifts in color reading as changes of tone and emphasis.
The situation of writing is also Michael Gottlieb's concern.
Street and store signs, packing labels, public notices, etc.,
make up the material of his color xerox bricollage, which
re-place the signs of the world at hand. Lee Sherry, whose
paintings are intense studies of color and richly textured
pigment with a nearly monochromatic visceralness, has
become interested in her pages of hieroglyphic-like markings
in the sheer graphicness of the linguistic sign. Susan Bee's
use of purely visual material in the context of bits of
handwriting and type, in her collages, turns these non-
linguistic scraps into ciphers, creating an overall feeling of
intertextuality, that is, different senses of textuality being

balanced against one another. My own "veils", which involve typewritten pages of various shapes in which writing is continued on top of writing for several layers so that the overprinting of new writing partially obliterates the writing underneath it, come from a sense of the act of writing, that energy having as its *byproduct* the visual image. Karen Eubel's use of overprinting, in contrast, is related to her interest in repetitive and optically dense visual structures—a typical page for her involves various offset overprints of the same pattern of a single letter, each overprint slightly out-of-phase with the others, and some using a quite beautiful variety of overprinted color. Johanna Drucker's marvelous books involve a constantly shifting use of typefaces and typesizes even within individual works—representing a giddy thrownness into textuality, the typography actually pulsing with the energized impulses of writing as practically a libidinal flow. That is, what appears as the interruptive quality of the typography doesn't so much have its roots in cut-up or program (the "imposed" form) but comes out of "trust in the intuitive aspect of the organism"; i.e., the construction collapses back onto its own necessity, a short circuit that refuses to allow for anything but an integrated thing. Finally, Robert Grenier, a writer, found that his interest in seriality made him more attentive to small units of writing and as a result he visually removed his writing from its normal vertical and horizontal inhabitation (placement) in page and book so that these particulars could be seen better both for themselves and in relation to each other. His work, *Sentences*, made up of 500 different sections printed on white index cards, allows for an unlimited variation in sequence, or, in another sense, for a 500-part simultaneous sounding.

HEARING 'HERE':
ROBERT CREELEY'S
POETICS OF DURATION

1. IS THIS A REAL POETICS OR DID HE JUST MAKE IT UP HIMSELF?

A person makes measure as they move in the world, hearing it and sounding that hearing. *I had been trying to make clear that words might be lived in, in this way.* Value resides in the particular constellation of sound-in-movement: not exactly event or occasion if these are seen as stop-frame, out of duration: 'actual' as acting in-the-world versus 'real'—*res,* thing, possessed state. *I am not at all interested in describing anything.*

This insistence on duration is simultaneous with life lived in—as—a body: framed not by this device but by this inexorable condition.

The italicized passages throughout this essay are quoted from Creeley. Each of the three sections draws primarily on one of the following books, respectively: *Was That a Real Poem* (Bolinas, CA: Four Seasons Foundation, 1979), "Mabel: A Story" in *Mabel: A Story* (London: Marion Boyars, 1976), and "A Day Book" in *A Day Book* (New York: Scribner's, 1972). Poems cited are from the "In London" section of *A Day Book.* Note that beginning and end punctuation of the italicized material does not necessarily conform to the original texts.

292

> These things
> seen from the inside, human,
> a head, hands
>
> and feet. I can't
> begin again to make
> more than was made.

Inexorable but audible: to audit, that is, not the things of a life but its conditions, so to measure the contours and scales by which—in which—we, as human, live: *as though time were a distance.*

Creeley has demonstrated this seeming double abstraction of scaling measures to be the literal *power of heart:* solace's generosity. Thus in Creeley there is no imaginable split between emotion and recognition:

> I ask, who is the man
> who feels he
> thinks he knows.
>
> I had felt
> the way accumulated,
> coming from that past.

Accumulating in an order of sensation: a feeling that allows thought as its motion, giving way in turn to knowledge. The pictures of the world are things we offer, in our way, to make our way, with or against one another.

> Things one sees through
> a blurred sheet of glass,
> that figures, predestined,
> conditions of thought.

I think of a friend who often expresses the wish to have his perceptions free of what he says are the interferences of

words. This is like the man who, unhappy that he could not
see well enough, tried to improve the situation by plucking
out his eyes. *Poems have always had this nature of revelation for
me, becoming apparently objective manifestations of feelings and
thoughts otherwise inaccessible.* If access to the world does not
conform to a preconceived notion of an empirical world—
the transcendental signified!—you're liable to find the disappointed believer decrying instances of such access as word
befogged, "the prison of language". If that were the case, we
would be our own jailers, and the bars of the jail not made of
iron but of sand: sandbars of an oasis that quenches the thirst
of those who drink at it.

> Ears hear. Eyes
> see everything.
>
> The mind only
> takes its time.

So writing becomes not the wish to express a self egocen-
trically but rather to hear—attend—the order of syllables in
the world and in so sounding find who 'I' as a 'self' am. *I
want to give witness not to the thought of myself—that specious
concept of identity—but, rather, to what I am as simple agency, a
thing evidently alive by virtue of such activity.* The concept of
identity being specious because it presumes a self already
conscious of, conversant with, itself. I 'know' myself, however, only in attending to the measures of the world, that in
such witness I am able to 'place' myself in an order of selves
that counts me as one. *I was born some years ago and I have
paid attention as I was able, to all that came to attention. . . .
"How can we tell the dancer from the dance."*
The field of language is coextensive with the field of the

interpersonal, call it the communicative field. The dawning of language in us already holds the impress of others: it is impossible to start to think without becoming totally possessed of this influence of others via language, existing prior to any visible, any noticeable, any imaginable, phenomena. In this way, the body gives evidence not of some primary subject but of a physical presence in the world. *In that literal situation of what one calls experience, the* outward, *call it, of the content of perception, a life is lived in the explicit package of meat one calls the body. A mind thinks of it, at first so intrinsically the organism itself that there is, apparently, no separation experienced. The eyes see, the mouth tastes, the nose smells, the ears hear, the hands touch and hold, the legs stretch and walk. Hair, skin, bone, the body fills, voids, heats, cools, sleeps, wakes. An interminable one of many, the thought of life apart from itself is vague, impossible to consider.*

Language is the literal territory of interpersonal exchange, call it intercourse. It is in this context that three central features of Creeley's poetry can be understood: the pervasiveness of lyric love poems in complete or vestigial form, the persistent address to the (a) second person—'you', and the virtually ever-present invocative use of the word 'here'.

For Creeley, the love poem becomes an occasion for envisioning the possibility of relation(ship) as a textual issue. Preliminarily, it can be observed that the 'you' of Creeley's texts operationally signifies the reader reading the poem.

> How the I
> speaks to
> you—
> over hills.

(The text, in the form of a book, is interposed between the

writer and reader: a hill that separates here and there.)
However, Creeley's 'you' seems to have a wider ontological
status, referring to any point of spatial or temporal displacement from a posited—you might say inherited—here.

> The *you* imagined locates
> the response.

'You' locates spatiality and temporality as vectors from any
fixed point.

Here/there, self/other are, in Creeley's poetics, projected
fissures rather than lived durations. In this way, the 'you' is
a masked 'I', not an actual other point but a felt exclusion
(from, that is, other bodies, but also from oneself reflexively
perceived as embodied, say, by seeing oneself in a mirror).

> You will never be here
> again, you will never
>
> see again what you now see—
> you, the euphemistic
>
> I speaks always, always
> wanting a you to be *here.*

The resolution of the projected otherness of others is a
matter of the power of duration, a sequence of actualities as
literal replacements, displacing displacement. Thus, the
hinge role that 'place' and 'here' have in the work: locating
the 'voice' of the poem and its material situation as a
duration that bridges the distance of 'here' to 'there', that
reveals a *mythic elsewhere was here all the time.*

> Think
> slowly. See
> the things around you,
>
> taking place.

'Place' in Creeley is always occurring as a sequence, as an order of events. 'Here' is never a point but always a series in time. The measure of that order being continuously *heard* 'here', in the language's enveloping continuity.

> *Here, here,*
> the only form
>
> I've known.

2. MABEL

There is, in Creeley, an insistent repetition of terms and names; his essays are filled with permutations of homologous formulations, consistently recited quotes. *There is a ring around my head, that crushes it.* The apparent lack of distrust of such historicizing is sometimes disquieting, although it is of a piece with the work's heroic claims. *Stuck with wanting to win, to prove it. Given world as destructive quicksand you had to find some purchase in, point of—struggling to get to mythic elsewhere was here all the time.* The terms of that heroism—a few "men" shaping the possibility for poetry in America—may seem out of place now, unnecessarily theatrical. This can partly be accounted for by the substantially greater visibility 30 years later of the tradition for which Creeley speaks, as *Sagetrieb*'s existence itself indicates. While this tradition and its current manifestations are hardly in the mainstream of official culture, the magnitude of related subterranean, ground level, and occasionally above ground anthologies, presses, magazines, and public readings is incomparably greater, and far more entrenched—a circumstance that Creeley has significantly helped to bring about. The difference from the current time is that, while an artist might develop a missionary drive in any circumstance, in 1950 there was little by way of organized alternatives to the established verse tradition to hook into. But the hegemony of Eliot and his kind in the 1950s only partly explains Creeley's necessities for parental forebears: *My own father died when I was so young I never felt that experience articulately, which is to say, I can never remember calling anyone 'father' in that precise way.*

I recall Creeley, about a year ago, speaking at the New School, commenting that he missed an heroic stance in those now writing, and my thinking, yes, what a relief to be rid of that, not to need that. It may be that others can significantly relieve one of burdens otherwise necessary to shoulder. I don't mean to saddle this person, so insistently of his generation and predicament, with the serpent's tooth of another generation's fervour. True to his poetics of the nonegocentric, these have been for him *conditions*, givens of his world. Far from blithely accepting such, he has ventured on an extraordinary investigation of how such conditions operate. *In this sense I am more interested, at present, in what is* given *to me to write apart from what I might intend. I have never explicitly known—before writing—what it was that I would say. For myself, articulation is the intelligent ability to recognize the experience of what is so given, in words.*

First coming to Creeley's work, *For Love*, I was initially put off by what, operating myself out of a time of intense awareness of the oppressiveness of sex role stereotyping, I found in his talk of "fair ladies", of the pervasive image of women as set apart, objectified. *So you got stuck with it too, trying to please the ladies—and why weren't they pleased. Histories of shifting discontent, maladjustments,* try again. *You put them where you thought they were, in your head.* Creeley's work attests to the experience of maleness as a social condition, replete with the troubling and problematic values that are so central a part of that role. *His parents had persistently told him of the need to* be a man, *in a great diversity of contexts. . . . The whole society had conspired, so to speak, to so create him, after his initial birth.*

That women in Creeley are set apart counts for him as the receding of human presence, of the possibility for it. That is, the image of women, in this literally *hetero*sexual work, is the image of the 'other', again that "mythic elsewhere" of projected displacement. So to come back to language as the territory in which this displacement/replacement occurs, and the matrix of points of 'I'/'you', 'here'/'there': *Why* you *never talk to me, why I can never make anything out of* you, *why* you *are never there when I want* you, *why I look for* you *and never find* you, *why I can never understand* you, *why it all goes wrong. . . .*

While the issue of sexual relations runs throughout Creeley's work and provides a major formal dimension to the nature of the love poems and the address to reader/other in much of the work, they are the explicit subject of Creeley's noncritical prose—*The Island*, "A Day Book", *Presences, The Gold Diggers and Other Stories*, and "Mabel: A Story". Of these, the most sustained interrogation of male sexuality is to be found in "Mabel: A Story". Mabel—*ma belle*—confronts a sexuality that has been given and, though perhaps not satisfactory, cannot be transcended. Give it to me, *is what he is saying, but tries to think of other words. The meat rises. Severed from the body, a series of steaks, it considers him mutely. Thus he is fed.* For Creeley, the sexual conditioning creating maleness appears to be correlative to the social conditioning creating identity, and neither is simply an ideological construction insofar as ideology is (mistakenly) conceived of as primarily a mental process. Indeed, Creeley's work provides continual demonstration of the physical ground of so-called mental events, and, in this sense, how language operates as a physical condition—that "blurred sheet of glass"—through which things "figure": life, again, "lived in the explicit package of meat one calls the body". These attitudes are not, then, "mind trips", as if the body does not so totally intrude into the world that the image of anything "without" the body becomes the best snapshot of it.

3. DAY BY DAY BOOK

After *For Love*, most of Creeley's books fall uneasily into the convenient cubbyholes of literary genre that his earlier fiction and verse allow. *Like many of my contemporaries I felt myself obliged to be an explicit craftsman so as to have defense against the authoritative poetry of my youth—whose persons I'd like now not to recall just that it's taken so long to forget them.* Freed of these constraints, Creeley has created works that sometimes synthesize and sometimes simply include literary and social and philosophical and psychological commentary, poetics, essays, narratives, lyrics, Spicerian "dictation", meditations, notes and fragments, collage, Steinian word-play, autobiography, and much else. It is difficult to understand the stylistic developments in Creeley's work if the "poetry" or "criticism" or "prose" is focused on in isolation from the rest. The best way to get from the more classical, and often unexcelled, lyrics in *For Love* to the great statements of the open field that *Words* and *Pieces* represent—an open field that seems to me a primary poetic domain for those currently active—is through the poetry in prose format: "Mabel: A Story", *Presences*, and "A Day Book" (the three works brought together in the English volume *Mabel: A Story*).

These works of prose poetry are usually seen in the tradition of such great works of imaginative prose as Williams's *Spring and All*, a text that has been significant, as well, in the current flowering of paratactic (serially disjunct) prose-format poetry. While Creeley relies in his prose on a more time-based sequencing of events compared to Bob Perelman's or Bruce Andrews's more constructive approach, there is a significant overlap in terms of narrative discontinuity and the resulting isolation/framing of individual semantic units. Robert Grenier's *Sentences* [Cambridge: Whale Cloth, 1978] is a unique realization of the possibility for such articulation of the sound of single sentences as autonomous and both semantically and acoustically saturated (the semantic and acoustic being coextensive in Grenier's work). Much of the new prose-format poetry uses autonomous units such as Grenier's in serial order within larger prose blocks. What is instructive about Grenier's individual units is the degree of independent articulation each unit can achieve without programmatic (or thematic) integration into larger formats: the units do exist in a crucial relation to one another, not durationally, as in Creeley, but simultaneously. In this sense, Grenier's work occupies a middle ground, useful to consider in this context, between Creeley's techniques and those of other recent poetry.

Creeley's insistent attempt to sound each articulation, to

stop it up short and let it be heard a second time, operates, then, to frame each sentence, or phrase, as somehow exemplary. *Insistent breakup of forms, things.* Perhaps the most characteristic indicator of this tendency is his often repeated "as they say", flagging, in a colloquial way, the thing said as well as the device: "as they say", as they say, and so on to one of those delightful transfinite regresses. *They* may well be *you* or very likely *I* that is, *we*. Creeley has a funny way of making it seem like he's citing, and in turn literalizing, clichés, when in fact he's manufacturing the sensation of hearing clichés out of word combinations not otherwise heard that way. You can see Creeley coming upon such bits of language he wants to cite in a process of something like journal writing in "A Day Book", a format that appears to give a more 'organic' placement to such gleanings. A similar process, however, occurs in his poems and can account, especially in the most recent work, for the multitude of insubstantial, watery ephemera that he is so drawn to include and, in the extreme case, seems to articulate nothing more than this process.

> I get
> a lot
> of writing
> done—

In the poems, the citational process is not limited to only sentences or phrases but often involves individual words, for instance, when they are broken over lines. The citational process is not primarily intended to call attention to the 'way' something is said—say its dialect or point-of-view—but to the sound as physical duration, as sequence of syllables. In this respect, note the plethora of off-rhymes, marvelously moronic at times, that bring to conscious ear the sound of the words as musical: *Bar talk. Bartok . . . , Sitting— / shitting* and so on.

In works like "A Day Book" there is little restriction on the type or order of material to be included. These things happen: *This, here. I am however young [old] writing at random—straining at particles of light in the midst of a great darkness.* These Gnostic-sounding "particles of light" are the specific conditions that make up (a) human life— identity, sexuality, but moreover a language that envelops these. In this way, the writing comes to desire to make actual its own conditions in/as writing by making audible the process of writing, or the vacancy of an inability to, in duration, as trace: *Like this—writing—fitful tracing.* Or again: *Syntax making articulate, i.e., coming literally to sound in the context, fact of fatigue and distraction.* And what principle relates, resolves, these gleanings, "particles of light": the ability, in "A Day Book", to accept the world as it comes, as an order that of itself coheres. *Finding then everything in due tone and order.*

> Pieces
> fall away dis-
> closing another place.

Place inevitably emerging out of whatever collation of pieces, always closing, foreclosing perhaps but only in the sense that life in time is always limited by the condition of time. So that this duration of particles, occurrences, particulars is, like Heraclitus's river, always flowing, always another river always *this* one. The river we live in as humans is our language—

Or is it water,
as ever, one feels the
flooding of?

"Liquid notes"—

NARRATING NARRATION: THE SHAPES OF RON SILLIMAN'S WORK

Narration doubtless preceded Acting and gave Laws to it.
                                                —JOHN DRYDEN

Think don't narrate.
                                        —BRUCE ANDREWS

The limits of adjacency are claimed; flagpoles flutter; in a faint sea breeze the buoy is boosted.

Out of a deep crease . . . & stationary orbit: a function made of hurl and laid with tarn. Beggaring for life's glimmer, indeterminate heliotropes on the slow boat to New Foundland. . . . There are no minutes, only moments, sewn together by this "self" same thread: a candle's whisk of tomorrow in the tailspin of cylindric episode. Or maybe two kilometers away . . . bedwetters, undigested skies.

How to get from A to C by way of, at the least, D. This is not only the story of a poem but of a life—bio*graphy*. The miracle is rather that you string together pieces and have a syntax comprehended, a life inhabited.

The pleasure in hearing syntax is like the pleasure in tasting food; in either case the alternative is sustaining, perhaps bracing, sometimes 'sheer'; but even the interstellar Hippy of the old lore likes to come down from time to time, for contrast. It follows, that is, by *dint* of: a demonstration that we live in a world made content a posteriori: an age of huts *(series makes syntax)* not bits. The body, so to say, is very nineteenth century; that we understand little more about it than a horse hay reminds me of the story of the writer who proved that discontinuity is a readerly fiction by riding on the subway. *It's* all connected and if you don't comprehend that it may be because it's not trying to persuade you that it is. Not that up is down—not so simple; more like sideways.

"That's not writing it's spelling!" I think it was Norman Mailer said of Erma Bombeck, or was it Golda Meir speaking Gershom Scholem. "That's not writing, it's spilling!"

Syntax is the order of words in a phrase or sentence (from the Greek for arrangement, to order together, as in tactics); grammar provides a set of rules that govern normative (a rule-governed normal) syntax. Or, as we like to say in the poetry business, "you broke it you bought it" i.e., you're gonna get hung with it. Which is probably fine with "you", just the ticket. You're hanging by it anyway. ("'Better well hung than ill wed.' . . . Better so, better well hung than by an unfortunate marriage to be brought into systematic relation with all the world", as J. Climacus put it some time ago.) I provide this explanation to put off such inhospitable and ungrateful concepts as "nonsyntactical" as if elephants, because they have trunks, cease to use their feet for walking. Should I choose to take my tie off, the one with the embossed seals that is so carefully knotted over my Adam's apple, I do not fall into a state of undress. I remain clothed, in some fashion or other, until I am without clothes and indeed then my skin still encloses me, until I disappear. (The real moral of "The Emperor's New Clothes" is that power is always naked and by force of that concealed by the modesty of a people who cannot bear to look at the spectacle without mediation; the Emperor is clothed, that is, by the self-protective squeamishness of the collective subconscious.)

If syntax is a neutral term for intrasentential relationships, narrative, in this structural sense, would be the term for intersentential relationships. That is, narrative is not intrinsically tied to causality, development, chronology, characters, setting—concepts that might be associated with narrative conventions within fiction or the novel. To make a narration is simply to make an account, and while an account is customarily given so as to picture an event in a causal-sequential manner, this is already a privileged assumption about the nature of the "event" narrated. Such conventions largely predetermine the nature of the reality accounted for by them.

The etymology of narration ("etymology is the hobgoblin of little minds" was it Noam Chomsky said of Louis Wolfson?) traces it to the Latin word for "a tale", which is derived from the past participle of *narrare*, meaning "to relate, literally make known", which in turn is derived from *narus* and *gnarus*, which mean "knowing, acquainted with". The root word, according to Rev. Skeat, is GEN, as in generate, beget (secondary form, *gno*—know). So, evidently from the first, narration has slept with epistemology.

Which brings us to Ron Silliman (this is an article about

Ron Silliman), whose work accounts for narration by showing how the sequencing of sentences engenders meaning and
how the world accommodates—is made particular by—the
ingenuity of narrative shapes.

Or again: Silliman writes tales, a word whose Anglo-Saxon
derivations include both the word for narrative *(talu)* and
number *(tael)*. By adding number (numerical structural
programs) to narrative, Silliman tells the tale of ourselves; or,
better, has awakened such tales from the deep slumber of
chronology, causality, and false unity (totalization).

Hypnotized by false unity, that is a theme Silliman's work
returns to again and again: the desire to read-in a unity even
where none exists. And so, in his own texts, detail is cast
upon detail, minute particular upon minute particular, adding
up to an impossibility of commensurable narrative. With
every new sentence a new embarkation: not only is the angle
changed, and it's become a close-up, but the subject is
switched. Yet maybe the sound's the same, carries it through.
Or like an interlocking chain: A has a relation to B and B to
C, but A and C have nothing in common *(series not essence)*.

Breaking the hold of rationalized narrative is not new with
Ron Silliman. One only needs to look at the opening of
Blake's *The Four Zoas:* "Four Mighty Ones are in every
Man; / a Perfect Unity Cannot Exist." And if the indulgence
of the juxtaposition is not incommensurable enough, let me
compound the problem by substituting Silliman's name for
Blake's in this passage from Donald Ault on *The Four Zoas:*

> Silliman forces the reader to come to grips with an
> experience of radically incommensurable explanations
> of the narrative nexus of events. On the other hand,

> Silliman implants signals which appeal to the reader's
> desire to find interconnection beneath surface incom-
> mensurability. The basic formula which lies behind the
> interconnection of these two narrative processes is:
> incommensurability does not entail disconnection; and
> interconnection does not entail unity. ["Incommen-
> surability and Interconnection", p. 298]

The "signals" Silliman uses to encourage the reader to find
"interconnection" are the structural programs that underpin
each of his works. Unlike Blake, whose signals are often
obscured by his mythopoetics, Silliman has relatively straight-
forward, usually numerically-based patterns that are, at least
in part, readily graspable. For instance, each new paragraph
in *Ketjak* has twice the number of sentences as the previous
paragraph and embeds all its words. The "logic" of his
narrative sequencing is experienced at the same time as its
effects. What differentiates this approach from a more ex-
perimental/conceptual minimalism is that the narrative rules
are not taken to be of intrinsic interest. Rather, they are used
to enhance the pleasure of reading the subject matter that is
processed through them. Silliman accentuates rather than
obliterates the distinction between structure and subject
matter, while at the same time making structure his most
insistent subject. The experience of reading a Silliman text is
less the coolly formal pleasure of looking at an architectural
plan and more the surprise of being in a building whose plan
becomes apparent as you walk through it.

Ketjak is one part of Silliman's tetralogy, *The Age of Huts*,
which also includes *The Chinese Notebook*, *Sunset Debris*, and
2197. *The Chinese Notebook* is organized into 223 numbered

paragraphs, a format based on Wittgenstein's *Philosophical Investigations*. The subject matter of this work is explicitly poetics—not only what it means for a text to be a poem but also why this particular text, in so many ways like an essay, is being claimed as a poem (and a section of a longer poem). But it is partly just the placement of *The Chinese Notebook* within *The Age of Huts* that makes it a poem. Poetry need not privilege a particular kind of language as poetic. In *The Chinese Notebook*, types of discursive discourse are explored by a poetic process: Silliman not only writes about, but also uses as formal devices, strategies of continuity, discontinuity, synchronicity, and format. Within its frame of poetics, other topics—sometimes the frames of the other books of *The Age of Huts*—emerge. Indeed, throughout *The Age of Huts*, Silliman recasts similar subjects into novel contexts, so that, for instance, when the topic of discontinuity/synchronicity comes up in *Sunset Debris* it can take on the erotic content that pervades that work: "Do sentences 'just come' or are they conditional, a logic of disorder, accumulative, sequential?"

In *Sunset Debris* every sentence is a question. This structure makes otherwise theoretical questions—which are quietly meditative in the environs of *The Chinese Notebook*—volatile, unrelenting, pleading. Who is the reader—*you*—reading the text? What assumptions do *I* make about *you* or *you* about *this*? As in a "mis"assembled jigsaw puzzle, autobiographical facts reside next to political inquiry, surface descriptions of landscape, overheard conversation, twisted clichés and jingles, imaginary aphorisms, place names and personal names, formalist self-scrutiny. Indeed, all these things are in all four parts of *The Age of Huts*, though with a different preponderance in each.

2197 balances out the more discursive concerns in *The Chinese Notebook* with a primarily intrasentential investigation. The poem is made up of 13 individually titled sections of 13 paragraphs or stanzas each with 13 sentences. Each section, then, is composed of 169 (13 squared) sentences and overall the work has 169 stanzas/paragraphs. The title is derived from the equation $13 \times 169 = 2197$. Each sentence in each section appears to be a modification of a similar sentence (or sentences) in each of the other 12 sections. Sometimes the modifications involve elaboration or fragmentation, sometimes syntactic permutations, and sometimes hybridization (parts of previously distinct sentences are detached and recombined). For instance, a sentence with the words "form" and "fill" shows up in all thirteen sections of *2197*. Versions include: "Only forms fill us." "Forms should not have fill." "Talking with the forms about the fill." "Forms fill." "The fill is a forms of coleus, canvas, barnwood, and skylights" ("canvas" and "coleus" are index words for another series of sentences, making this an instance of hybridization). "Forms stood on the sidewalks waving to the incoming black-clad fill." "The mereness of fill is not form." "This dream forms in the summer song of the fill." Evidently, the text has been generated from a group of core sentences [169, 1 in each stanza/paragraph, the author has subsequently informed me]. Like an inscrutable object of reference, we get many different views—some apparently incommensurable—but never the whole-itself. The structural metaphor of *2197* is playful and suggestive: "Locating prior concept atop difficulty." It baits with a lure of totalization, a unified and idealized picture, while providing only partial glimpses.

One of the thirteen sections of *2197* is entitled "The Four
Protozoas", referring to Blake's *The Four Zoas*, which is itself
a Biblical reference to the four living creatures who together
make up the human form in Ezekial's dream. In the midst of
Silliman's own tetralogy, the suggestion of four basic elements—with its echo of ancient Greek physics—is less a
numerologically oracular assertion than a wry comment on
lower limits—at least four. At least that's how I interpret a
motto that occurs twice in "The Four Protozoas": initially
Silliman writes, "Only struggle defines us"; before the
section is concluded this is transformed to "Only struggle
defines." This is the principle of narrative process rather than
narrative fiction. Definition is a posteriori, arising from a
poetic practice in which the reader is acknowledged as
present and counting. It is, accordingly, not reductive to a
single world viewed, but participatory, multiple.

> "Perspective" . . . is a product of the drive toward the
> suppression of multiplicity into unity, a drive which we
> have seen is overwhelmingly strong in Newton. . . .
> Thus what Blake's *Four Zoas* narrative constructs is,
> from the point of view of Newtonian narrative, an
> impossibility: a series of eccentric, mutually incom-
> mensurable universes which intersect precisely at their
> lacunae. [Ault, "Incommensurability", p. 299]

Rationalized narrative, in its presuppositions, is "A specific
ontology hushed, search[ing] for the world", as Silliman
points out in "The Four Protozoas". In contrast, Silliman
has produced a writing in which that search is replaced by a
material engagement.

In "Skies", a section of his ongoing *The Alphabet*, each
sentence is about the—or a—sky. These sentences "intersect

precisely at their lacunae"; they do not build a more and more commensurable picture but exist, despite this unity of subject, as separate, partial *and* complete.

> Newtonian narrative presupposes that behind the text lies a single unified field . . . whose essential features do not irreconcilably and incommensurably conflict with one another but can (in theory at least) be fully captured through systematic analytic explanation. . . . Both "Single vision" and "Newtonian narrative" aim toward making explicit the coherence and completeness of the narrative world of the text . . . and towards realizing a pre-ordained "end" or closure which resolves conflicts into a unified whole. [Ault, "Revisioning", pp. 2-3]

The Age of Huts demonstrates incommensurability not only within works but among them. Extending this further, Silliman conceptualizes "The Age of Huts" as part of a yet larger, as far as I know unnamed, superstructure. To understand Silliman's work it is necessary to look at both the shape of the canon (the external relationships of shape among the works) and how this shape is reflected within the individual works.

By backtracking to Silliman's early *NOX* ("Chronology is false consciousness" was it Harpo Marx said to Margaret Dumont?), the continuity of his work with the reversibility of macrostructure and microstructure becomes apparent. Each page of *NOX* is divided by a printed cross into four sections each of which contains a short (one to four line) poem with a distinct style and shape. The "action" of the work is the relation of the four poems on each page to each other, multiplied by the relationships among the fifteen pages of the book. By not homogenizing the text into a single voice or syntax, the separate elements are able to interconnect with each other through the readers' mediation. The isolated units come into a part-to-whole relationship not by altering the components but by incorporating them into the common poetic project.

As a highly schematic prototype of the work to come, *NOX* reminds that Silliman's structures can be read as political allegory for a society that is nonauthoritarian (playful and provisional structures) and multicultural (the absolute right of difference). Not that this is ever made explicit in *NOX*. In fact, the scale of such a reading contrasts with the delicate word-to-word and syllable-to-syllable displacement ("velopes / alism // *now hear this*") that are typical of the poem. These implications are internalized into the fabric of *NOX*—"a plaid etude". Yet, once recognized, the interpretation gains all the more power for not being demanded.

Let me abruptly jump ahead in Silliman's chronology and sketch the shape of *Lit*, his most recent work as of this writing. Twelve sections, twelve formats, each structured around some variety of twelve ("L" being the twelfth letter of the alphabet):

I: Twelve paragraphs, increasing from one to two to five and then, by plus ones, to twelve sentences each. The first few sentences of each paragraph are only one or two words, with larger paragraphs building up sequentially into very long, complex sentences with increasingly embedded, baroque style. The number of words in the sentences in the last paragraph, for example, goes from 1 (in the first five sentences) to 4 to 11 to 13 to 26 to 34 to 67 to 104. On closer count, this turns out to be a numerical sequence in which the number of syllables in each sentence is equal to the sum of the previous 2 stanzas' sentence count starting with 1 syllable and stopping at 144 syllables (12 squared and the 12th in the sequence). (This is called a Fibonacci series and is used by Silliman as the numerical structure for *Tjanting*.)

II: Twelve stanzas, a sentence a line, with the number of sentences in each stanza proceeding by Fibonacci progression, as in I, from 1 to 144. Sentences are fairly short, often only a couple of words and only once slightly exceeding a single line of typescript. So the feeling is of a steadily increasing accumulation of quick hits ("Numbers harden." —definition of a tale?); sharp visual details, often with structural connotations ("Web visible because it reflects the sun."); delirious (or serious or cited) assertions, aphorisms, headlines, slogans ("Punk is a petroleum product."); plain statement, naming ("The rooster."); decontextualized dialogue ("How can you think that."); "factual" and political reference, observation, irony (Reagan's "There you go again."); poetics ("Syntax presents the illusion of depth [pork stomachs]."); author self-reference ("Silliman is wrong and I can prove it."); idle word play, cited from a new commodity's brand name ("Nissan stanza."); sex ("Orgasm is a consequence."). (This kind of serial subject matter is similar to that in I.)

III: One long sentence arranged into 145 lines (12 squared plus 1: a delightful "mis"count), running-in similar kinds of subject matter as previously, commas where periods had been and only once at the line break, the strong effect of the enjambment to make it seem one long stream of associations in contrast to the clipt autonomies in serial order in I and II.

IV: Twelve prose paragraphs of twelve sentences each.

"This is narrative (you will die)." The relative uniformity of the paragraph lengths makes each a set piece; easy to become familiar with, keep in mind the inter- and intra-paragraph arrangements: a feeling of decorum, stateliness. "Lit, then whispers, flashes out" being a description of the emotional valence (in Stein's sense) of each paragraph.

V: Four sequences of twelve numbered sections each with three one-sentence verse lines (the total number of sentences is, like IV, 144). The sentences are mostly simple and declarative. The effect is similar to *NOX*'s schematic perspicacity. The groups of three suggest stanzas and paragraphs, but the double spacing between lines, and the lack of overt sound or meaning overlaps from line to line, emphasize the discreteness of the line-sentence units. "The simplest thing (a paragraph) has begun to melt."

VI: One long paragraph of 144 sentences. The subject matter is more obviously unified than in the earlier sections. Each of the sentences apparently refers to an aspect of Silliman's one-term move to San Diego for a teaching job. Because of the unity of the subject, this section comes as close as Silliman gets to a conventional narrative account. But the absence of causal and chronological connections among sentences, or explanations of settings and names, or attributions of attitudes or remarks, makes the "underlying" subject elusively unplanar and multifaceted, refracted into 144 synchronizing parts rather than caught and held in an ever more single image.

VII: Six stanzas of 12 lines and 24 sentences each (144 sentences total). The stanzas are typed across the horizontal axis of the page to fit the double-length lines. This is the most direct use of page scoring in *Lit*. The line lengths suggest ragged right prose, an impression underscored by the absence of periods at the line ends except at the terminus of each stanza. The second section plays with this confusion by opening with "New paragraph: old tricks" when of course the format, appearances to the contrary, is stanzaic. Is this a difference that makes a difference? There is another, subtler dynamic here as well: In the more gradual tonal discontinuities between sentences, the length of the para-graphic stanzas, and the strategies of opening and closure, Silliman appears to be alluding to the highly conventional-ized "prose-poem" style about which he has elsewhere said, "if it looks like a prose poem than it is not" ["What Is the Prose Poem?"]. Certainly, these last lines suggest a parody of that unnameable mode, or, at the least, a wry nostalgia for the fantastical unity of conventional short fiction: "A dense mist settles over the small white homes on the hill." "In the kitchen two sisters are dancing to the Stones while the calendar on the wall still shows July." "The old parrot gives a squawk." "The tiger stares through the bars of her cage."

VIII: A brief quote from Thoreau on the need for "a thousand themes" as distinct as a text can sustain. Written on the twelfth day of the month, this is a kind of reductio ad absurdum of *Lit*'s criteria of twelveness, although it's similar to Ray DiPalma's fecund text-determination method in his *Birthday Notations*, which is composed entirely of quotations written on the day and month of his birth.

IX: Four 12-line stanzas of 3 words each (144 words total). The short lines seem enough to induce the experience of lyric poetry and Silliman goes with that—the first line being "Wild gesticulation, wide"—but immediately under-cuts in the next with "receivers." and continues more in the latter vein through the highly controlled and "lovely" poem(s).

X: Has basically the same twelve-step Fibonacci progression as II but with several wrinkles. There is both prose and line format, some of the lined stanzas do not have any periods for the first time in *Lit*, and the tenth section, counting as "55", is actually five separate eleven-line stanzas with only one terminal period at the end of the fifth stanza. The internal complexity of this structure gives the text a quirky, quixotic feel. "These sentences occur in this order. I hate what narrative does to time. The garden's grown into a jungle." The final prose paragraph, with its 144 sentences in amusingly varied serial order, both caps and dominates the section as a whole.

XI: Twelve twelve-line stanzas, no periods, with a recurring pattern of six-, seven-, or eight-word lines. A return to normalcy—"semi-gloss wall". Each line is as much a sentence as previously punctuated ones, more than many. So verse = prose (there is, strictly speaking, neither prose nor poetry, Silliman has written ["What Is the Prose Poem?"]). There is no line-to-line enjambment in this section (an explicit exception is the two lines where the metaphor in the structure of autonomous lines is spoken: "To mean anything, to mourn anything, two / People terrified to speak of love.") Unlike, for example, the sentences in the final prose paragraph of X, each of the lines is evenly matched in length and content; there are no one- or two-word lines and no lines of purely transitional content; neither is there any of the pseudofiction of VII. "Sighing, declarative sentence makes wrong judgment or none." Everything is equivalent: "Espousing freely into air bag (sic)"—an odd comment on writing poetry, given the reference to James Schulyer's

Freely Espousing—to "Too tall antenna on a lone house"; or these stanzas make them so, make them heard as. The power of language: "Tough blue stanza Z-80 shuts engine off."

XII: Twelve twelve-section paragraphs that alternatingly decrease (to a series of one- to three-word sentences) and increase (to ca. hundred-word sentences) in sentence length. Because of the gradualness of the increase or decrease, the constraints and possibilities for sentence length are brought into focus. The shorter, simplified sentences tend to name and declare, a series of snapshots, while the very long sentences have a wildness of imagination related to the exuberance of their syntax. Yet, lest we be carried away by their exhilarating sweep, Silliman ends one ". . . that new syntax equal to the living could just as well lie."

The air steams with August heat, modicum of ectopian respiration. My preconscious is crowded with shapes and they're beginning to crawl. I can barely think my own thoughts. All I've ever been *authorized* to do is eat shit. Eyes stutter, ears bug out, mouth stiffens into brace. Plain brown wrapper around semblance of an echo of an act. Bunting puns, fronting stuns. *More than this.* The reasons, enumerated, cannot be asphyxiated. Get off the wall & into the hall. Which is not origami. Having ideas a kind of conduct [George Burns]. Not enough. "Mouth closes slowly over friendliest of . . ." WHAT then. WOA, Nellie Belle! "Everything is syntax (there is no meaning apart from the world)." "The sun steams into the sea."

This "writing whose value is not that it has none, but the image presented, craft-centered, of what working could be, the care in the word."

References

Ault, Donald. "Incommensurability and Interconnection in Blake's Anti-
    Newtonian Text." *Studies in Romanticism* 16:3, 1977.
———. "Revisioning Blake's Four Zoas." MS, nd.
Bombeck, Erma. *Life Is Always Greener over the Septic Tank.* New York:
    McGraw-Hill, 1976.
Burns, George. "Our Virtual Friend Gerald", *Aesthetics.* MS, 1983.
Climacus, Johannes. *Concluding Unscientific Postscript to the Philosophical
    Fragments,* S. Kierkegaard, Responsible for Publication. Copen-
    hagen, 1846.
Chomsky, Noam. *Conversations with the Invisible.* San Juan Chamula,
    Chiapas, Mex.: Np, nd.
Marx, Harpo. *Harpo Speculates!* Casablanca: Hungadunga, Hungadunga,
    Hungadunga & McCormick, 1961.
Meir, Golda. *My Life.* New York: Dell, 1975.
Scholem, Gershom. *Major Trends in Jewish Mysticism.* New York: Schocken,
    1961. See especially the discussion of *gemantria* (the calculation of
    the numerical values of Hebrew letters and words and their corre-
    spondence/substitution with words and phrases of equal value) and
    the related "science of combination".
Silliman, Ron. *The Chinese Notebook.* MS, 1975. Excerpts published in
    boundary 2 V:2, Binghampton, NY: 1977.
———. *Ketjak* (1974). San Francisco: This, 1978.
———. *Lit.* MS, 1983. Sections in *The Difficulties* II.2, Kent, OH: 1985.
    Quotations in the final section of this essay are from *Lit.*
———. *NOX* (1972). Providence: Burning Deck, 1974.
———. "Skies". Sections in *Sulfur* Nos. 3 and 4, Pasadena: 1982 and *This*
    No. 11, San Francisco: 1981.
———. *Sunset Debris* (1976). *Roof* No. 7, New York: 1978.
———. *2197.* MS, 1977.
———. *Tjanting* (1980). Berkeley: The Figures, 1981.
———. "What is the Prose Poem?" Talk given at New College of
    California, San Francisco, November 1, 1982.
Skeat, Walter. *A Concise Etymologic Dictionary of the English Language.* New
    York: Capricorn, 1963.
Wolfson, Louis. *Le Schizo et les Langues.* Preface by Gilles Deleuze. Paris:
    Gallimard, 1971. A good English account of the book is Paul
    Auster's "New York Babel" in *The Art of Hunger*, London: Menard,
    1982.

UNDONE BUSINESS

The publication of a complete and textually accurate edition of *The Maximus Poems* makes possible consideration of the poem's literary and historical context and its implications for current writing.

Olson's influence since the time of his death in 1970 is based as much on the impact of his poetics as of his poetry. Essays like "Projective Verse", "Proprioception", and *Call Me Ishmael* propose a theoretically charismatic alternative to the overly confining prosodic tenets of an official verse culture that aspired to police writing as doggedly in Olson's day as it does in ours. Olson's ideas of what poetry could be are in many ways more usefully provocative than much of his poetic writing—an observation that should not disguise that Olson's engagement with making poetry stands at the center of all his work.

Charles Olson, *The Maximus Poems*, ed. George F. Butterick (Berkeley and Los Angeles: University of California, 1983). George F. Butterick, *A Guide to The Maximus Poems of Charles Olson* (Berkeley and Los Angeles: University of California, 1980). George F. Butterick, *Editing The Maximus Poems* (Storrs: University of Connecticut Library, 1983). All page numbers, unless otherwise indicated, refer to *The Maximus Poems*.

Olson's commitment is to poetry as the most ambitious possible activity, exploding the containers of form by its outward thrust. *Maximus* never errs on the side of caution or conventional literary values (closure, smoothness of transition, propriety of fit). *The Maximus Poems* stand squarely against a literary ideology of rationality, preconceived unity, and stasis as the prime arbiters of the real.

Begun in 1950, *Maximus* has a boldness of gesture and visual enthusiasm for the page that, along with the work of other contemporary writers, makes a sharp contrast to the staid elegance—verging on claustrophobia-inducing syntax and subject matter—of much of the published poetry of the period. *Maximus*'s staggered line arrangement and ample use of white space represented an exultation of the page as a place to enact a living movement. Olson's articulation of the visual dimension of writing as something distinct from its aural/oral dimensions is more akin to Mallarmé than to many of his otherwise innovative contemporaries. *Maximus* insists on the semantic value of the spatial arrangement of the words: no meaning but in space, materialized on a physical page with printed marks. This, in turn, relates to a poetics of the body (proprioception)—the projection of the body's experiences onto the page, for instance in the physical marking of the ink as an extension of the hand. Such an articulation goes significantly beyond Olson's organicist explanation of line breaks as measuring "breath". The effect of the visual layout of *Maximus* was to foreground the page as field—more a process of material construction than Olson's more limiting breath metaphor allows.

Maximus not only challenged the staidness of received formats but also of conventional subject matter and syntax—

incorporating lists of provisions and land records, long quotes from other sources, personal and ephemeral diary entries, dates of composition, etc. By these and other means, Olson breaks down any easy distinction among writing genres—saga, chronicle, journal, essay, myth, narrative, geography, cosmology, natural history, lyric, epic, list, notation, schemata. The difficulties sparked by this refusal of a unified genre and attendant unified syntax are among the most original and valuable contributions of *The Maximus Poems*. By foregrounding the fragmentation of the text into incommensurable parts, Olson decisively rejects the rationalized narrative of conventional rhetoric. The competing ideological materials and the surplus of indecipherable passages and obscure references work as Brechtian epic devices to defamiliarize, to pull the reader away from the intensive and uninterrupted reading (consumption) of the text. In this sense, the length of the book operates to prevent any fixed or final or outside image of the poem's meaning; rather, the length tends to locate the meaning in the reader's periodic reimmersion in the text, with its multidirectional vectors and eddies. Sustained exposure to the difficulties of this writing has the potential of breaking down the reader's resistance to its intractabilities. Like the transformative effect of the final minutes of one of Jonathon Edwards's hours-long sermons, the mind finally snaps, giving way to another state of consciousness, a different way of reading.

Though the analogy is shaky, the impact of first seeing the large, allover pages of *Maximus*, with their agglutination of found materials, might be compared to first seeing paintings by Kline (with their black strokes against white canvas suggesting the field of action of the page) or combines

by Rauchenberg (with found elements stuck onto the form).
Olson's eye-catching work may seem less liberating, however, if the more radical, and ear-catching, precedents of
Stein's syntax, Reznikoff's use of found materials, Zukofsky's prosody, Oppen's polis, or Gillespie's vocabulary[1] are
considered. Olson's achievement becomes more conditional
if so contextualized—but such a contextualization cannot be
assumed for readers of this work either now or in the 1950s.
It should, however, be no surprise that the outwardly
directed, grandly scaled heroic gesture is more prized in our
culture than more intricately formed, perfectly realized,
introspection. Olson was not the first writer to break down
genres, or reject received literary forms—that he does not
claim to be is an integral part of his work. That *Maximus*
may appear so bold is at least partly the result of our culture's
literary and historical—call it "species"—amnesia, on account of which such precedents as there are get repressed or,
worse, explained away by justification. In the end, Olson's
lack of fussiness about his own breaks from established and
alternative poetic practices, and his willingness to completely abandon what he had rejected, is both original and
exasperating.

The Maximus Poems has a size and conviction of voice that
is able to confront hypocrisy and conformism loudly and
decisively. Yet the risk of an heroic stance is that in the very
boldness of its gestures it may lose substance. Olson's

---

1. See *The Syntactic Revolution* by Abraham Lincoln Gillespie, ed. Richard
Milazzo (New York: Out of London, 1980). Gillespie (1895-1950) made
extensive use of neologisms, idiosyncratic punctuation, constructed syntax,
and lettrist elements to create a total prosody more extreme than that of
Stein or late Joyce.

project—*push*—was to find an alternative to the discourse of
a single, rationalized voice acting with predetermined knowledge—trappings, in his view, of the "Western Box". For
this reason, he was attracted to Keats's concept of "negative
capability", which he interpreted as acting decisively in the
face of uncertainty. Maximus and the other protagonists of
The Maximus Poems represent "Actual Willful Man" who is
unafraid to act even where no sure course is charted. This
goal is less to restore a preexisting order than to "find out for
oneself".[2]

> *Maximus of Gloucester*
>
> . . .
> Half Moon beach ("the arms of her")
> my balls as rich as Buddha's
> sitting in her like Padma
> —and Gloucester, foreshortened
> in front of me. It is not I,
> even if life appeared
> biographical. The only interesting thing
> is if one can be
> an image
> of man, "The nobleness, and the arete."
> . . .
>   [p. 473]

While Olson breaks with the restrictions of biographical
persona ("It is not I"), his alternatives are personae of epic
scale, the heroes of *The Maximus Poems*—men of action—sea
captains, pioneering settlers, mythic characters. By "image

2. Some of these concepts are usefully and lucidly treated by Robin Blaser
in his essay "The Violets: Charles Olson and Alfred North Whitehead", in
Line No. 2 (Burnaby, BC: Simon Fraser University, 1983).

of man" Olson may intend but certainly does not achieve an "image of the human": almost all the heroic figures in *Maximus* are male as are almost all the authors of Olson's mastertexts (as well as most of Olson's commentators, as, alas, here). "Arete" means "manly virtue": virility. Women's voices—by which I mean not a product of biological gender but of socially-mediated attitudes, circumstances, syntaxes—are completely marginal to *The Maximus Poems*. The image is of men speaking to men—and all who fall outside that discourse are simply inaudible. The image is of the man of action ("my balls as rich as Buddha's") sitting *in* (and acting *on*) the female "field" (where "field" is also an image of the page). This sexual metaphor is further explained by the more explicit gender reference in *"The View"* [p. 225]: "the arms [of her] / of Half Moon Beach, / the legs / of the Cut".

The heroic, for Olson, must encompass certainty and uncertainty, the global and the local. While he rejects the idea of a single heroic voice as narrator or protagonist, Olson never rejects the heroic, which persists in *Maximus* in its scale (conceptually, and in the new edition physically), proclamatory syntaxes, "larger than life" stance, microcosmic sense of place, and so on.

> This, is no bare incoming
> of novel abstract form, this
>
> is no welter or the forms
> of those events, this,

> Greeks, is the stopping
> of the battle
>
>   It is the imposing . . .   [p. 184]

In *Human Universe*, Olson comments that the Sumerian *Epic of Gilgamesh* is "an incredibly accurate myth of what happens to the best of men when they lose touch with the *primordial and phallic* energies which . . . make it possible for man, that particular thing, to take up, straight, nature's force."[3] Characters like *Maximus* 's Carl Olsen have not lost touch with these energies:

> . . .   Up to then he was a giant
> of the experience of being
> a man, and so scared was I
> of his reputation (as one was
> of all these great fishing captains)
> . . .
> It is a pleasure to report . . .
> that there are men still . . .
> who are of this make.   [pp. 475-76]

This type of celebration of male bonding needs to be sharply contrasted to the claim made for some other writers as significantly exploring "femaleness", that is, psychic and syntactic structures that may arise from the social circum-

3. *Human Universe and Other Essays*, ed. by Donald Allen (San Francisco: Grove, 1967), p. 23. Italics added.

stances of women. Olson does represent some of the psychic and syntactic structures that may arise from male social roles. The problem is that for Olson "maleness" is patriarchally assumed to be an "all-inclusive" term for *significant* human experience by dint of an *unacknowledged* reduction of the nonmale to insignificance. Yet there is nothing new for writers of the "Western Box" to valorize virility—it is much less a break with the value systems of the West that Olson wishes to get beyond than a nonphallocentric perspective would be. Olson's critique of logocentrism fails to cut just this umbilical chord—and as a result he projects, like a man taking a Rorschach test, phallocentric values onto the non-Western/archaic sources that were to be his escape route.

The problem may be Olson's insufficiently radical interpretation of "negative capability". For Olson, the implication of the unattainability of certainty is that one must go on and act decisively in its absence. But there is a deeper sense in which doubt can cause cessation: one doubles over, paralyzed: one *hesitates*. Negative capability suggests not only the need to "know for oneself" but also to *not know*, to accept the limits of knowledge and of action. Yet Olson's commitment to "putting the hinges back on the door of Western Civilization" is a harkening back to the fiction of a prior order. This groping for occult explanations in the archaic is an instance of Olson's refusal to accept the limits of knowledge. Perhaps the more chastening lesson to be learned from the archaic is of our own ignorance and of the value in acknowledging it. That is, acknowledge that we can see in such worlds from which we are cut off only projections of ourselves writ large. The lesson is not of archetypes but of shadows and haze.

In breaking with rationalistic discourse, Olson sets up a false dichotomy between the authority of breath and parataxis and the stasis of the periodic sentence and formal metrics. All attempts to put forward one side of a metaphysical dichotomy just ensnare one deeper in the "Western Box". Olson's relation to language was that it must be shaped into an "image of man"—words put to the use of this image, instrumentalized in its name. Phallocentric syntax (by which I mean a social or symbolic construction not necessarily related to biological gender) values the declarative more than the convoluted, grandiosity more than humor, assurance more than confusion. Olson's overly literal insistence on breath and place too often distracts from the enactment of line and location as facts primarily of a text. Olson's heroic stance bypasses the syntactic revolution already achieved, by the start of *Maximus*, by Stein, Zukofsky, and others. The heroic stance translates into a will to dominate language rather than let it be (heard) (though note that Olson resists this encroachment in, for example, *The Distances*). In short, the "humanist" claims of the heroic help evade the responsibility for creating a prosody not based on received idealizations of speech and the willful man.

Yet it would be misleading not to place Olson's stance in the context of the malignantly bland conformism of the 1950s and of a left opposition eager to celebrate the worst aspects of statistical rationalism on both literary and political fronts. Many of the most powerful poems in *Maximus* speak out grandly and magnificently against these unholy alliances:

> Let those who use words cheap, who use us cheap
> take themselves out of the way
> Let them not talk of what is good for the city

          . . .
          As the people of the earth are now, Gloucester
          is heterogenous, and so can know polis
          not as localism, not that mu-sick (the trick
          of corporations, newspapers, slick magazines, movie
              houses,
          the ships, even the wharves, absentee-owned

          they whine to my people, these entertainers, sellers

          they play upon their bigotries (upon their fears

              . . .
          I speak to any of you, not to you all, to no group, not to
              you as citizens
          as my Tyrian might have. Polis now
          is a few, is a coherence not even yet new (the island of
              this city
          is a mainland now of who? who can say who are
          citizens?

          Only a man or girl [though sic] who hear a word

              . . .
          Root person in root place . . .   [pp. 13-16]

But such moments are not the stock-in-trade of *Maximus*,
indeed are deliberately limited so that the other types of
material can speak their pieces. Yet after reading a poem like
"Letter 3", it's a letdown to read so much of the uncompel-
ling material that gives *Maximus* its bulk. Obviously, to be
disappointed is to have expectations; the prejudices I bring
to reading make me want to be able to count on every word
to make a meaning that inheres on the page. The escalating
plethora of proper names, chronologies, unsubstantiated
references and quotes, shipping inventories, geographic data

constantly distract: lead away from any grounding of the poem in the actual experience of the words. Or rather, the poem is an experience of distractions. *Maximus* is not an example of "intensity throughout the system" and one perception as often as not is quite distant from the next.

Certainly Olson, despite his dual allegiance to intensity, consciously breaks from the close-knit finesse of much of the poetry he most admired in an attempt to excavate, to create an open process. He intends a degree of discomfort as the reader is led to a world, and a vision of human history, beyond the page. The significance of Olson's alternative to the homogenizing, totalizing rhetoric of conventional literary practice is as much political as aesthetic. Olson attempted to create a work that would be as all-encompassing as that projected by the rhetoric of rationalism—a language, as Don Byrd puts it, "inside of which life can be conducted". Both the passionate language of "Letter 3" and the formal strategies of *The Maximus Poems* are infused with this attempt at counterhegemony (that is, a full-scale alternative to the dominance of the ideologies of rationalism, stasis, etc.). But it may be that the epic demands of such counter-hegemony led Olson away from a strategy of maximal textual heterogeneity in order to hold onto the unity of the heroic conceit and the unity of *Maximus*'s historical and geographical—thematic—concerns. These compensations for the text's structural ruptures undercut the realization of an intensity of readerly experience that does not rely on traditional tactics such as closure and uniformity and plot but rather is the *product* of heterogenous compositional methods. The lure of countertotalization is that it masks its own complicity in the assumptions of totalization: it is less a

departure from these assumptions than a regrouping of
them.

My balking at *Maximus*'s failure to grip my attention is
partly a response to the poem's insistent refusal to allow itself
to be readily consumed and disposed of. An argument can be
made in defense of *Maximus* in terms of the value of
boredom as an antidote to the fetishizing of aesthetic experience. Yet this sacrifice of the reader's experience—no matter
how consciously it is made—it too great because just this
sacrifice is the one that need not be made, and yet all-too-
often is made—in the name of Instrumentality, Conceptu-
ality, Representation, Clarity, or History. This is the *ph*allacy
of the heroic stance, grounded as it is in the anthropomor-
phic allegory of language as the stride of a man, with all the
attendant idealization of "speech syntax" and a voice of
authority. The poem ceases to be an arena of action (or
inaction) valued in and for itself, realized by its own internal
necessities (which is *my* understanding of composition by
field)—and is instead a repository of indications, specially
marked references leading everywhere but to its own durational integrity. *Maximus* is as far from the word-effacing
practices of conventional writing as could be. Yet its scatter-
shot information too often leads away from acknowledging
the specific tonal values of the textual materials at hand in its
effort to *use* these materials as tags for Olson's many
geographic, philosophic, mythopoetic, and historical ideas.
The result is a dissemination and dilution of meaning. In
contrast, where *Maximus* glows is just in the moments Olson
allows for intensified flashes:

> I have had to learn the simplest things
> last. Which made for difficulties.
> Even at sea I was slow, to get the hand out, or to cross
> a wet deck.
>
> > The sea was not, finally, my trade.
>
> . . .
>
> I have made dialogues,
> have discussed ancient texts,
> have thrown what light I could, offered
>
> . . .
>
> Tokens.
> But sitting here . . .   [pp. 56-57]

The Maximus Poems suffers from an information overload.
Ideas and tagged concepts are plugged into the poems rather
than emerging from them. There is so much melodrama of
ideation that it tends to overshadow the considerable melo-
poeia. Too often, *Maximus* abandons its task of mapping
territories unbounded by the rationalistic and offers in its
stead legends for such a map: sacrificing here for there by
substituting abbreviations for realizations.

Olson's sources are numerous and well documented by
Butterick and others. The range is marvelous: Vedic, Norse,
Native American, Greek, Gnostic, . . . But while the
promise of *The Maximus Poems* is to create a collaged
"hyperspace", such a transubstantiation remains largely
theoretical—undone business. Unlike Blake, whose prophetic texts appear to be a model for sections of *Maximus*,
Olson does not reembody myths so much as point to them or
try them on for brief stints. The design of *Maximus* encour-
ages referencing to a mythopoetic stratum rather than
trusting the words to allow this dimension to come into

being as the poem. The recurrent use of code words or
phrases—names and symbols with loaded meanings—does
not create an experience of the meaning of these references,
leads less to hearing than to deciphering. The multitudinous
documentary material with its plethora of unidentified names
and Gloucester lore—given the foregrounded rejection of a
single frame, as in *Moby Dick*, in which such details can
accumulate—are left to stand or, more commonly, fall on
their own devices. Such materials rarely undergo the kind of
prosodic transformations Reznikoff achieves for similar
material in *Testimony*.

It is not unusual for an epic poetry to be interfused with
historical, geographical, theological, and literary references;
nor is this necessarily distracting. Traditionally, the references of epic poems become unfamiliar with the passage of
time and place; with Olson, the obscurity is built-in as part
of the formal strategy of the work and diminishes only with
a specific education in Olson's personal sources. Insofar as
there is a claim for the wider relevance of these sources, this
can be justified on either hermetic or culturally hierarchical
grounds. The case could be made that the figure of a
seventeenth and eighteenth century seaport (Gloucester)
does not really work as a microcosm of colonial America
(and all that image, in turn, is meant to stand for)—that it
does not hold up under all the historical, geographical, and
mythological weight that is put on it. *Maximus* totters under
the strain of casting history into an image rather than letting
it emerge as a multiplicity of not necessarily reconciled
images. The poem falls prey to the impulse to justify
America by the appropriation and overlaying of privileged
texts (such as the Hesiodic myths, so specifically rooted in

their own geographical and historical context) that are ingeniously contorted to appear relevant but are only relevant with the wildest leap of a Gnostic imagination. What is finally interesting about Gloucester is not its generalizability to the fictive generalization of the American experience but exactly its ungeneralizable specificity. No doubt Olson understood this as well as anyone could—but an image held him captive and it was as if history was repeating itself inexorably.

When *Maximus* flounders it is at a scale that puts most other poetry to shame. But it makes me want more, more instanter. There would, however, be no point in an abridged *Maximus* since, for whatever else, *Maximus* cannot be separated from its "difficulties"; the power of the book ultimately lies with them.

> I looked up and saw
> its form
> through everything
> —it is sewn
> in all parts, under
> and over   [p. 343]

These observations may help to explain why it can be more interesting to read Olson's talks and essays, and to read some of the material about his work, than it is to read long stretches of *The Maximus Poems*. The background information provided in Butterick's *Guide* is more than a textual appendage to the poems. Perhaps the reason Olson was so fortunate to get the sort of extraordinary textual scholarship that Butterick provides is that the work requires—comes alive with—this attention. Butterick's two books not only elucidate thousands of otherwise inscrutable passages but also chronicle the drama of bringing a textual order out of a manuscript chaos. This process is surprisingly interesting and a necessary ingredient in the reader's process of discovering what Olson was after. *The Maximus Poems*, like all good poetry, insists on collaboration by the reader; but unlike the imaginative collaboration required by a Stein or Zukofsky, many of Olson's poems need a *scholarly* collaboration to make them intelligible. With Butterick in hand, one can begin to construct backward from the poems, taken as legends, to some idea of the omitted maps. (This accords with Olson's enthusiasm at Duncan's characterization of *Maximus* as a magic recipe to be followed [*Guide*, p. 196].)

Of course, there are many *Maximus* poems that are unencumbered by the need to be deciphered, where the themes of *Maximus* are allowed to create their own space, unhaunted by the ghosts of reference.

                                                          I, dazzled

        as one is, until one discovers
        there is no other issue than
        the moment of
                        the pleasure of
                                    this plum,
        these things
        which don't carry their end any further than
        their reality in
        themselves   [p. 46]

On these occasions, Olson dispenses with loading the poem up with what he wants to say beforehand and lets the meaning be found in the writing. This happens in poems where the shards that fascinate him are allowed to play musically among themselves without need to be supplemented by the type of information in the *Guide* (for instance, on the first page of "Physically, I am home. Polish it" [p. 456] as well as in "A *Maximus*" with its giddy jumble of names and terms [p. 193] and "out over the land scope view . . . " with its oscillations of the local and the cosmic [p. 296]).

Olson knows the precarious difficulty of writing poems—and living a life—that strayed from the accepted corridors of communication. *Maximus*'s tales can resonate with this knowledge:

> I tell you it's cruel. . . . No ship can live on Cashe's in a storm. . . . The night was black and the captain was off his reckoning. . . . The crew of course was down below. They said it was all over before they knew what was up. . . . They got up on deck, dazed-like, and there she was, a complete wreck. The man at the wheel was lashed but he said afterwards when he felt her go over he thought it was all up with him. He held on for dear life and never lost grip as he went through the water. But it's a terrible strain on a man and he was pretty nigh gone. . . . He did finally come around all right. It was about the narrowest escape ever heard of for a vessel. [p. 189]

This is the untold, or hidden, story of *The Maximus Poems*.

Maximus fares best when it is released from the demands of information, its cargo load jettisoned: when its content is not like vitamins added to bread which has had its bran removed. There are many such poems at the beginning of *Maximus* I. With the addition of 29 more poems to *Maximus* III in the new Butterick edition, this volume of the poem literally takes off into a sea unmanned by mythic sea

captains (and even the huge retinue of extras begins to
wane). There is less the Let-Me-Bowl-You - Over-With-
Myth-And-Cosmography and more

> Wholly absorbed
> into my own conduits to
> an inner nature or subterranean lake
> the depths or bounds of which I more and more
> explore and know . . .
> . . .
> keeping my attentions as clear   [p. 585]

It's surprising the degree to which the final movement of
Maximus is imbued with a sense of dailiness, of the passing
of time as marked by the page, where themes emerge only in
the context of this close notation of the ephemeral, punctuated by the shifting times and dates of composition. It is a
kind of poem one would associate more with Whalen or, in
a more urbane way, with O'Hara than with Olson: yet it is
in these poems that the sweep Olson tried for elsewhere is
most sweetly achieved—as miniature. No longer the heroic
warrior, simply—

> I live underneath
> the light of day
>
>   I am a stone,
>   or the ground beneath   [p. 633]

—for a poet, the page—its measures and its musics, in
which, unbeknownst, "one suddenly is walking / in Tartar-
ian-Erojan, Geaan-Ouranian / time" [p. 633].

> Imbued
> with the light

the flower
grows down

the air
of heaven   [p. 386]

. . . the air alone
is what I sit in

among the edges
of the plagioclase   [p. 385]

THE TELLING

For what Laura (Riding) Jackson has had to tell, poetry is insufficient. "Deficient", she insists; *The Telling* her first major work after renouncing poetry in 1938 as being linguistically incapable of truth telling. For writers serious about the possibilities of poetry it has been difficult to react; that (Riding) Jackson intends this difficulty is evident from her vehement refusals to allow her views to be taken as the basis of a new way—a "medicine"—for poetry.

There is an unsympathy—a quarrelsomeness at times—that runs through *The Telling*, and is accentuated in some of the book's appended material. This is not a quarrelsomeness for its own sake, but the result of the prophetic—sometimes oracular—mode (Riding) Jackson has chosen to write in: "preachment". There are few styles of, to her, contemporary avoidance that escape censure—from rock music and left politics to all manner of "professional" thought. *The Telling*, indeed, echoes the critique of Rousseau's *First Discourse*—that "art" and "intellect" have replaced "virtue". (Riding) Jackson decries the obsession with doctrines, the new,

The Telling by Laura (Riding) Jackson (New York: Harper & Row, 1972).

success in the place of "articulating the human reality with truth"; it is professional learning—e.g., the poetic craft, specialized poetic form itself—that interposes itself between us and the truth of the mutuality of our one being.

Her insistence in *The Telling* is that in speaking it is possible to tell one another of that in which we each are not another—the "Before" that is in the "Now", spoken as "Subject" to all "Subjects". Of the many things that prevent this truth-telling of ourselves is the self-satisfaction of carving out a voice that is distinct, actualized by its difference. "Telling differently for the triumph of difference, and not for truth's sake." Poetry dwells on the description of the distance, whose extolling, it is imagined, is a penetration into the deepest roots of humanness. This dwelling in the less-than, on the forms of our present lives, is a diversion from the fact of our "self-sameness in Being".

Since it creates a "literary reality", poetry is limited by its craft. "The liberty of word that poetry confers is poetry's technique not truths." (Riding) Jackson's mode of writing in *The Telling* is able—unlike poetry, she says—to have a place for the reader in it: a speaking ideal of "normal" diction, one speaking to another of the mutualness of both, all, in being ("a method of our speaking, each, our All"). Each section of *The Telling* is—this is my experience of it— the enunciation of a shared fact; I find myself in it not in the sense of relation of personality (foibles, longing, &c) but ontologically, by the fact of my human being. (And yet in her sternness and insistence on this ultimate seeing, her rebukes of all our human failings, perhaps too much—this "all"—is asked of us—does not her very unsympathy shut out?—for there is connection also in the recognition and

acknowledging of such failings in our fellow human beings.)
Although (Riding) Jackson's prophecy/pretension does not
allow her to admit any predecessors in this self-actualizing of
words—she says there are none, that the personal concreteness of *The Telling* is diverted by such comparisons—still, I
thought of Dickinson (e.g., "The world is not conclusion"),
of Kierkegaard's *Purity of Heart* and *Works of Love*, of
Wittgenstein's *Philosophical Investigations* (which, like *The
Telling*, is a critique/renunciation of an earlier work and
method), of Oppen (not "gesture" but the "actual" "which
is ourselves"), of Ashbery's recitals. Of *Walden:* "There are
probably words addressed to our condition exactly, which, if
we could really hear and understand, would be more salutary
than the morning. . . ."

In the supplemental material to *The Telling*, (Riding)
Jackson cautions against confusing endings for completeness. This work, dedicated itself to self-completeness, brings
to completeness the promise of Laura Riding's poetry. The
turning required for this completeness is, perhaps, an un-
expected one; its faithfulness to itself—to language, to
"us"—is manifest. "And the tale is no more of the going: no
more a poet's tale of going false-like to a seeing. The tale is of
a seeing true-like to a knowing."

THE CONSPIRACY OF "US"

I don't believe in group formation, I don't like group formation, but I am constantly finding myself contending with it, living within it, seeing through it. "Okay, break it up boys." First, there is the isolation of the atom, looking for some place to feel housed by, a part of, & every which way the people passing seem to have that—"see it over there"—"look!". But every group has the same possibility for insularity as each individual: this new "we" having the same possibility for vacancy or satisfaction, a group potentially as atomized in its separation from other groups as a person from other persons. This is the problem of family life. Property, territory, domain. But, "for us now", group (family, aesthetic, social, national) is merely another part of our commoditized lives—for we consume these formations, along with most other things, as commodities, & are ourselves consumed in the process. ((Putting aside here the extent to which political groupings and parties would be different from groups of "artists", also the place of groupings based on class oppression on the one hand and minority oppression—women, gays, mental patients—on the other.)) So we use groups as badges—shields—as much screening us

off from the intrusion of outside, others, as sheltering us
from the sheer invasiveness of it, them (& so allowing us a
place to occupy, inhabit). I don't so much think that such
shelter is a fraud, unnecessary, as much as "let's look at it,
call the strictures into question, understand that we *can*
reshape": a call against paralysis from a sense of boundaries
fixed without, or before, our having had a chance to
participate in their making. "The danger is that our demands on each other will trample what we really feel." The
danger is that we will hide ourselves amidst the shuffle to
proclaim who we are.

We're afraid to say poetry, afraid of the *task*—that's why
simply having the goods—"Oh he's gifted as hell"—is never
enough. I want to see more than fine sentiments beautifully
expressed "in the manner of . . . " "He's really picked up
on me" but sadly, not on *us*. One might as well go back to
fruit picking. It's hard to talk about content these days,
everyone pointing to the trace of their ideas as if *that* was
"it" but we don't want mere conceptualizations. "*But*, I
mean, that person is really saying something", which is the
wrong way of making the point. But: enough of empty
vessels for sure. It's necessity which makes the form, which
then inheres; not just any "constructs" but the ones we live
by, the ones we live in & so the ones we *come upon*—
    "Getting it." "Using it." "Pretending." "Imagining."
"On the inside track." "In contention." "An authority that
genuinely speaks from its heart, letting us know that here
. . . " "Great hips." "Thyroid problems." "Oh how come
you done that." "Ain't that *Christian* of you." "Grace."
"Grave." "Maria of the *fleurs*." "An open cavity, about

three to six inches from the back of tongue, who . . . "
"Naturally." "Over-intellectual." "With too much *effort*
. . . " "Over-emotional." "Grecian." " . . . which at times
one only wishes would give way to some greater sense of necessity, like why bother to write it in the first place." "From
up here, the low-lying clouds obscuring the view . . . "

Language-centered writing and other art-historical epi-
thets. For instance, you're right that the need for recognition, given that the work is important, does demand that
action be taken. Cuts are made but not without enormous
confusion on all sides—what's in common within & different
from without both get exaggerated. A kind of blinder's
vision begins as we look at the world in terms of the
configurations being made. "At a given time we responded
to each other's work, were there for each other." "To the
permanent removal of everyone else after, simultaneous?"
No. These things arise in practice, have a practical value.
((Imagine a world in which people allied along lines of hair
color. Or what unified a group of artists was their use of a
given shade of blue, or that they live (or grew up in, or went
to school in) the same place—the impress of a common
environment a constant to facilitate art-historical apprehension. How does Richard Diebenkorn get seen by those who
think of nonfiguration as the key issue of his generation of
painters? & *wasn't* it the key issue?)) But the "final" cuts
have not—will not be—made. Only cuts for "here" &
"there"—

The identification of "younger" poets "coming up" by a
group or community can imply the beginning for these
people of inclusion within a paternalistic hierarchy—an
initiation into it.—Simply, the walls must be stripped down

& new ones constantly built as (re)placements—or rather this is always happening whether we attend to it or not. We see through these structures which we have made ourselves & cannot do even for a moment without them, yet they are not fixed but provisional. . . . that poetry gets shaped—informed and transformed—by the social relations of publication, readership, correspondence, readings, &c (or, historically seen, the 'tradition') and, indeed, that the poetry community(ies) are not a secondary phenomenon to writing but a primary one. So it won't do to just "think about the work". But it still needs to be explored what the relation between "normal" and "extraordinary" poetry is—& why both need to be more valued in some respects and devalued in others (snobbery, elitism, cliquishness, historical over-selfconsciousness, self-aggrandizement, &c)—especially at a time in which there is an increase in the number of people engaging in art activities—not just a few "men" "out there" doing the "heroic" work. —That poetry, with written language as its medium, is, in fact, the exploration and realization of the human common ground, of "us", in which we are—"that holds our sights within its views".

Or what we have is a series of banana republics with internecine (i.e. inner) conflict as to whose to "be the" THE of the court, all that fading with jocular regularity as we paddle our gondolas down the canals of time and look back at the many remnants of period mannerism. You want to name names? I feel very bloated at last & want to take this opportunity to thank everyone. I wish I had a quill pen. I'll take a dime for every time they . . . "I mean some of this stuff really knocks you out." A great place to take your date, &c, I mean it really impresses boys. "You wanna know something—I'm glad what they done to you. . . . " The foundations of a linguistic empire on the coinage of a distinctive and recognizable style—"& that means don't hone in on my territory" "& that means *you*" is about as crucial as the opera of Luca Della Robbia. But not to stop there. "We" ain't about no new social groupings—nobody gotta move over—*this is the deconstruction of team.* This is *looking at language*, which *is* "us", & not creating the latest fashion splash of the "up & coming".

What happens, which is what it is when something happens & you say "oh, look at that ————"—already having arrived in your mind as a ————. But not just to plug in—"oh I got it let me dig some out for you—" The skips on the record which our pounding feet accentuate, making the needle dance out of synch to the rhythm our bodies seem to want to keep . . . —keep us honest. "Honest"? But not to "groove into", it's to make the words that come out *that* way more aware of themselves & so we more responsible to them, not that we "say" them with whatever capacity our "gifts" allow us but that we *mean* them with a twice told intention that puts "mere facility for images & transitions" in its place & puts "poetry"—a guild without members, only occasionally one or another of us finds ourselves there, or not "ourselves" but rather "those syllables so ordered . . . " & *we* mere spectators, out in the public field, watching *that*, now already behind us. . . .

FIVE/ FLESH

BLOOD ON THE
CUTTING ROOM FLOOR

Imagine that words have a life of their own, radiocontrolled by an automatic pilot called history. Imagine, that is, that it is not we, as Humpty Dumpty liked to think, that control our words but our words that control us. Control? Well, let's say, say more than we ever intend to say, do more than we know what to do with.

Imagine, that is, that writing is an artificial intelligence—*intelligence* in the sense of having a power over mind, *artificial* in the sense of transpersonal and nonhuman (it neither breathes nor bleeds, nor ever has, though its origins issue from flesh and blood).

To understand language as artificial intelligence is to conceptualize writing as a kind of psychic surgery—knitting together pieces of deanimated flesh until, like the monster in Mary Shelley's *Frankenstein*, they come alive. Has there ever been a more lucid (or lurid) description of the relation of writer to text than this from Shelley:

> My imagination, unbidden, possessed and guided me,
> gifting the successive images that arose in my mind
> with a vividness far beyond the usual bounds of
> reverie. I saw—with shut eyes, but acute mental

vision—I saw the pale student of unhallowed arts
kneeling beside the thing he had put together. I saw
the hideous phantasm of a man stretched out, and
then, on the working of some powerful engine, show
signs of life, and stir with an uneasy, half-vital motion.
Frightful must it be; for supremely frightful would be
the effect of any human endeavour to mock the
stupendous mechanism of the Creator of the world.
His success would terrify the artist; he would rush
away from his odious handiwork, horror-stricken. He
would hope that, left to itself, the slight spark of life
which he had communicated would fade; that this
thing which had received such imperfect animation
would subside into dead matter, and he might sleep in
the belief that the silence of the grave would quench
forever the transient existence of the hideous corpse
which he had looked upon as the cradle of life. He
sleeps; but he is awakened; he opens his eyes; behold,
the horrid thing stands at his bedside, opening his
curtains and looking on him with yellow, watery, but
speculative eyes.

As Karl Kraus has observed, "The closer the look one takes
at a word, the greater the distance from which it looks
back." Or as Shelley goes on:

I thought that if I could bestow animation upon lifeless
matter I might, in the process of time (although I now
find it impossible) renew where death had apparently
devoted the body to corruption.

I propose Dr. Frankenstein's creation as a central image
for a poem because, in the blasé sophistication of the
humdrum, there is all-too-great a willingness to domesticate
that which is beyond our control and in so doing cede that

measure of responsibility we can assert. This may begin to suggest the inadequacy of a word like *imagination* to convey what is going on in a poem, or the kind of poem I'm interested in, since it's all too adequate to describe most poetry.

Nor am I suggesting that language is a given entity apart from the world. Rather I am speaking of that language which comes to be in the world as the condition of a specific place, a specific negotiation by a writer that does not appropriate words but invests them. Not that the words inhabit us (only) (or as much as) world inhabits us through these words. Always the hard part—whether it be in a poem or essay—is to leave the mechanics (language operates so, can do this and this) and enter into the engendering. Language is not self-determining (this is the always wrong-headed call of a perspective based on the idea of the arbitrariness of signs) nor is it determined by forces wholly external to it. Rather, language is a living necessity making place and time in the only world in which any of us lives for any lifetime. We are confronted by language as much as confront with it; its shapes arise from the way we handle that which occurs.

The description of a poem's making as a kind of psychic surgery emphasizes that poetry is a *technology* that makes, not exactly, as William Carlos Williams had it, "a . . . machine made of words", but more like a *flesh* made of words. If *flesh* seems too organic a metaphor, it is not intended to oppose a *social* construction with a *biological* one but to point to how *self* is as much a social construction as a poem. The practical implication of these observations is both to debunk the association of technology primarily with scientific rationality

and to deepen the conception of what fuses a poem composed
of discrete pieces into a whole greater than the sum of its
parts.

Although the root of *technology* is *techne* (the Greek word
for practical knowledge, craft, or art), in our culture art has
lost its legitimacy as producing knowledge. The exclusive
association of "scientific method" with knowledge production is reductive and represents a dominance of the
ideology of science over other knowledge-producing investigations, which are generally agglomerated together as
aesthetic. Art proposes and pursues *methods* of acquiring
knowledge that are alternative to scientific models.

In terms of writing and technology, two major topics
might be considered: the technology of writing and reading
and the effects of technology on writing and reading. The
most important modern technological development for
writing and reading has been the combination of inexpensive
printing and photocopying with increasingly efficient type-
writers/word processors. These developments—a kind of
second Gutenberg revolution—have made available to
writers the means of producing their work independently,
without going through capital-intensive, centralized publishers. At the same time, they potentially make available to
readers access to a wider range of contemporary writing than
ever before. Specifically, the minimal cost of book production enables "literary" and other writing a relative
freedom from constraints imposed when the largest possible
audience is sought (constraints that may inhibit the choice of
syntax and style as well as subject). Nonetheless, the
potential benefits of this technology have not been fully
realized due to distribution problems, attitudes toward publishing originating in relation to older printing tech-

nologies, and the continuing limitations of literacy levels and reading education.

Even more fundamental than understanding new technologies for the reproduction of writing is understanding the nature of writing as such. Alphabets, for example, remain perhaps the most formidable technologies human culture has produced. Readers can usefully be regarded as operating highly sophisticated technology. Yet little attention is paid to understanding the effects of alphabets and other reading and writing technologies. The technology of writing has many more dimensions than are "read" by most users; the technology is not fully "accessed". Poetry has an important, if often vacated, role in supplementing minimal reading values and in this sense can be understood as among the most useful tools for making alphabet technology available.

A cautionary note is necessary here. Compared to the alphabet or even inexpensive reproduction technology, the word processor threatens to become more a tool of industrial Taylorism than a means of increasing access to the many semantic strata embedded in writing. The current plethora of word processor ideology is the latest attempt to domesticate writing—not in order to inhabit it but to trivialize it. The word processor has about as much chance of instructing us about the nature of writing as the threshing machine had to instruct us about the nature of soil. The analogy is specific: for the relation of soil to vegetation is comparable to the relation of writing to human consciousness. The pen is mightier than the word processor in that, in comparison to what the pen makes available in respect to fully accessing the potential of alphabet technology, the word processor offers a microscopic efficiency and a number of severe handicaps.

The relatively uncritical acceptance of the word processor

is another chapter in the ascent of efficiency over and against other human values. The indelibility of ink, with its intimations of an extension of the blood through the finger tips and the related gesture of making a mark, places writing in a different dimension than that of the etherealized, all-too-correctable space letters occupy in a cathode ray tube or liquid crystal display. Since the alphabet is a visual and tactile technology, the specific types of visual media used potentially affect writing and reading as much as the differences among drawing, lithography, and etching affect the meaning of an image.

Certainly, the ability to make changes in a text more easily is a valuable efficiency and may make writing less intimidating for some people. But this efficiency tends to obliterate the positive value of "mistakes", which are a purely negative factor in the commercial and industrial and "educational" contexts in which most writing is processed— an attitude about correctness that makes writing intimidating in the first place. Spelling searches may save time; they also will produce even greater spelling standardization than at present; and will tend to eliminate all that can be gleaned from wading through a dictionary distracted by alternative word choices, or just distracted, *weighlayed* before returning to the "text" proper. Grammar searches are likely to enforce centralized styles of composition, further eroding both conscious and unconscious participation by users in determining language forms. Of course, machines do not cause these problems; word processors may permit a far greater degree of decentralization of spelling, grammar, and style making independent publishing and writing easier to accomplish. At the same time, word processor *ideology* reinforces the idealization of "clean copy"—a defleshed, bureaucratic and interchangeable writing.

No doubt some writers will use word processors to counter just the negative tendencies sketched here. But the potentially liberating aspects of a technology need to be considered in the light of how that technology is employed in society overall. Industrial word processors (the operators, that is; the same word stands for both the machine and its users), with no choice over the writing they process, face an additional, even more ominous, set of problems. Because word processors make possible a desocialization of the workplace leading toward cottage industry piecework, organized labor action is severely limited. Atomized workers at geographically distant terminals compete for who will take the lowest wages while constant monitoring of characters typed per hour prevents slowdowns or plugouts. The potential for control is unprecedented—and this control regulates a physical rigidity of posture for the worker that is far more restricted than that of a typist or assemblyline worker.

Just as planes and cars did not replace walking, and alphabets did not replace orality, word processors will not replace older writing techologies. For every real gain a technology provides, there is a real loss. Rather than "replace by improvements" the more accurate image is "supplement with new modalities". Only when it is understood how and why technologies are harnessed for social control and exploitation can it begin to be possible to change these uses and put the technologies in the service of positive social transformations.

Machines will never replace writers, anymore than, as the story goes, they replaced cowboys: machines won't take that much abuse.

Poetry is potentially the most powerful technology to realize the multidimensionality of reading values—to sound the sonic, measure the lexicon, and refuse a standardization and regimentation that deafens us to the living past in language and diverts us from enacting living presents— decentered and plural—*for* language.

But these living presents may be more than can be accounted for; rather than being the devourers of words, we may find ourselves devoured by them. The latter scenario is the legacy of the willful refusal to recognize the power *in* words; that power cannot be overturned or mastered, but it can be heard and channeled. When you put bits and pieces of language together you get more than the sum of the parts, the process resembling Dr. Frankenstein's stitching together pieces of flesh and engendering not dead matter, not an abstractly arid and random collation of parts, but a simulacrum of human being and a being in its own right. This is the story of the poem, its internal narration, as the kidneys and liver and heart narrate the body's story. We are, then, systematically de*lude*d—led from play—by reductive understandings of such techniques as collage or juxtaposition or parataxis. The problem with *juxtaposition* is the emphasis on a possibly arbitrary relation between two elements, placed side by side, which tends to undercut the overall system of relationships—the total prosody—that makes a poem a whole. That is, every part of a poem relates to every other part—the parts are fused, coalesced, grafted together. *Collage* and *parataxis*, while accurate descriptions, may minimize recognition of the degree of overall musical and thematic construction. In this context, Denise Levertov's term, organic form, was an attractive alternative to *free verse.* The problem, however, is that it may suggest a unity of naturally harmonious parts—again a biological as opposed to cultural unity that misses the interpenetration of these aspects in creating the *social flesh* that is the poem. As Sergei Eisenstein writes in *The Film Sense* [trans. and ed. Jay Leyda; New York: Harcourt, Brace, Jovanovich, 1975], "the image planned by the author has become flesh of the flesh of the spectator's risen image" [p. 34]. But Eisensteinian montage is also a limiting case since it suggests the primacy of a thematic "image" ("single, unifying, and definitive" [p. 70]) determining—presumably in advance—the choice of elements to be juxtaposed. Insofar as this image is understood as "single, recognizable, and whole" [p. 16], it precludes thematically and ideationally nonidentical material. ("Each representation is, in the image sense, individual, dissimilar, and yet identical thematically" [p. 34].) This would necessitate making a distinction between the "common denotation" of sharply conflicting elements that is the essence of Eisensteinian montage, and some other, less iconographically representable, whole. Irreconcilable material, that is, may produce an unforeseeable (indeed unseeable) fusion that is not an image in the Eisensteinian sense.

Dysraphism may be a useful term in this context. Medically, it would mean a congenital misseaming of embryonic parts—*raph* means seam, a rhapsodist being one who stitches parts together, that is, a reciter of epic poetry. So different parts from the middle, end, and beginning—it's a 4-D image—are fused together to become one entity.

These considerations hold open the possibility of a maximum *differentiation* of parts—style, vocabulary, syntax. You start with the integrity and autonomy of parts and find the whole in them. What made Dr. Frankenstein's creature a monster was just the reverse—starting with a preconceived whole and tailoring the parts to fit.

Reconsideration of the possibilities of the part-to-whole relation will allow further alternative prosodic techniques to the common and positivist rhetorical techniques of "ego" unity and rationalistic expository unity. At the broadest level, the part-to-whole relation means the relation of one text to another, one poem to another, and one book to another; the idea of the interweaving of all of the work of a single author and beyond that of the related interweaving of the works of different authors. This is common enough as a reading practice, as when one skips through a number of books at the same time. As a writing practice, there is the collaboration of writers on a single work as well as the appropriation by a writer of other texts. In these and other ways, the endpoints of a given poem or a given author are radiated outward. On another level, the part-to-whole relation concerns syllable to word, word to line and word to phrase, phrase to line, line to stanza, line to poem, stanza to poem, poem to book, and so on. Within this conceptualization, the territorial integrity of the poem begins to break down under a shifting focus that suggests a number of places in which the membranous line that may be called closure or poem's end can be invoked. What is the smallest or largest discrete unit of a text? Where does mine stop and yours start? Every cesura, whether the line break or the last page of the book, opens up to a possibility of continuing (rereading the book, going on to another) or *stopping*. For the practicing poet and practicing reader, the concern does not so much have to be with an increased definition of prescribed boundaries as with how these provisional limits—horizons—are invoked or provoked: allegorically as the continuities and fissures of a life (Lyn Hejinian's *My Life*, Robert Creeley's *Pieces*), structurally as the component parts of meaning-generation (Ron Silliman's work), narratively as the progression of story (Laura [Riding] Jackson's *Progress of Stories*), historically and geographically as the creation of a place (Charles Olson's *The Maximus Poems*), and so on.

The poetics of part to whole cannot help but expose motivations for, and principles of, unity and the mechanisms by which they are approached. Louis Zukofsky's *"A"* manages to do this with the metaphor of a life's work. Its carefully composed articulation of distinct movements, as in a symphony, permits maximum differentiation section to section without recourse to a single thematic or syntactic underpinning to create unification. *"A"* seems exemplary of a genuine negative capability for fusing a poem together: significant for each of its endings and completions; serial, in the Spicerian sense, more than thematic.

Consider a work composed of a number of autonomously distinct pieces that nonetheless functions as a whole by articulating the relations among the parts—that is, has an overall configuration whose music is composed of differences. But what are the possibilities for a whole that is not constructed along narrative or overtly thematic/historical lines? I've pointed to some limitations of an overly explicit or regulatory constituting framework—whether called coherence, closure, or unity ruling out possibilities for heteroclites, anomaly, oddness. One alternative image to the uniplanar surface of "ego" or "ratio"nally-organized writing is of a möbius textuality, aspiring not toward the arbitrariness and accumulation of juxtaposition but rather the fusion of social flesh. That is, the succession of displacements involved in a möbius rather than otherwise rhetorically-unified poem are not centrifugal but centripetal, do not displace from the site of the poem but enact an emplacement *as* the poem.

Of course, any movement, any duration involves displacement, which can be more or less disguised. The poem can acknowledge its duration as an emplacement, as *metaphor*, insofar as metaphor means to transfer. So we get to duration in a poem by a series of substitutions or replacements that don't *stand for* or in *place of* but themselves embody that moment of time. Duration, then, becomes not a series of constantly postponed absences but the site of the con*fusing*.

So the poem enters the world, and each of us beside it, facing it. It keeps beat not to an imposed metrics but to the marks of its own joints and the joints of the reader's projection. The poem sounds as music the marks of its continual newness in being made; and the only mark of its past, of its having been made, is the blood on the cutting room floor.

LIVING TISSUE / DEAD IDEAS

Think of dead ideas as deposited in language and writing, as the compost heap in which present language and writing grows. Suppose dead ideas as comprising an historical unconscious lived out as perception, as smell and taste, as speech. Imagine consciousness resounding with an inexhaustible repository of ideas, as a cave to be mined. And consider poetry as that mining, so the incorporation of dead ideas (call them prior texts) into a work is not simply collage or a familiar, almost comforting, defamiliarization technique, but the spiritual domain of poetry, its *subject* (subjectness) percolating through.

Ideas not dead then, though their origin is past. Or ideas dead only in the way a culture may die, be lost, its people vanish without records or monuments or memories. Ideas, then, not so much dead as submerged, melted, transubstantiated, absorbed; everywhere informing but no where fully explicable. Yet such ideas are neither solace, as a past to which we can turn, nor tools to represent the present. In this sense, dead ideas are not the stars but the heaven in which the stars gleam, not tools but tolls.

This sense of "dead ideas" turns the phrase into an

oxymoron; for ideas cannot die though we may seek to kill them. Kill them in rage that we are mortal but they are not ("the body dies, the body's beauty lives"). Or kill them in that perverse homage we call display: hold up, inspect, collect (as the father kills the moth for his son in Stein's *The Making of Americans:* "caught him and killed him and pinned him"). Here is the root of what, ungraciously, I call ideational mimesis: that ideas are static objects that can be accurately portrayed. The controlling impulse to "catch and pin" collects much more than the putative idea; the desire to represent overwhelms the idea represented. Thinking, which is the living tissue of ideas, their flesh, consists not in representations of concepts but in a fabric or nexus of relations. Ideas are always syntactic and prosodic, con- stituted by the interaction of different kinds of elements— scenic, associational, historic, economic, tonal, . . .—and as such are never reducible to one type of image.

So a second sense of "dead ideas", suggesting a rule of always-already formulated concepts, habits of agreement running roughshod over newly formulating vistas. Call it a *necroidiocracy*, ideas stiffened by rigor mortis wounding flesh with their rigidity and technorationality: the arrogance of logic and the perniciousness of the "common sense" stereo- type, each disguising its biases in the shadows of its neutrality.

Language is the first technology, the extension of the body outward toward an articulation, *forging*, of the world, which is immediately transformed by this act, hence a *forgery*. As Stein so majestically shows in *How to Write*, ideas are to be enacted not entombed. Words, that is, do not signify ideas; rather, ideas are forged in the ovens of historical language practice, which means as visual representations and as sound.

There are so many prejudices against the possibility of a nonarbitrary relation in verbal language among sound and ideas, sound and meaning, that discussions on this matter risk being defensive or oracular. (The disassociation of ideas or meaning from the visual representation of verbal language—the graphemic—is perhaps more pervasive and many of the arguments I use here about sound are equally relevant to this issue.) Sound is not simply a neutral mechanism for designating differences. Even in the semiotic model, sound's semantic dimension must be seen not only as a product of negative differentiation onto which meaning is "attached" but also as consisting in the positive effects of the "mechanism". Onomatopoeia is the most tangible example of the nonsystematic dynamic of sound as meaning. A *tweet* is readily conceded to be more than a sound whose meaning comes only from its difference from any other sound. *Plate* would not do as well and though *twit* might perhaps that accounts for its own dynamic of sound and meaning. But while *tweet* and *twit* are understandable as nonarbitrary sound choices, it is more difficult to see how this could equally be true of *true* or *of* or *or*. What twits! So fixed on seeing an overt mimesis as the only possible mechanism for the relation of the semantic and the sonic, we fail to *hear* the infection of the other variables—associational, iconic extension of mouth shapes, psychogenic, sociogenic, . . .—for which we have no clearly defined concepts. As Walter Benjamin writes in "Doctrine of the Similar":

> The similarities which one perceives consciously . . .
> are, when compared to the countless similarities per-

ceived unconsciously or not at all, like the enormous
underwater mass of an iceberg in comparison to the
small tip which one sees projecting above the waves.
. . . The perception of similarity is in every case
bound to an instantaneous flash. It slips past, can
possibly be regained, but really cannot be held fast,
unlike other perceptions. . . . the concept on nonsensuous similarity . . . indicates that in our perception we no longer possess what once made it
possible to speak of a similarity which might exist
between a constellation of stars and a human being.
Nonetheless, we . . . possess a canon on the basis of
which we can bring towards clarification the obscurity
attached to a concept of nonsensuous similarity. And
that canon is language. . . . The question is: how can
[the] onomatopoetic mode of explication be elaborated
. . . [to] establish an underlying meaning for [the]
assertion "Every word—and the whole of language—
is onomatopoetic." . . . Language is the highest
application of the mimetic faculty: a medium into
which the earlier perceptive capabilities for recognizing the similar had entered without residue, so that
it is now language which represents the medium in
which objects meet and enter into relation with each
other, no longer directly, as once in the mind of the
augur or priest, but in their essences, in their most
volatile and delicate substances, even in their aromata.
. . . So speed, that swiftness in reading or writing
which can scarcely be separated from this process,
would then become, as it were, the effort or gift of
letting the mind participate in that measure of time in
which similarities flash up fleetingly out of the stream
of things only in order to be immediately engulfed

again. Thus even profane reading, if it is not to forsake
understanding altogether, shares this with magical
reading: that it is subject to a necessary speed, or rather
a critical moment, which the reader must not forget
at any cost unless he [or she] wishes to go away
empty-handed.

"Human beings invent language themselves from the
sounds of living nature," quotes Benjamin in an earlier
essay. Anson Rabinbach explains that "Benjamin's view of
the primacy of the sensuous, onomatopoetic in language,
over its semiotic, nonsensuous character in speech and
writing" is "a rejection of the theory that language has an
arbitrary relation to its objects."

What is being proposed is not a "crude" materialism such
that vibrations in the air are given metaphysical status.
Sound, like the graphemic, is a principal tool of communicative (and noncommunicative!) activity and, as such, invests
the social field with an horizon of meanings. When sound is
used for communicative purposes, the communication already entails not only the extra baggage of its material form
but also of the history of its communicative use in a similar
form as well as otherwise, for instance, its use as music or
musing. There is no *origin* that can be identified; only the
echoes that we continually cover and uncover.

It is as if the picture of an idea holds us captive, locking us
off from language's body, its soul, its stare.

Poetry enacts ideas more significantly in its line breaks
than in whatever tags there may be to the presumed subject
matters of the humanities or social sciences. Poetry starts
with sound as a positive, rather than as differential or
negative, value: sound as engendering meaning, its corpse—

begotten, *gnosis*, knowledge. No ideas but as sound. Are
there *purely* visual ideas? Sure, just as olfactory, or tactile.
Synaesthesia. *Thought* as mediating among these, supra-
ideational. To sound the language, make it resound. Soul is
an echo chamber for the universe's peals.

As against other writing practices, poetry explicitly holds
open the possibility of producing, rather than reproducing,
ideas. Beyond that, it may make this production of ideas
audible—in measuring and placing, sounding and breaking;
and visible—in page scoring and design.

Certainly, the majority of what is presently written as
poetry makes no greater claim to engage these possibilities
than any other type of writing. Yet, in a deeper sense, all
writing, at least passively, inexplicitly, produces ideas: not
the ideas referred to, however, but the ideas produced by the
mode of discourse. Style and form are as ideological as
content and interpretation.

To understand a text as ideological, and to understand the
ideology as a matter of syntax as much as subtext, is to raise
the problem of interpretation. Whatever is the strongest case
for an interpretive method—Marxism's unique recognition
of historicity, or psychoanalysis's unconscious, or poetry's
sound—there is always the presumption of an Archemedian
point of greater vantage. But this Archemedian point provides not an absolutely greater vantage but a *vantage for*, as
with all instrumentalities, involving a trade off. Any truly
ideological epistemology must account for the interest component of any knowledge-producing process, an interest
component that necessarily screens-out in order to screen-in.
The implication of specialized theories of literary interpretation tends to be that they have a vantage the text lacks; a

result is that interpretation may take a form similar to that of the physician-patient or anthropologist-native relationship. But what is a political or cultural criticism to do with a work that already contains the very critique it wishes to make? Allow its interpretive method to be critiqued in terms of writing practice, or ignore or negate the challenge? What if the natives are not only hostile but also have developed systems of interpretation—call them art—that are more sophisticated methodologically than those of the decoders? Utter sighs and squint while saying "artifact"? (It is less useful to understand how non-Occidental/Oriental "art" resembles modern art than vice versa, but only if this allows the transformation of our concept of *both* art and artifact.)

The tables will be turned on any cultural theory that suggests its methods have cornered the market on interpretation, or, as I like to call it, interpenetration,—that treats the literary object as necessarily passive, reduced to the level of cultural or social artifact. Of course, many literary and cultural works *are* passive. But imagine a literature that proposes its own interpretations, enfolding these in sequence with interpretations of these interpretations, that takes as material for interpretation and transformation not just ideational content but the full range of semantic properties revealed and reveiled by the writing. By *literature* I mean *verbal art*, specifically that subset of art pertaining to writing. Within literature there are both more active and more passive tendencies. Passivity is not necessarily unintentional, however; literary and other cultural production is often passive by design, to facilitate digestion. There are no clear divisions in a distinction between proactive and reactive literature; there is a dynamic of overlap and undertow among any such categories. A simple criterion is suggested by a test of utility. For a self-interpreting, proactive literature provides instruction in how to read the ever-present social texts of the culture, while the reverse is true only in a more obscure and arcane way. The necessary conceptualization of texts in terms of their common roots as cultural production or social exchange will, in the process, also usefully undermine a privileged status for any interpretive method. But such a leveling to the open field of culture can only be a first step, an initial break with received hierarchizations and Olympian authority in an attempt not to overthrow the possibility of truth but to begin to participate in truth's constitution. Marxist critics have justifiably insisted on the privileged status of their interpretive framework; one accedes to this privilege not for abstract or metaphysical reasons but pragmatically, because one sees the Marxist story as a tool necessary for the transformation of current social and economic conditions. The interpretive privileges of a proactive literature are equally pragmatic (though not limited to these concerns); for example, such literature will tend to discover techniques of semantic production and exchange that cannot be revealed or investigated in any other manner, that is, that are not able to be articulated in expository forms of discourse.

Literature * is the best word we now have for a writing

Poetry is, technically, the better word insofar as it is understood as including all "literary" writing. However, the *social* fact of the professionalization and *genre*ization of writing makes the term *poetry* stand less for its literal definition than as a type of literary writing distinct from other literary or aesthetic writing. Adopting a remark of David Antin's, poetry could be understood as *literature* that goes "all the way".

that critiques itself not only at the level of represented ideas but prosodically, acoustically, syntactically, visibly; which is to say gives these dimensions equal methodological weight as it gives to more traditional notions of semantic content. (Sadly, the bulk of literary writing purveys ideational mimesis as zealously as the bulk of nonliterary writing; in this sense most literature cannot be distinguished from most criticism.) Any writing practice that, for example, fully internalized the implications of the relation of sound to meaning would, for all practical purposes, be stigmatized as literary, even if it proposed itself as critical or interpretive.

The increasing credibility given to the "idea" that the "formal" dynamics of a work are knowledge-constituting has done little to undermine the hegemony of techno-rationalized discourse as the arbiter of the "real" in official, popular, academic, and Marxist contexts. Within the academic context, a scholarly degree is conferred only after successful performance of the rites of ideational mimesis, a.k.a. a dissertation and oral defense. The code word here is "documentation". This becomes grotesque when the subject matter of such a dissertation suggests the limits of its own style of exposition. (This may be a key to the perverse prose style that has been the product of much routine high-theoretical criticism in America—a tortured syntax that leaves the reader hoping for an early confession and release.) While many intellectuals would be happy to sympathize with the view that scientific rationality is not the only knowledge-producing method, this is usually, and the meta-phor is apt, lip service. Scientists, not literary or other artists, are brought in to give authority to public policy com-missions; formally investigative poets are excluded from teaching jobs in "creative" writing programs. And even the most radical literary or cultural or political theorists write for publications that as a policy exclude any writing—critical or literary—not subscribing to the principles of ideational mimesis. At present, the only forums for such writing are those edited and published by literary artists.

The kinds of theoretical contributions that poetry can make by virtue of its mode of inquiry can be retrospectively codified in expository forms. But such forms necessarily undermine the acknowledgement of the ideological implications of their style—a highly ironic situation if there is a simultaneous debunking of the "value-free" posturing of literary critics who claim to be doing nonideological interpretation.

At one point in his book on *Literary Theory*, Terry Eagleton remarks that at Cambridge students quickly learn that it doesn't really matter what you say, however oppositional or outrageous it will be accepted blithely if written in the conventional matter. This is an unintentionally ironic moment, for *Literary Theory* illustrates the point. If, in what follows, I seem to single this work out, it is because while I agree with many of Eagleton's political and cultural positions, I find his sins of omission all the more egregious. However, my comments are not particular to Eagleton but apply as well to a vast assortment of literary and cultural theory and criticism. It is commonly said that such work has become both too self-preoccupied and insufficiently occupied with its object of study; in contrast, I would say such work is not self-preoccupied enough; that is, not sufficiently occupied by the fact that its mode of writing reflects its historical material circumstance. Contemporary and past literary practice can contribute theoretical tools to cultural studies; by ignoring these tools, cultural studies parochializes its endeavors and stunts its achievements.

And there is no doubt about it, Eagleton's book represents a complete shut-out of contemporary literary practice in the universe of discourse relevant to his topic—whether called literary or political or cultural theory. His argument that literature doesn't exist has the practical effect of neutralizing or negating the value of activist literary practice while at the same time adding to the valorization of literary theory without literature, even if in his version literary theory has become cultural or political theory. There is little in Eagleton's thesis to give comfort or support to a proactive, oppositional literature, little that is relevant or pertinent to the working of a literary artist. Indeed, true to the thesis that literature does not exist, neither artists nor artworks have any significant role and are virtually never mentioned in the volume.

Eagleton's Oxford and Cambridge academic context has reasonably led him to question and reject the legitimacy of not only the literary canon preached to him but also any possible literary canon. What he seems to miss is that because his dons insisted on an essentialist definition of *Literature*, it does not follow that if this definition is false, *literature* ceases to have any useful meaning. By giving so much credibility to this academicized notion of literature, Eagleton's reaction formation leaves him even more deeply entrenched in an academic perspective. I do not cede to dons at Oxford or Cambridge, Yale or M.I.T., the power to so taint a word that it can't reasonably be used without reference to *their* use of it. The argument reminds me of those who wish to give up words like *syntax* or *reference* or *truth* because some people claim an overly restrictive meaning for these terms. Rather than looking to F. R. Leavis for the final word on the meaning of *literature*, it would seem more relevant to go to the producers of literature, for whom the word does not necessarily mean the Great Works but rather may be a provisional term for a kind of work engaged in.

Eagleton's argument is a ghostly cousin to the familiar claim that all culture is bourgeois culture, a claim Raymond Williams puts gracefully in perspective in *Culture and Society*. By emphasizing the diversity within culture, Williams resists any attempt to stigmatize all or parts of culture as subservient to the dominant ideology. Presumably, Eagleton wishes to designate "Literature" as that part of culture which can be so stigmatized. In contrast, Williams is at pains to show how the common "intellectual and literary" tradition, like the common language, is a shared inheritance, with divergent and conflicting tendencies, and not a product of any single class or sector, *even if one wishes to lay claim to it.*

While I agree with Eagleton that literature is a functionalist term suggesting more a way of reading/regarding than a definable kind of work, the paradox is that something like literature is necessary to learn how to read/regard in a literary manner. There is a difference between reading all "signs" in an aesthetic way and works that shape and deepen such reading. To abandon the term *literature* is to abandon this crucial fulcrum point. Eagleton does not so much dispute as disregard this bottom-up concept of literature. His concern is not for how specific literary artists work or how they use the term literature but what *Literature*—a term reified by its isolation from networks of readings, magazines, publishers, correspondence, etc.— meant to the New Critics. The literature that Eagleton wishes to dissolve is always the canonized *Literature* of educational institutions, and he makes a convincing case for the "rise" of this *Literature* and for the class bias of any claims made for it. The problem is that this argument removes literature from the struggle to resist *Literature*. Rather than challenging received notions of *Literature* in an effort to encourage activist and oppositional literary works, Eagleton imperiously sinks literature into the morass of pop music and the color coding of traffic lights.

It's hardly an argument against a *term* that it is socially rather than "objectively" constituted. Eagleton's remark that "literature does not exist in the sense that insects do" is the giveaway. Of course, all Eagleton intends to say is that there is no objective, value-free sense of literature, that this designation and valuation is always ideological. But this is also true of *insects, fiction,* and *ideology,* with no sense that the use of such words is problematic or that the entities that they define, if not transcendental, are nonetheless *real*.

Eagleton's thesis has the macabre effect of finishing the dirty business started by the arch-villains in his scenario, the New Critics. Their hierarchization and decontextualizing sanctification of the literary work, their refusal, that is, to see literature as social facts, is notorious for checking activist and oppositional tendencies in reading and writing practices. Eagleton, the unconscious coconspirator, provides the death blow.

It is not literature that is overvalued but science and

technorationality. What is needed is not a *deliteraturation* of reading values but a *reliteraturizing* of writing values.

Eagleton's position reminds me of a story told about W. C. Fields. Fields was complaining that the studio was run by Jews. "But the studio bosses are all Catholics, Mr. Fields." "Catholics!" Fields snapped. "Worst kind of Jews." "Literature! Worst kind of New Criticism."

What is most distressing about Eagleton's position is that it links up to a pervasive tendency in contemporary literary criticism to read literature as examples of literary theory. First we have the possibly reductionist, possibly edifying claim that the author is dead; now literature is supposed dead (or submerged, i.e., drowned). Eagleton's attack on "close reading" is troubling because he does not demonstrate the inclination or ability to read closely, to let the specific experience of reading a work effect his thinking. Indeed, in his reading of Walter Benjamin, he shows an inability to account for the warps and gaps and shifts in Benjamin's writing style. The qualities that make Benjamin's work literature are for Eagleton obstacles to be overcome. Eagleton's practice of ideational mimesis allows him to find in literature and literary theory only "ideas" detached from their material grounding in a writing practice.

The fallacy of ideational mimesis is that it treats ideas like objects that can be "caught and held", that tries to contain the dialogic mode of philosophic inquiry in brief topic sentence summaries rather than as unfolding in a writing (or dialogic) production/exchange that must be entered into, not observed. (Eagleton's one-and-a-quarter paragraph grotesque of Husserl (complete with F. R. Leavis lurking in the bushes) is a case-in-point.)

Eagleton does not allow for literary practice influencing

literary theory. At most, he uses early twentieth century texts as tagged illustrations for more recent theory, aggressively ignoring that literary practice goes on and shapes any viable cultural or literary theory. He is silent on the aporia between literary theory and literary practice (and its shadow aporia between writing theory and writing practice). Literary examples are scarce and always secondary, stock citations of the Dante, Shakespeare sort. They are never used to make or rethink an idea but merely as nonessential illustration, any number of other citations would seem to do as well. The few modern literary works Eagleton does cite were completed by the late 1920s; this in a book about post-1945 *literary* theory. Eagleton usefully insists that all theory is at heart political theory. By denying an activist role for literature, he undermines any serious radical critique of language practices.

These grumblings are not intended to set up a distinction between the aesthetic and the political, but rather to prevent a neutralizing aestheticization of the political. If we lose the designation *literature*, and by extension the broader term *art*, we lose the motor to politicize writing, to transform it, to make it answer the call for an acknowledgement of its ideological construction in its textual practice. It has been an important lesson that an understanding of the causal role of history must not preclude the role of historical actors and of subjective resistance. Analogously, an understanding of the role of economic and social processes in determining literary production and literary evaluation must not preclude the pragmatic contributions of individual literary works toward an increased realization of exactly what it means for all texts to be political and social.

Literature, as with the other arts, as with sociology, or

history, or philosophy, exists not as an abstract category but in concrete situations determined by audiences, publications, social formations. A work is literary partly because it is situated in this arena of discourse and association. As a result, the designation of literature has a very special political utility, for it provides access to a unique social network in which political issues can be raised. It is a mistake to underestimate the political power of this arena or the strategic loss in not differentiating literature from the broader field of cultural production.

The concrete social usefulness of art should not be dismissed, as when Eagleton remarks "in a society like ours . . . literature has ceased to have much practical function at all." One practical function of literature, though not a *deliteraturized* writing, is the continual formation of utopian content, either as story, in Fredric Jameson's sense, or as textuality. As Perry Anderson observes, "Raymond Williams has reproached the classical utopian impulse for a tendency towards an escapist simplification of the existing world, and insisted on a more exacting need for a feasible institutional specification of any socialist future beyond it, which will always involve *greater*—not less—complexity than the arrangements of the capitalist present." One such complex realization of what a political culture could be and do is represented by investigation into social and political dynamics of sound, syntax, and narrative: political theory exclusively adopting the discursive practices of ideational mimesis must be understood as part of the escapist simplification that must be overcome. Sophistication is needed in terms of form and content, and that sophistication includes understanding these terms as interdependent. That is, sophistication is needed in the cultural and not just in administrative and economic areas. This extension of Williams's observation should also serve as a rebuke to those who wish to defame as elitist any artwork that aspires to complexity. Perhaps we can reinterpret Pound's remark that poets are the antennae of the race to mean ideas embodied as poetry construct a new polis in the site of the old: no longer postponed, *enacted.* Then poetry's pealing would be a toll from that "other" world calling for its truth to be established in *this* one.

Current literary practice, far from being negated by the recognition of its ideological construction, is liberated by such formulations and can provide models of ideological critique more radical than otherwise available. Literature— art—is the workshop for such models, the research and development sector of culture. It is no accident that cultural work done under the banner of literature has provided the basis for many of the insights of leftist thought. Historically, poetry—as often as not institutionally broken-off from the dominant discursive practices of the political thought of the time—has provided a necessary corrective to the crudely rationalistic drifts of much social radicalism and its theory.

There has never been a more urgent need for literature, for in this culture it is primarily in the realm of literature that alternatives to the stale formulas of ideational mimesis and positional writing strategies are being realized. Literature, however, not just in the sense of verse or fiction or essays. I am proposing a literature that would go beyond modernist closure of form and self-containment, excluding the social except by analogy or adjacency. Further, such literature would also reject the trivialization of meaning and the paranoia or trace and deferral that is the hallmark of much so-called postmodernism in the visual arts, a tendency that has no significant counterpoint in contemporary literature largely because there is no "market" to create and support it. In contrast, much "postmodernism" in the visual arts is not only as fashionable as it is profitable but also, astonishingly, seems readily assimilable into the context of left cultural/political studies, especially insofar as it gives the critic the upper hand as political decoder of "nonart" art. I am proposing a dialectical material writing, decentered and democratic, not vested in the authority of a rhetoric dictated by Capital but part of a "collective struggle", as Jameson puts it, "to wrest Freedom from the realm of necessity".

Much "poststructuralist" as well as Althusserian literary analysis has sought to point up the hidden fissures in a seemingly unitary text, perhaps further showing the disguised ideological or psychoanalytic unities beneath it, the text's "core ideas". This question persists: What is the interpretive stance to be toward a work which unmasks its own discontinuities, flaunts its core ideas as candy coating, and insists throughout not on its deferred meaning but its enacted meaning? Not that such a work transcends its historical/ideological situation; fully contemporary with its readers/critics, and anticipating their interpretive methods, such work subverts the privileged status that may be lorded over works "regressive" of their interpretive horizon.

That literature of which I speak is not unitary, does not insist on closure; but neither does it thwart or drain meaning. Yet if it resists the lure of positive (or expressive) totalization—that is, unification of a represented world view—it acknowledges the fact of negative (or structural) totalization. By "negative totalization" I mean a projected vantage point against which all ideologies can be critiqued, a negative horizon or dialectic that can, like history for Althusser, never be represented, yet, despite this refusal of reduction, is *there*.

On the spectrum of theory to practice, literature falls squarely in the realm of theory. Literary workers have as their natural allies literary, political and cultural theorists and commentators. All share the common craft of writing. Critics and theorists have the same need to consider contemporary writing techniques as cartographers or economists or sociologists have to consider methodological changes in their field. Cartographers now recognize that the technology of Mercator projection effects what they chart. Literary or political theory that ignores the relevance of its material base as writing composition, unquestioningly replicating received stylistic models (often comparatively cruder than Mercator projections!), engages in a denial of theory by theory. (Literary artists as a group are hardly exemplary in this area—too often they put themselves above theory or cultivate an ignorance of it and of the methodological implications of their craft, while projecting a picture of critical thinking as monolithic and antiimaginative.)

What I am suggesting, in summary, is that the theoretical contribution of literary practice is often categorically excluded from the theoretical arena because of the "realist" and ideationally mimetic biases of the writing practices of such theory. A proactive, oppositional literature can encourage a useful reflection of the historicity of writing practices, at the same time proposing alternate models that provide a way out of the trap of ideational mimesis and a deeper understanding of the relation of ideas to writing. At a conference sponsored by the Humanities Institute, "a forum for interdisciplinary exchange in the human sciences", and speaking to a section on "theory and methods", it should be no great surprise that I close with the possibility of a more reciprocal relationship between political, cultural, and literary theory and contemporary literature.

REFERENCES

Anderson, Perry. *In the Tracks of Historical Materialism*. Chicago: University of Chicago Press, 1984. Page 97 is cited in the text.

Benjamin, Walter. "Doctrine of the Similar". Translated by Knut Tarnowski. *New German Critique* 17 (1979): 65–69.

Eagleton, Terry. *Literary Theory*. Minneapolis: University of Minnesota Press, 1983. See Introduction, Chapter 1, and Conclusion; pp. 16 and 10 are cited in the text.

Jameson, Fredric. *The Political Unconscious: Narrative as Socially Symbolic Act*. Ithaca: Cornell University Press, 1981. See Chapter 1; p. 19 is cited in the text.

Rabinbach, Anson. "Introduction to Benjamin's 'Doctrine of the Similar'". *New German Critique*: 60–64.

Rasula, Jed. "The Compost Library". *Sagetrieb* 2:1 (1982):190–219.

Williams, Raymond. *Culture and Society: 1798–1950*. New York: Harper Torchbooks, 1958. See Chapter 5 and Conclusion; p. 321 is cited in the text.

Six/ Catechesis

AN INTERVIEW
WITH TOM BECKETT

What's the relationship, to your way of thinking, between surrealism and "language writing" as compositional mode? I'm struck by the rapid juxtapositioning of image as well as voice in your work. How about Ashbery as an influence in this regard? "Matters of Policy" might be a relevant text to go at.

I guess I have ambivalent feelings about the expression "language writing" "as a compositional mode". I could speak of my own work, or specific other's work, but feel uncomfortable generalizing since what seems more compelling is to understand (be troubled by) the situational dynamics of categorization and characterization rather than accept them as intrinsically useful: to see how they can engender a fruitless competition, on the one hand, and a destructive historicism of style and trend on the other. (Fredric Jameson, in discussing Barthes, points to this in terms that remind me also of my article, "The Conspiracy of Us". He writes that insofar as a literary writing "marks my affiliation with a given social group, it signifies the exclusion of all the others also—in a world of classes and violence, even the most innocuous group-affiliation carries the negative

386   An Interview with Tom Beckett

value of aggression with it. Yet the objective situation is such that I cannot but belong to groups of some kind, even if they turn out to be groups that wish to abolish the existence of groups: by the very fact of my existence"—class, time, place; by the fact of the work constituting a readability, a factitiousness, at all; by the fact of its distribution and hence readership—"I am guilty of the exclusion of others from the group"—even if it were only of one, group in the sense of aspect—"of which I am involved.")

Certainly, I do see the magazine, $L=A=N=G=U=A=G=E$, and my own work, as expressing certain shared views about reading and about the constituting power of language, about seeing language itself as the medium of the work and foregrounding that medium. And yet this is not a movement in the traditional art sense, since the value of giving an aesthetic line such profile seems counterproductive to the inherent value of the work. If a larger common profile is called for, I would choose the social project of writers committed to a transformation of society at a large-scale social level, of which writing can be an important arena in terms of its investigation of the nature of meaning, how objects are constituted by social values encoded in language, how reading and writing can partake of noninstrumental values and thus be utopian formations. These political dimensions to poetry (and more generally art, and more generally to a way of regarding—reading—the world, which can be acted out at every level from personal relationships to conduct at the Job) seem to be worth bringing to the fore. They involve more a movement to change the nature of reading values, and not only reading values applied to poetry.

In contrast, the setting up of schools of writers based on associated aesthetic styles and pushing the group identity of the common denominator of these associations seems to me a misplaced energy in the face of the larger social project I am suggesting. Of course, poetry activity in a given period can be grouped into different tendencies in ways that trade off elucidation for the repression of difference; this defining process is inevitable I suppose. But what come to be the predominant ways of characterizing, insofar as they are restricted to stylistic analysis, are bound to miss out on even closer affinities that cut across styles and even genres or mediums, not to mention emphasizing the dissimilar characteristics of projects that may in fact have many shared assumptions and repressing the often volatile, hostile, contradictory differences in writers viewed for the sake of the paradigm as similar.

And what's the value of giving this flux up—except perhaps to further divide an already marginal and beleaguered bunch of highly individualistic, somewhat paranoid (in the sane sense: to be beside one's mind is at least to be close by), often harried poetry writers (= poetry readers).

Furthermore, in $L=A=N=G=U=A=G=E$ and in my writing I've tried to explore the possibility that it is not necessary to narrow one's work down to a single style and I feel that the advocating of a *way* or *style* of writing would contradict a more important principle that would criticize the fetishizing of any single style as a *preferred* method of generating meaning; which is not to say that individual persons, fixed in time and in a body, do not gravitate toward the limits of their situation as expressed in the limits of the style(s) they use to express or produce meaning. But it is foolish and counterproductive to put forward a stylistic School since this would rapidly be reduced to simply another fetishized style. What might be put forward, though, is this larger social concern, along with an analysis of style, which is what could be called the putting forward of reading values not (divisive) writing values. Perhaps this would allow for a greater interchange among different types of writers, and indeed other cultural workers, instead of the disastrous movement toward increasing specialization and parochialization of reading. In that context, understanding the characteristics defining any of our own writing practices and interests could contribute to a dialog and not instead be the pretext for shutting one off. The former process is a refusal of the ghettoization of poetry with a recognition that all meaning and all communication occurs through a particular set of conditions (contexts, desires, sexual/ethnic/aesthetic traditions, audiences). It is not the valorization of style, and certainly not a style, that is fundamental, but the recognition that meaning is possible only through styles. The poem needs less to be viewed as a fixed end, an *objet d'art*, and more as a transforming agent whose exemplary features are to be used by the reader in her/his researches into the nature and products of the production of meaning.

You ask about my being influenced by surrealism. I actually feel quite ignorant of French Surrealist poetry, assuming that ʋu have in mind Breton, Eluard, Aragon, Arp, and so on. I've read some of this work, but only cursorily and in translation. I do know considerably better the Surrealist painters, but neither the writers nor the painters (Magritte being an important exception), while of course of interest, have seemed important to me in terms of

my own work, apart from the great significance this work
has had for contemporary art generally. Though at the same
time I can see how my own development may have brought
me, as if through the back door, to a proximity with their
work.

My basic conflict with both the theory (of Breton's) and
the practice is the underlying psychologism and the reliance
on symbolic, allegoric, or "deep" images. For me, images,
especially of this type, are suspect, or at best wildly humorous
as *constructions* (fabrications), not revelatory as "psychic
automatisms". I don't believe in automatic writing either as
a literal possibility or as an utopian or propagandistic literary
value. And if anything, the kind of "dream logic" juxtapositions that characterize much surrealistic work seem to
me a candied souping up of traditional literariness, especially
insofar as the surrealist technique has been drawn upon in so
much post-war American poetry (of what has been called
"the bird flew through my pillow" sort). Such "dream"
time and space seem to me to accept the normal narrative
space of the poem and to distort it; in that sense it is
insufficiently synthetic. I guess it's a certain kind of depth of
field that surrealist eery dreaminess highlights that I would
prefer to see diminished or framed.

While surrealism often seems to put forward allegorical
values at the expense of the primacy of the materials of
writing, my own interest in poetry of this century would be
better traced along lines involving Stein, Beckett, Zukofsky,
Riding, Creeley, and *many* others, as indicated by the poets
I've written about or cited a lot (or will), who've seemed to
me in some way exemplary. Sure, Ashbery, too, where
although the image generation is fairly fluid and the transi-

tions elegant, a framing mechanism is still active, though most especially and usefully in *The Tennis Court Oath, Rivers and Mountains* and *Three Poems*. I'm not here thinking so much of personal influences but of writers who seem to me significant in terms of the recent historical tradition in which my work might be placed. Influence is a different and more byzantinely complicated matter involving crucially a wide range of contemporary work, much writing from before the present century, not to forget works old and new which I have disliked or am ambivalent about, or that I've never read (Algernon Charles Swinburne?!). But even more specifically, I don't feel exclusively influenced by work done in the genre of poetry, of equal importance is both non-poetry literary and nonliterary writing; I feel a reductive characterizing in thinking only, for poets, in terms of the "verse" tradition since as far as I'm concerned the relevant tradition is writing, which is quite a bit wider. As to impact on my work, the other arts, too, have been very important, very formative to my thinking. Certainly looking at Pollock and Louis, say, not to mention Kandinsky or Braque or Schwitters or Gorky, etc. etc., had much more influence on my ideas than reading many poets with whom I feel an affinity, while the surrealism of Dali's "The Persistence of Memory" was a model to work against.

An exchange between Clark Coolidge and Barrett Watten at Coolidge's talk at 80 Langton Street in San Francisco seems relevant to all this. Watten cited Stein's *The Making of Americans* as a similar instance of work which "goes on". He suggested as an alternative the possibility of breaking the "carrier frequency", of stopping. Coolidge: "Why stop? Am I going to stop breathing?" Watten: "To stop would be calling into question. Doubt." Coolidge: "Doubt goes all the way through. You live in doubt. Negative capability." For me, this doubting, this STOPPING is all important ("STOP! in the name of love, before you break my heart"! with the all important credo as addendum, "Think it over".) I don't want to produce an unending flow of dream/ psychic/automatic material or images, but, as in Brecht (I would relate my own interest in many of the longer poems to trying to create something analogous to what Brecht meant by *epic*) to break out from the propulsion/projection—but the questioning, the stopping, built into the structure of the poem, seems to me crucial to seeing the constituting nature of language, which is the reading value I've been suggesting, and that indeed this stopping/framing allows the *music* of the poem to be heard, the music being hearing the sound *come into* meaning rather than a play with already existing meanings by way of meter.

I'm not interested so much in disconnected bits (the paratactic monochrome) but rather how these bits form an overall weave, so that it's a kind of spell-creating but where the spell is continually exposed or surfaced. A poem like "Matters of Policy" is exactly about this process, how conventions and language itself induce trances under which we glide as if in automatic pilot. And how we live in this spellbound way—it is our making and our unmaking, the source of beauty (and the magicalness and majesty of beauty) and also of alienness (towards each other and towards the world we so rarely and fitfully realize we make). Certainly the relentless theme of how language socializes us, but so often without a trace of this socialization that would illuminate, like the phosphorescence of an all-permeating world-soul made manifest as world-body, our self-sameness in being and our communal project that is the socious that shapes not only our thoughts but our very bodies.

The nature of the image I am thus proposing is not so much surreal as critical, analytic—an analysis that is inextricably bound up in making visible a fabricating mechanism, so that the manufacture of the fabulous and the ordinary are indistinguishable parts of desiring production (to use the phrase of more recent French theory). Mine is an interest more towards focusing attention on the constitutive nature of conventions (which works out as well to attending to the syllables of each line and the parameters of each work) than presenting a *surreality* with claims to the absolute. So that the poem itself becomes a machine that spells and dispells illusion upon illusion, so that illusion's engendering may be witnessed.

Surrealism is to be credited with opening up new possibilities for images and perhaps more crucially for the transition from image to image (unit to unit) in the total organization of a poem—opening up, that is, the domain within which we now work. Artaud allows for this in his 1927 attack on the Surrealists, "In Total Darkness"— "The imagination, the dream, that whole intense liberation of the unconscious whose purpose is to raise to the surface of the soul all that it is in the habit of keeping concealed, must necessarily introduce profound transformations in the scale of appearances, in the value of signification and the symbolism of the created." I also think of some remarks made by Robert Desnos (for me, with Artaud, one of the most interesting writers in some way associated with this grouping) twenty years later. "It seems to me that beyond Surrealism there is something very mysterious to be dealt with, that beyond automatism there is the intentional, that beyond poetry there is the poem, that beyond poetry received there is poetry imposed, that beyond free poetry there is the free poet."

To what extent do you make use of "found language" in your work?

You're dealing in all cases with a material, language, that is in the most fundamental way *found* and that fact has got to mediate any response to your question. So what you get is different types of found materials: I would reject the normal dichotomy between inside and outside in these cases. But that also makes the idea of appropriating language from other written sources as basic an activity to writing as memory or overhearing or describing. There has been so much attention to how photography freed painting from the necessity of representation, but I think a similar point needs to be made about the relation of movies to writing. As writing focuses its attention less on recreating characters, place, and story—presumably based on "found" situations, cities, people, etc.—and more on types of style and vocabulary and argument, part of the investigation, of the work, requires using other texts as material to incorporate into a poem. But this is no more special or easy than is the situation of the photographer who in a similar sense uses the found materials of the world to take pictures of; the problem is still not only *what* to shoot but at what angle, what part, what exposure, etc. So in my work there are quotations from a vast array of sources, and just as many made-up quotations that sound like they are from a prior text. There are lines from other poems, and echoes of lines; remarks from letters (my own and others') or memos from the job; things heard and misheard. Much of this is very specific, though some is not conscious—things that stick in the head but the source is not remembered. And, more, there are words or phrases suggested by prior sources, though in the form they appear in the work they would be totally unrecognizable. "The originals are not original" starts a quote Bruce Andrews and I use in our collaboration in *Legend*, which is based on the idea of deriving a piece exclusively from prior texts—but again often so reworked that they bear no resemblance to anything else. The idea of getting all the material in a poem totally "spontaneously" from my "self" seems boring to me—my interest in writing is to be able to incorporate material from disparate places—I'll get fascinated with a particular word I've found somewhere, or a particular type of rhetoric or professional lingo and want to use that.

There is actually an interesting tradition of the "found" in American poetry—with Olson and the finding of a "place" or Reznikoff making use of legal documents in *Testimony*, found event, or Zukofsky's use of prior texts for a very specific kind of syntactic material and resonance. I think the whole persona conceit capitalizes on a sense of "finding a voice" which to me is finding altogether too much too fast, and getting stuck with it. I'm not that interested in myself— in recounting facts and observations about that; though how the self gets formulated as an article of socialization seems to me insufficiently explored. So I'm interested in the situation—the ontology—of the person in the world and what constitutes that. How the self in circumstance is inseparable from it, that is, not an independent actor. But at the same time how withoutness is a primary fact of serialized experience that needs to be acknowledged before it can be adequately critiqued or dispelled.

In your essay "Three or Four Things I Know About Him", writing apropos of Surrealism and the Beat Movement, you state: "What is needed, now, is not the further dramatization of far-outness but the presence of far-inness." Can you elaborate on this?

I think what I explain as "far-outness" in that essay is the gesturalizing of nonconformity or anticonventionality, whether this is reflected as rejection, formally, of literary convention, or theatrically, of bourgeois lifestyles. Such negations are preferable to the complacent comforts of the well-heated, furnished poems that populate *The New Yorker* or *Antaeus* or Atheneum Press; it is probably necessary as an originating passion to write in reaction to the smugness of social and literary conventionality and it's neither something I am free of myself or have stopped being interested in in others' writing. Certainly, for example, agit-prop has its own commendable values. But it's not as much as poetry can do; after a while the liberation of a dadaist or beat stance can open up the door to the construction of a positively constituting poetry which is not essentially reactive but generative. The alternative of getting stuck in the reactive is a theatricalization of possibilities that waves banners such as "nonsyntactical" as if syntax were other than the order of strings of words, rather than simply working with, if to describe it, nonnormative syntax. (Richard Kostelanetz has generally put forward this kind of reactive "experimentalist" line, actually calling Stein in his introduction to the otherwise

wonderful new Yale Gertrude Stein "nonsyntactical"—an
appalling remark to make of someone who wrote "I am a
grammarian", meaning she wasn't being *anti*grammatical
she was discovering what the grammars of our language *are*
by making them. This is of course one of the predominant
misunderstandings that we thought $L=A=N=G=U=A=G=E$
would help to end; nonetheless I was recently introduced by
an art critic friend as a parasyntactical poet! Well, I thought,
para, next to, at least I'm *close by;* and perhaps indeed that is
our relation to language, to be next to it, but the writing is
very much inside. The irony is that if you actually hear or
notice the syntax then there's a temptation to call it *not*
syntax, an internalized *sense*orship (to use Bernard Noël's
term) that very effectively turns into nonsense most adver-
sary or utopian or alternative views.) Ray DiPalma puts it
this way: "It's creating *the focus that generates* that concerns
me. Not so-called revolutionary ideas reduced to connoisseurship."

Let me give an example of what "generative" might
mean. I think of some of my poems as a series of remarks,
either in the aphoristic sense or in the sense of observations,
constructed items, etc., occurring at the level of phrases or
sentences. These can be interpreted in multiple ways: they
are each, perhaps to say, polyentendres (that is, any given
remark can be taken as true, ironic, false, didactic, satiric,
fantastical, inscrutable, sad, funny, my view, someone else's
view, and so on). Polyentendres suggest the continuous
choices of interpretation that confronting the world involves
(though that is a matter of semblance only—structural
affinity to other forms of creation). Polyvalences and poly-
rhythms occurring overall throughout the poem create a

music of the text, a music that has to do with both the rhyming/comparing/vectoring of possible meanings, creating *chords* of the simultaneous vectors of the several interpretations of each polyentendre, and with the combination of these chords with other chords, durationally, in the sequence of the writing, and simultaneously, in the overall structure. The overall "sound" of the work is actually more important to listen for than the linear prosodic sequences, since the relation of the "chords" reinforces the sound resonances and echoes creating an intense overall vibration that adds a dynamic dimensional depth to the sound of any given linear movement.

What is your sense of the relationship between poetic theory and practice?

Theory is never more than the extension of practice.

This question seems to break down into the relation of "writing" and "writing about" or critical/discursive writing, or essays, or philosophy, and poetry. Yet those distinctions tend to collapse when you push them, which is not to say that they don't operantly define different styles of writing and, perhaps more accurate to say, different contexts of reading and different readerships. Ron Silliman recently suggested to me that you could speak of a *primary* writing addressed to the most general possible audience and a *secondary* writing addressed to a more specific audience; so that while poetry like *Tjanting* would qualify as the first, writing about gentrification for a community newspaper would be the second. One thing this illustrates is that to talk about "poetic theory and practice" is to distort the question of the relation between theory and practice, in which poetry and poetic theory might both be considered theory, in contrast to the active organizing possibly involved in writing in an activist community journal. A project of $L=A=N=G=U=A=G=E$ was to shortcircuit the either/or styles of criticism and poetry, to publish writing which talked about other writing—reviews, notes, letters, responses, etc.—in as actively written a way as any poem could be, that is that took the writing itself to be at issue, at play. And then, to what degree is any writing not "writing about" and even about other writing; and then, aren't all texts autonomous to the degree that they are read for themselves? But still, in this interview am I not engaged in a different activity than I am in the section of "poems" that appear elsewhere in the magazine? Or am I simply working in relation to a different literary form; it's not necessarily *what* I am saying that is different. For a long time I was under the sway of an idealization of poetic thinking; I attached myself to the conceptual purity of such approaches as Stein's "Composition as Explanation", "Lectures in America", and *How to Write*, works that demonstrate there is no writing, no explanation, without composition. The deeper truth is that composition underlies all modes and moods of address and is not the exclusive domain of the "poetic", though all writing certainly does not acknowledge this condition, its conditionality. Different modes of writing, assuming as they do not only different potential readers but also modes of reading, kinds of information, and areas of investigation, have different domains of communicative and social power, and different limitations of these powers. The relation between the communicative and social power of a mode is always a complex one: the depth of communicative power of some recent poetry is severely restricted in terms of its social power by very limited dissemination, while it is the restriction of the full dimensions of communicativeness, by a suppression of the acknowledgement of "modeness", that allows for the mass distribution of much writing whose social power is thereby secured. It seems important to me to break the closed circuit of a *forced* social insularity (the poetry is *marginalized* but it is the least marginal of all writing!) not by writing a different kind of poetry but by taking a variety of other occasions to speak, to underscore this process of discrediting just what is most of credit, and to try to illuminate the nature of whatever discourse within which one finds oneself, to allow its forms and potential coercions to become apparent—to agitate, to question authority, not only in the poetry magazines but in the workplace, the academy, the corridors of intellectual debate. The work of the poetry that most interests me to read—and to write—at present is not something that will wait for popularizers to champion and misconstrue in the process of art-historical aesthetization; all the work must continuously be ours to do.

How did L=A=N=G=U=A=G=E *come about? Could you delve into its history a bit?*

Before actually starting the magazine with Bruce Andrews in 1978, Ron Silliman, Bruce, and I had talked and written to each other about the need for a magazine to extend the work we, and others we were interested in, were engaged in. This was also an extension of conversations I had had with Susan Bee [Laufer], who ended up designing the magazine.

What we imagined originally was something we just could not afford—a book-format quarterly with poetry, discussion and commentary and reviews, as well as work from artists in other media. In a sense, *L=A=N=G=U=A=G=E* was one piece of this larger project, which to some degree did come into being in a modular way—if you think of *This*, or *Roof*, or *A Hundred Posters*, or *Tottel's* as other parts.

At the time of the initial discussions about starting a magazine, the three of us were all very involved in correspondence with a variety of people on many of the things that later appeared in *L=A=N=G=U=A=G=E*. The impulse for the magazine was to make that kind of exchange, and presumably other kinds we were not privy to, more public, to share the thinking and conceptualizing with as large a group of people as we could interest, including people who might be more interested in the "thinking about" than the actual work (the poetry) itself. At this point there was no forum for the discussion of the issues we thought most current in terms of poetry writing. Reviews of poetry tended toward the contentless and were generally written in a totally bland style, not that that has changed much. I imagined a "writing about" in which the stylistic practice would be just as active as in the poetry: a mix of journals, letters, statements, reviews, articles, theories, and political analyses. (Bruce and I relate a bit of this background in the "Pacifica Interview" which is published in the supplement to Volume Four.)

But to pursue your question about "history" on a different tack, the sort of critical writing that *L=A=N=G=U=A=G=E* was in large part committed to publish very much picks up from Stein's work in this vein. For me, she remains the preeminent literary theorist of the century. Indeed, many more recent and better-known literary theorists have not even begun to catch up with what she was doing. Certainly my own writing and thinking on the overlap between philosophic and poetic practice fixed on Stein, in whom I found a culmination of what had awakened me in Dickinson and Thoreau—the absolute refusal to make compositional and prosodic questions secondary to "content". So that one of my earliest works of, to give it a name, "composition-centered philosophy" was a long reading of Stein in the context of Wittgenstein's *Philosophical Investigations* [*Three Steins*, MS, 1972].

Charles, one frequent criticism of many of the contributors to L=A=N=G=U=A=G=E *in general and you specifically is that the theoretical essays you write, say, are considered to be more "alive" than your poems. How do you feel about this?*

The issue doesn't arise for me in that the people who actually can read and respond to my poetry aren't going to think that. I would imagine if someone said that that he or she wasn't really interested in *any* of the work and that this was just a more strategic way of broadcasting this opinion. There is an annoying bait in this type of disassociative discrimination insofar as it's fueled by a valorization of the Poet who only writes Poetry (in the narrower sense of the verse tradition), since it is out of fear of this type of criticism, of being typed as a theoretician in mutual exclusion to being a Poet, that I think causes many poets to retreat from expressing themselves in modes other than verse, as if to include non-"poetic" subject matter or diction in one's

writing taints the purity of the project. This view you
suggest seems primarily a negation of the whole activity,
both, perhaps out of a sense that it punctures the privileged
domain of poetic discourse, and challenges the self-imposed
limits of what the vocabulary and style of poetry are. So I
would think the person who makes this point doesn't know
where to find the poetry. Whatever "critical" writing I've
done makes sense primarily in terms of the "poetry", is one
and the same project. In general, the work in $L=A=N=$-
$G=U=A=G=E$, like the poetry which is discussed in it, has
developed in relation to the materials of the medium of
writing. It is inconceivable that what you are calling the
theoretical essays could have developed without an active
poetic practice informing it and framing it: they are none
other than an extension of that practice. Even in terms of
development, these works occurred *after* a significant
amount of the poetry had been written. It's a mistake to talk
of the *independent* value of the "theory"; or anyway it's a
fatuous conception of what the value of such work is, a
theoreticism I would reject. "I'm interested in reports from
the field, but not the field." A poetics can only be "alive" if
its poetry is—and indeed I suspect, as Pound has argued,
that the converse of that is equally true. If one of the things
that has characterized my critical work is the use of writing
methods basic to the practice of my own poetry, the dichotomy of quality you are setting up is all the more suspect.
I'm used to hearing that the thoery is not theory at all but
only (?!) poetry—i.e., not systematic, not sufficiently explained; one might imagine professional critics exactly re-
versing your equation. But on a personal level your question
is more prickly since how can I really answer an evaluative

charge? The work is there and speaks: anyone who is interested is likely to find some of the work—"poems" or "essays"—more telling than others. But to break the work down into two basic types seems to me not founded in actually reading the texts and tuning into the primary unity of them—and in that sense is based on a misreading of the essays. "I like his drawing but not his color." All that I am is in my work.

Okay. Let's go at a text. Could you speak to The Occurrence of Tune? *What motivated that piece? And were there any special procedures involved in its creation?*

At the end of the notebook which has the first draft of that poem is a quote from Oppen: "We want to defend / Limitation / And do not know how". Which still seems to me a suitable epigraph for the work. Basically it's a transcription from a notebook I was using in the Spring of 1977, all the material was written in a "journal"-type way and edited over the summer. I think the piece is so much about "motivation" that it's hard to single out a strain apart from the confluences expressed there. That somehow questioning, interrogation, emptiness had their own music and would suffice—you didn't need anything else to go on. But as far as compositional procedures go, this piece really just happened, I don't now remember having anything overall in mind when I was writing it, though obviously as it evolved I began to see the shape and worked toward that. I spent a long time reading and rereading it after it was finished, mostly cutting things out that didn't seem to work, but this involved a lot of attention to a small amount of excising, since most of the work is as it was originally composed (and still I can remember the many weeks of editing better than the writing itself). Four short sections—the ones with line breaks—which I imagined to be the "tune" of the title, were published in *Roof IV* but otherwise, apart from some xeroxes, the work hasn't been seen, since the person who was originally going to do it as a book just never got off the ground. Susan Bee and I have just now published it as a collaborative project, through Segue Books, in which the text is interspersed with her pictures.

It has been interesting to reread the work, in proofing, and puzzle through many of its idiosyncrasies. I'm struck with how often I have to spend quite a bit of time rethinking a quirky piece of punctuation or spelling and how it is working through this process that opens up the content of the text for me. Struck both by how much what I myself wrote I've now forgotten about and how the choices that confound me now push back as key elements in my current reading of the work. How much this work seems about that process too: tune being the variety of ways meaning congeals, not so much as a plotted act of creation but rather, retrospectively, as the accumulation of occurrences, occurrences being nonsystematic formations, accidents in the literal sense. For me, writing is a process of engaging the unrealized (and therefore a production of the real). Starting a new poem tends to be pushing against a powerful field of inertia; that's why so much of the work is about motion, resistance, connection, flow, fissure. Not only don't I know what I'll write in the next poem, I don't know what I'll write in the next line of a poem I'm working on. (One of the things that interests me about line breaks is the pulse of energy involved in the connection at the end of one line and the beginning of the next, like a spark jumping a break in a cable). So writing is a startling uncovering of meaning by the very fact that it is a production of it, a making of it word by word.

I had a conversation recently with a friend who said that he found his work insufficiently expressive of his sense of the world, what he actually thought and had to say. The style with which he was working seemed to have a life of its own and it's as if he was working out what could be said from within that. He said he was making an effort to make his writing more reflective of his thinking and perceptions. Hearing that I realized I have no conception of what I have to say which I then want to put into writing, but that the writing itself shows me what I have to say, and it's always news to me, even years later, as in rereading this poem. It's not the horse pulling the cart of writing but the writing that's pulling me; and I find out who or what *I* am, or what I have to say, by reading it. So really here the cart *is* pulling the horse. That sense of not sufficiently expressing what I have to say or express is inimical to this process of production. The meaning or expression does not accompany the writing, as if the process is split, but is the writing. *The Occurrence of Tune* is an exploration of some of these issues. Perhaps to see what *inspiration* could be: not putting a prethought meaning or perception into words but rather arriving at either or both in the activity of writing itself.

In what regard does a sense of "limit" enter into the work or your work in general?

Well, completely—that there's no limit to limits and blockages, stoppages, jam as depth of field, as the abstraction/condensation of poetry, as if a dam were the poem's hydroelectric power/intensity source. So it's both a subject matter and a formal concern. What, after all, is the subject matter of poetry? Certainly limitation is right up there, *as* the body, time, place. Here you have a subject matter that actually raises itself in formal terms. I'm a bit leery of what gets called self-referentiality in poetry because of the possible self-consciousness in that—"here I am writing this on yellow paper, and you, the reader, looking at this script become type" and so on. I tend to want to cut that out. *The Occurrence of Tune* was partly a work in which I left in, made a piece around, what I would normally think to edit out. But the point is that what's significant about issues of formal limitation as a subject is *not* the self-comment on the object you can get, that's almost a distracting byproduct, but rather what this says, manifests, works out, about communication, about what and how one person can mean something, what the limits of that are. So it always seems ironic to hear someone say, well I'm not interested in aesthetic issues, I'm interested in emotion, or life, since if you can attend to the writing in the right way these so-called aesthetic issues stop being comments about writing or the poem itself and become investigations into the possibilities of and the realizations of communicating or acting or being in the world. Everybody has their ends, the things they can make do with. What's the subject matter of poetry? The way a person walks across the room, listens to him or herself, the patterns of the water as it falls, the color of the sky. One reads these words to see how a person measures their day, or how it could be measured. Everything is contained when it is apprehended; language is limitation. One sees certain things, or constructs them. And a limit is just the measure at hand.

Do you have an active sense of "voice" which could be said to condition your work?

The question that always interested me was how could language be made more conscious of itself, a question of the making audible of knowledge otherwise unreflected or unconscious. This making audible being the music of the poem. *Voice* has seemed just the most obvious way of avoiding this, since it is inextricably tied up with the organizing of the poem along psychological parameters. Unlike terms such as *limit* and *measure*, voice becomes a self-constituting project, both from an external categorizing point of view and from an internal compositional one. To try to unify the style of work around this notion of self is to take the writing to be not only reductively autobiographical in trying to define the *sound* of me but also to accept that the creation of a persona is somehow central to writing poetry. I say reductive because any characteristic ordering of language that creates a sense of voice is very much a construction out of an horizon of possibilities. I don't have *a* voice; though I can create a consistent stylistic voice in writing, or let some habitual pattern of composition bleed in from, for example, speech, and call that voice. But habitual orderings in writing, the patterns I tend toward or fall into, do not have a privileged status as self-disclosing, much less as text-generating—though they tell something of course, and I do attend to my preoccupations and obsessions. So I don't want to enfold the variety of language I use into the category of voice, any more than I would want some autobiographical gestalt to be imagined as the cohering principle among diverse elements of a single poem or among poems. Such principles of interpretation or composition are the product of a series of exclusions of relevant features of the work as much as inclusions of other features. This relates to what I was saying earlier about an aversion to characterizations of schools of writing. What is the basis for the idea of individual voice as a privileged structure in the organization and interpretation of poems; that is, when does writing stop being composition or song, incorporating at times fictional or real events in the author's life but not necessarily expressive of it at the level of form or content? When, that is, does a certain type of consistent tone among a series of discrete texts become valorized with the ontological status of voice as self, as we see in Expressionist and Romantic theory? Voice becoming self-individuating rather than, for example, reflective of a period or of each poem individually or of a common stylistic practice or of even broader notions of human speech, all of which make competing claims on the notion of voice. It's a mistake, I think, to posit the self as the primary organizing feature of writing. As many others have pointed out, a poem exists in a matrix of social and historical relations that are more significant to the formation of an individual text than any personal qualities of the life or voice of an author. I do not wish to discuss the well-known position about the "death of the author"; but there is no question that authorship is a concept that has been given much more significance than it merits, and as such is an obstacle for reading and writing to overcome; even though I do not feel that it makes sense to carry these views to the extreme of cancelling authorship as a factor completely, making a text exclusively the product of a discourse or a period, since in crucial ways a poem is as much a resistance as a product, and for the moment at least the individual is the most salient concept with which to describe the site of this resistance. The valorization of the author function, in its current guises as voice, persona, autobiography, and self-expression, hierarchializes a complicated constellation of variables including structure, social context, genre, method, politics. One of the things I wanted to explain in my piece on Mac Low is how his work challenges this model of what he would call ego organization. I'm not interested in precluding, in my own work, any of the variables of writing, per se, which is why I say I am interested in a multidiscourse, polyvocal writing practice. *Islets/Irritations*, the book I have most recently completed, is partially organized around the idiocentric occasion of each poem, rather than the more sociocentric approach in *Controlling Interests*: in each poem the coherence that *it* requires is worked out in a way that doesn't necessarily apply outside its specific occasion. This is also what interested me in doing short poems in the new book and in general accounts for the exogamic appearance of the whole with a different shape or parameter to each poem, different voices, different measures—to have an over-all text without an overall format or style.

I'd like a fuller understanding of your notion of "author-ity". You ended the Mac Low essay with what seems to be a key point ("That it is architectures that shape the world, but we who must fill them up."). Who is Charles Bernstein and why is he implicating all of us in these strange things he does?

I wonder myself. What a person is is certainly a theme throughout my work and the formal dimension of that concern in a text is the question of author-ity. It's the topic, for instance, of "G—", of my dialogue with Ron in *Legend*, of the cover motif of *Poetic Justice* etc., etc. It's a running issue in *Controlling Interests*: the self constituted by a matrix of language that envelops an individual like the swaddling clothes in Rousseau's *Emile*. So is the *self* the impression of a mold or the particular form of maladaption to it, or what? Individuals are in essence that which is maladapted, idiocentric, resistant; it is in that sense that we get to know another only through the identification and appreciation of their peculiarities as particularized—mutant—and not as instances of some generalized feature of some genre of humans.

The reason there may be some value still in the author function is that the *I* in a text operates as a very pertinent measure of the constituting capacity of language. It's like a radioactive tracer in physiology, where a radioactive isotope replaces a stable chemical element in an ingested substance allowing the course of its activity to be scanned formally, the *I* allows the language's formative capacities to be scanned. —So I hope the reader does feel implicated because I want to show that *I* as a social construction, a *product* of language and not a preexisting entity outside it; that *I* is first a *we*. We're implicated in each other from the first!

SOCIALIST REALISM
OR REAL SOCIALISM?

I'm just beginning as a writer. In a lot of ways the role of ideology and the point of view that seemed to pervade James Sherry's and Bruce Andrews's talks, while they were interesting to me, were out of my reach. What I write now is conversational. What is the path beyond conventional writing, beyond what you would find in the ten best-selling novels? As a writer, how does one progress beyond it?

It's not a question of going beyond the dominant modes of writing but of taking a different course. The styles of best sellers are highly technical, requiring a great deal of commitment to produce them. You don't just stumble upon such styles, you have to make a conscious effort to master them. I wouldn't, as a general rule, say no one should take that course. It could be that someone might write a best-selling novel and it would be a valuable thing for them to do: it would be a good novel and a good piece of social practice. Although, I find that hard to imagine. I can say why I'm not

Italicized questions and comments are from participants in the Institute for Policy Studies program from which this text is transcribed.

Socialist Realism or Real Socialism?

attracted to doing that type of writing. I'm extremely stubborn about what I write. I only want to write things the way I want to write them. I think that quality of stubbornness, of wanting to do exactly what I want to do . . . I don't put that forward as a virtue, although I certainly don't feel it's not a virtue, but I don't feel it's necessary to put forward these kind of views in a holier-than-thou or a bohemian dirtier-than-thou way. These are simply things one does, finds oneself able to do. And I'm not able, perhaps, to do anything different than what I do.

So it's not going beyond conventional writing styles as much as finding alternatives to them. Unfortunately, there is an almost total marginality—invisibility—of any sort of writing that does not use the conventional styles. No widely (or even moderately) circulated publication in this country diverges from the dominant forms of verbal discourse— except in their advertisements! Even within the left, conventional viewpoints about writing reign to the almost total exclusion of anything else. *The Nation*, for example, restricts its poetry publishing to academic style or "populist" realism. At the American Writers Conference, organized by *The Nation*, there was a virtual shut-out of any of the traditions of "the new American poetry", or to put it another way, any writing that does not employ conventional grammatical, narrative, or expository parameters to express its meaning. Strangely, there was a significant degree of 1930s-style distress about early modernism, without any seeming awareness, much less cogent argument against, contemporary modernism. As far as I could tell, these attitudes were publicly questioned only by George Lakoff, the linguist, at his panel.

Is it rhetoric you're trying to get away from?

I've had a very negative feeling about the word *rhetoric* as opposed to the word *poetry*. But in this context it may be worthwhile pushing the term rhetoric just because it is unsettling, to dispel some of the idealism in the preference for *poetry*—as if somehow they're rhetorical but we're not. We're all rhetorical in everything that we write; to take responsibility for a text is to understand that all texts are rhetorical, are involved with persuasion. In some way, persuasion is a more interesting term for thinking about poetry than is communication. I'm looking to be persuaded by my own words and by the language. That's what happens when a poem works—I am persuaded by it, not communicated to.

Rhetoricians of the eighteenth century didn't think in terms of sentences, the written unit of grammar, but periods, a spoken unit. Sentences encourage conciseness and simplicity to give the effect of clarity, but rhetoricians weren't concerned with diagramming sentences so that you have a subject and an object rapidly following upon each other; rather, the period, as opposed to the sentence, was something that had to do with sermons and speeches that went on at length and had various curlicues, much like the period upon which I am presently working, which isn't really a good sentence in that it would be uneconomical if you started to look at it that way, but which has its flows, its various ups and downs, its breaks, which moves in time rather than being an abstract grammatical entity, so that you can lose yourself in its meanderings until, when the suspension is sustained just so long—*then I say to you that you will be saved.*

The period doesn't work by pithily communicating a message, you're left hanging as to what is to be the point because the subject might not come till the very end. I admire the openness and expansiveness of the prose styles of the eighteenth century. Most of these qualities have been lost in the movement from the material practice of the period to the *idea* of the sentence, with its ostensive subject-verb-object relation, and the attendant boasts of communication and "value-free" writing. I think we might have been in a better spot when it was more apparent that all writing really is rhetorical.

What do you see as the role of the unintentional and of the accidental, which Allen Ginsberg, in his talk, presented as central to poetry. What is the role of craft?

There are lots of different ways that people come upon what is interesting in their writing, including unintentionally. Very often the unintentional may be a useful way of breaking out of programmed thinking and writing. Craft, in the sense of achieving intentions, is everything, but it is insufficient; accident is inspiration, but you're responsible for every word.

A related issue, raised by Ginsberg, is the role of the individual and his or her psychological and physiological processes in the creation of art. From a political point of view, I am interested in understanding art ideologically, that is, in terms of social considerations. Rather than thinking of individual artists and what they have in their minds to do, it may be more valuable to think of how artworks reflect struggles and conditions that exist in the society or culture as a whole. Even within an individual author's work there are contradictory things going on, which the author may not have control of, which may be unintentional, but that as readers we can try to understand. People don't suddenly invent a poetics all on their own. Any poetics has to do with a large number of other writers and other political, social, and class factors that have contributed to that process. Such a perspective is an essential ingredient in any political analysis of art—to undermine the idealization of the individual artist as existing in eternity and expressing the universal truth of his or her life. Whereas in fact we don't have that much control over what we create. We have some control, and that control is a crucial thing. The role of the individual isn't so much expressing his or her individual self, but rather resisting various flows, ideologies, and habituations. And I would suggest that listening—attending—is a better model for such resisting than emoting or expressing.

In contrast, much of the arts is concerned with securing a trademark style, or, as they say in poetry, finding your own voice: insidious processes. But you don't have to use art as an example. Just think of someone who's somehow found the "way" they are and then makes a determined effort to be that way—a frightening business. It's like "communicating": "I'm going to COMMUNICATE with you." Well, I don't want you to communicate with me, just be there, or say what you think: don't mediate your behavior to conform to being the *way* you are. Such an idealization of personality is not so different from the idealization/fetishization of style. There is a great deal of explicit and implicit social pressure on artists in creating their works, and an individual can resist only to a certain degree and at some point necessarily succumbs. But it's the way in which they succumb, the angle of submission, that is often interesting.

The success of an artwork doesn't have so much to do with your identity, which you are expressing through it as if it were a prosthetic self, but rather what you're actually able to manage to *do* at a pragmatic level out there on the page. You can have the most interesting inner life in the world and not be able to produce an interesting poem, and you can have a seemingly bland inner life—whatever that may be— and produce the most beautiful poems in the world. It's not a question of your inner life, it's a question of what you're writing . . . alas. Otherwise, it would just be possible to live this terrific life, which the poetry would just come out of. I could just go on automatic pilot in that journal-keeping way and it would just work. That would be a relief; it would make for a lot less depression, and a lot less work (which is always objectionable!).

Is that your objection to Ginsberg's poetry?

In terms of his presentation here last week, I disagree with his valorization of breath and of the spontaneous. I don't object to those things as a practice, necessarily, but as a prescriptive theory: the idea that there is something more "natural", i.e., patterns of breath, than what you might construct. That I'm able to write something based on my breath or based on twelve reworkings from a story in the New York *Post* is not a relevant criterion of value. Ginsberg is saying that when the poetry comes out of breath, or out of meditation, then it is better; but the process from which he derives his material doesn't make it more interesting. For example, his comment "ideology is only an abstraction from phenomena rather than phenomena itself", rather, that is, than the brook, the tree. There's no such thing as "phenomena itself" apart from ideology. Ideology, I would almost say, has more the status of substance than do so-called objects, because it is the system through which we constitute objects.

It seems to be an anti-intellectual view.

Anti-intellectual in a totally ideological way! Something that claims to be anti-ideological but which is essentially a religious belief or an ideological structure of belief is one step more intellectual than I'm willing to accept. I'm not claiming any of us are transcending our ideologies, our particular historical circumstances. There are limits to consciousness of consciousness. I don't think that just by saying things that are prohibited, which Ginsberg advocates, that you break out of ideological structures. Nonetheless by working in this area Ginsberg has done something of the greatest importance. In this respect, perhaps anything I write is possible only by virtue of the work Ginsberg and others have done.

What do you mean by ideology?

Ideology is often used as a pejorative term, much the way rhetoric is used pejoratively—false consciousness. But, again, I don't think we need to use these terms pejoratively because it creates the idea that somehow you have ideology but I don't. Louis Althusser has argued that even should a classless society come into being, people would still see things within the context of ideology. When you scratch an ideology you find a culture, when you scratch a culture you find a mythos. It is possible to see various aspects of the ideological process and possible even to liberate oneself from some compulsive behavior governed by ideology. But this is not a process that gets finished once and for all, followed by a return to somnambulance. It is a dialectical process involving critique and then critique of the critique. And that is a process in which poetry can play a part.

I gather that you believe we have some sort of freedom to "create" the world through language, an ability possibly appropriated by the institutionalization of certain rules for language = thought. Well, I agree, and yet it doesn't quite feel that way very often. It's like Samuel Johnson's remark about predestination—all logic is for it, all experience against it.

It is NOT that grammar, per se, which is an abstraction, a projection, is repressive, but that societal conditions are repressive and that these repressions are *reflected* in grammar, can be spotted in that particular mapping. It is not the grammar that creates the constrictions on thought but the nature of human social organization, often as a result of species survival/adaption, often as part of the hierarchialized system of rewards that have developed and the explanation for which is to be found not in analyzing grammar but in historical materialist studies. But such studies are locked in, often, to given sets of conclusions that they cannot break out of by virtue of the presumptions contained within the language of the investigation.

What is the writer's responsibility to the reader in terms of being intelligible?

None. A writer's responsibility is to make sense . . .

. . . to himself or to herself.

Not to him/herself, to make sense, period. Not *to* anybody. To say it makes sense to somebody . . .

How's one to judge whether someone is making sense?

When someone is making sense the one to judge is the person whose *making* the sense.

So in other words it's the writer for him/herself?

Well, but "for him/herself" is . . .

You're the only one who has to understand what you're writing, as far as you are concerned.

No, I don't think you understand it necessarily. There's no claim that you need to understand your own writing, nor does anybody really understand, at least in some absolute way, their own writing. They wrote it, they don't necessarily understand it.

But you're the only person your writing has to make sense to.

No, I'm not the only one. For one thing, your writing doesn't "have to" make sense to anyone. But what I'm saying is that when you're writing your responsibility is to the text itself and that the text . . .

Oh, the text makes sense of itself?!

Well, not *of* itself, the text makes sense. See, what I object to is this imposition of the idea of communication as conduit between two people. That's an imposition that comes only when we have these kind of constrained conversations where somebody is saying somebody else isn't communicating. The problem may not be that someone isn't communicating with you but that someone is annoying you, someone is saying something you don't like even if what you don't like is the way they're saying it. But then we raise these matrices of concern that revolve around the idea of communication as a circuit between two autonomous points. That to me is an unnecessarily theoretical—intellectualizing!—imposition onto the human situation that creates an artifical set of values about what human activity consists of. I mean I'm not concerned whether you communicate with me, I'm concerned with whether you get off my back, for instance. I don't want my boss to communicate with me, I want him or her to pay me more money. George Lakoff has written an interesting paper on the assumptions implicit in the conduit metaphor of communication, especially relevant considering what a buzz word communication has become. Not the least of the assumptions is the premise of these preconstituted individuals who are terminal points of an enclosed channel. That's why I object when you say it makes sense "to me" as opposed to "to you". Why talk about making sense *to* anybody and not *of* something. By this, however, I do not mean that "sense" is some linguistic universal; on the contrary, different experiences, different social circumstances, will radically alter the sense a reader makes of a text. But that's not only an *individual*, a psychological, process but also a social one.

I might accept what you're saying as far as communication being a conduit, but I want to relate this back to something you said earlier—that we have responsibilities to something out there. If what you're saying is to have any real value in terms of taking it out to the streets, in building some kind of revolutionary movement, in furthering class struggle, then this has no place, then you are not fulfilling your responsibilities as a writer. You can dismiss me as being simplistic and as only trying to see goals. The comic book that came out, Marx for Beginners, *that had very cutesy little drawings and simplified sentences and vocabulary, probably did more to further the class struggle than anything Gramsci wrote in his prison cell late at night in pain.*

I've said that people have multiple responsibilities that can't necessarily be neatly packaged together. A person's political responsibilities cannot be fulfilled by any kind of writing no matter how popular or how obscure. It's a mistake to superimpose political or ethical responsibilities—the necessity for social *organizing*—onto textual practices in any kind of literal way; it's a confusion of realms. For one thing, there is a great danger in proscribing irresponsibility, "bad" politics, and so on, in art because these things may reveal the dark side of whatever "enlightenment" is the order of the day; in any case, there's no nonreductive way to identify such qualities. Another problem is that this confusion of realms bolsters one of the more common beliefs of our time—that only *mass* communication is of any genuine significance. Unfortunately, the left has not always extricated itself from this prejudice. Too often the argument seems to be that the content of mass communication is the only issue. There is something suspect and elitist about anything short of (or not aspiring to be) popular, much less (the Revolution forbid!) obscure. At best, one sees (a sometimes grudging) acceptance that literature addressed to a clearly identified oppressed group need not have an appeal beyond that group; but at least it should be popular throughout that group! A Leninist distrust of decentralization runs counter to any limited-interest cultural activity, especially if the audience is dispersed; although such activity, which enhances the realization of human diversity and eccentricity —spiritual values—has been greatly facilitated by the new reproduction technologies. There's surely the need, and the possibility, for more than one type of cultural activity. Commendable as *Marx for Beginners* is, I wouldn't want to live in a world that allowed no utterance more complicated than can be made with two-syllable words.

Moreover, there is an instructive value in working with— reading *and* writing—texts that offer alternatives to the directional, unifunctional, hierarchialized structures that dominate both Capitalist and Communist societies. We have got to understand that the failures of socialist revolutions are related to failures to break with these structures. It is not enough, as has often been said, to just switch the operators of the same state/corporate machine: the machine itself must be dismantled. But it is also not enough simply to *say* that. It is, however, possible to offer glimpses of other ways of putting things together, a different scale of values; this can be called utopian content. Such content can be realized only by a total de/reorganization of the formal norms embraced by both realist/populist and academic writing. Insofar as the American left rejects divergence from this dominant discourse, it rejects the need to envision such alternatives. In so doing, the prospect is diminished for social transformation that does not sacrifice pleasure and diversity and freedom of activity and expression to the abstract necessities of instrumentality. " . . . constant labor of one uniform kind disturbs the intensity and flow of a [person's] vital forces, which find recreation and delight in the change of activity itself" [Marx, *Capital* I:14:2].

Then you should be honest with what your goals as a writer are, and they are to yourself.

Not to myself, that's what I don't understand. What is that "to myself". When I'm sitting down and reading I'm not thinking "Gee, this makes sense *to me*." I'm not thinking about "me". I'm not thinking about "you". I'm thinking about "it". No more than Noam Chomsky, when he's trying to figure something out about depth structure versus surface structure is thinking, "Gee, this makes sense to me." I'm doing this work that has a particular integrity to it and also has a limitedness to it based on being written by a particular person in a particular time and place. It simply makes no sense to say you communicate to yourself; I reject the self-conscious deformation of that terminology. At the same time meaning (aesthetic *or* scientific) is never a universal, translinguistic thing. The conduit metaphor misdirects our attention from the social determination, and hence partialness, of meaning onto a decontextualized, dehistoricized transmission of a message from one individual to another (A to B). So we think if we're not talking about communicating to "B" we must be talking about communicating to "A", oneself, as if masturbation is going to be the next metaphor.

Isn't it appropriate to ask of a text, what is it saying?

Absolutely, and no less so with apparently intelligible texts, where a great deal of work has to be put into figuring out what's being said that's hidden.

But some of the essays in L=A=N=G=U=A=G=E *do not seem to be concerned with being clear.*

Clarity is a particular technical effect of writing; a writer has no more responsibility to be clear than a painter to use blue. Yet, clarity has this mystique of being the *raison d'être* of . . .

It has the quality of being a liquid.

It has the quality of being a liquid but it is not a liquid. It has the quality of being transparent but it is opaque. It's just the particular form of opacity that as an optical (I should say, textual) illusion we see as transparent. That's a very powerful thing to use. And you ought to know that you're being used by it and exactly how you're being used by it. Clarity is the most extremely rhetorical property of language. "I don't want you to be clear with me . . . I want you to do the dishes!"

I don't accept that. When you write an essay, you probably refine it many times over. Clarity I define as the opposite of clutter, which leads to impurity, externality, and error.

I like all those qualities, at the technical level, at the aesthetic level.

When we talk about clarity we're talking about something being understandable.

No, I don't think they're the same thing. One understands many things that are not clear. Clarity is an effect operating on the reader that has more to do with hypnosis than understanding. We think something is clear, but it's more like slickness, it's like gloss. It's a very attractive affective quality. I don't put it down either: to achieve clarity is a considerable technical accomplishment. It's a particular tool. But I say expose these tools, see how they operate, who they serve. Walter Cronkite has clear prose about the news. Clear about what? Clear about what he chooses to say, very unclear about what's actually happening in the world. I guess Walter Cronkite is not with us anymore, but whoever is telling us these facts in such clear tones is essentially an obscurantist. There's a clarity in the struggle of the Polish or Salvadorian people without them having to say a word, certainly without the need for a clear prose style with good transitions and parallel structure.

What progress is being made toward bringing about an improvement in regard to the use of language? What's the prognosis?

"There are probably words addressed to our condition exactly, which, if we could really hear and understand, would be more salutory than the morning. . . ." Over a hundred years after Thoreau wrote that I can't think of anything more true. To wrest meaning from the abuse it receives daily: without that there won't be any value in political change. But I can't say whether we're better off in respect to these issues now than people were 500 years ago; and I'm not sure what difference it makes whatever the answer. The potential means of our greater liberation are also more effective means for our suppression. It's a continuous struggle to take control over language, to take it within our own hands and make it mean what we want it to mean, like Humpty Dumpty says in *Alice in Wonderland*. That process is hard to measure in historical terms. At any given point when something meaningful is said or enacted then that is a concrete instance of success.

You spoke of Ginsberg's contribution to breaking the molds. My question is to what extent, how many molds have we broken?

For every mold that is broken, a new one springs up in the midst like Athena out of Zeus's brow. This is a time of great transformation, development, and achievement in the practice of writing in North America. Yet, in North American society as a whole active participation in the shaping of language by its users diminishes everyday. That's a very disturbing, but not inevitable, process that must be fought against.

Wouldn't you say that when you write the way you want to write you're reforming the use of language?

Yes, but the problem is one of scale. It's hard to be optimistic about the "larger" picture. The language changes, there are spectacular particulars; but greed and property remain, perhaps with changed names. Yet discouragement is as much the bogeyman as avarice. Any action begins in articulation—an articulation that doesn't wait for the "right" words to express itself but speaks of its situation with the conviction of reflection as much as assertion. Every instance is an actualization.

CHARACTERIZATION

CHARLES BERNSTEIN: I found this in *The New York Times* for October 5th on the back page of the first section:

BILL BERNBACH
1911-1982

He said,
"The real giants have always been poets
men who jumped from facts
into the realm of imagination and ideas.

He elevated advertising to high art
and our jobs to a profession.

He made a difference.

Doyle Dane Bernbach

428

I don't know how much that costs—

TOM MANDEL: Oh, a fortune. $15,000, anyway.

BERNSTEIN: "Bill Bernbach, 1911-1982. He said, 'The real giants have always been poets. *Men* [laughter] who *jumped* from facts into the realm of imagination and ideas.'"

RON SILLIMAN: You mean, like "jumped back" [laughter].

BERNSTEIN: I've never been able to figure out what it is I have to say about this, but something. "He elevated advertising to a high art . . ." He elevated advertising to a commercial art is really what he did. ". . . and our jobs to a profession."

MANDEL: But it's more than that he created commercial art. Elevating advertising to a high art would actually mean that he was among those "men"—that generation that made advertising work. In other words, that made it possible to manipulate, to totally identify needs, and do the work of targeting who you were going to address with your satisfactions of those needs. Before, advertising had simply been publicity.

BERNSTEIN: And "Doyle Dane Bernbach" right here, no commas—for those of you who are doing proofreading. It's one of the biggest agencies in the U.S. You would have seen thousands of images from them.
    I love the way they use "flush center": it's a very class look. Of course, if I were a different kind of person I would discuss this *difference* here: making "Doyle Dane Bernbach" very small here, and these two black lines . . .

So this to me is a really interesting instance of characterization. How do you make something seem classy, something that's actually very offensive to many people, even people who read *The New York Times*. And I think they did a very good job with it, even though it's really kind of weird.

"He made a difference." What I especially like about the characterization of this is *this* is not a piece of advertising. This is a tribute to a man we love. You can't even see "Doyle Dane Bernbach" from a distance. If they were really advertising, obviously they'd make it really big.

I've always objected, actually, to the characterization of myself as a poet, much because of the way they have "He was a *poet* . . ." This idea of the poet being singled out. In fact, I've noticed recently that when you want to say somebody does something . . . I saw a bathroom poster for "Jim Morrison, an American poet". Obviously he was a great American musician, not a great American poet. It's as if you want to say that Zukofsky is a great American poet, you would say that he is a "great American musician". Somehow, to be characterized as excelling in your field they want to jump you into another field.

MICHAEL PALMER: It's interesting, too, that when Zukofsky is characterized as such, to distinguish that kind of "great American poet" from "the great American poets", let's say like Robert Frost, who people actually know about, it's then followed parenthetically by "a poet's poet". It's a removal from the domain of the nominative, somehow. And so it's at once "poet squared" but also "poet diminished."

BERNSTEIN: You see this in respect to some American

playwrights wanting to say that what they're doing is opera. Robert Wilson, in *Letter to Queen Victoria*, which he called an opera,—it was, to me, one of the best pieces of theater I've ever seen. But it had to be called an opera because it was so good.

SILLIMAN: There was a review in last Sunday's paper: "A 3-D movie good enough to be 2-D" [laughter].

BARRETT WATTEN: You better look out or you might start doing a performance piece, Charles [laughter].

BERNSTEIN: So thinking about how writers tend to get topped off in this trivializing way as being "poets", I've always preferred the term "writer", which is more neutral, which refers anyway to the medium, since there is some difficulty in separating out what the difference is between poetry and writing.

Or else I tend to like the most perverse types of characterization, the ones that can't possibly be accepted because they imply . . . That's why I'm amused by David Bromige's "dialectical materialist". That's a great term for poets because nobody's ever going to say, "The new dialectical materialist poets are doing exciting stuff in San Francisco." It just has too much baggage with it, whether or not it's more accurate than other terms. It's interesting just as a difficulty.

Last night, reading "Words and Pictures", I quoted from Williams in terms of the poetics of sight, when he talks about catching and holding—"The Lily" was caught and held, and quoted from Richard Foreman saying you have to kill something in order to catch it and hold it, and I suppose that's my basic hesitation about characterization, that it's naming, it's defining. At the same time, there isn't any escape from some degree of characterization, of talking about, of pointing to. But there can be different approaches to it. Essentially any kind of characterization involves a system of metaphor because you're characterizing something *by* something else. It's always a partial view. Or it gives a different view but at the same time it obscures other parts of it.

To me, one of the most significant examples of taking over a systematic characterization is the way Marx takes over the metaphor and characterization of political economy from bourgeois economics, which is what, in *The Mirror of Production*, Baudrillard criticizes him for. Essentially he feels that Marx falls short by accepting certain words that characterize social life in terms of value and instrumentation. That by continually using terms like the production of value, he characterizes society in terms of production as the only inherent value that can be defined, and thus accepts the whole world of bourgeois economics rather than doing a thoroughgoing critique of it. And yet it's Marx who did do the most thoroughgoing critique of the economy of his time in the West. And it suggests to me not so much that he was in error than that there's an inherent problem with all criticism and with all characterization.

So for myself in writing criticism I've often found an odd situation of focusing in on certain terms which always imply more than I would like. I spoke of this last night in criticizing the terms I used in "Words and Pictures": sight, optics, focus, vision, perspective, reflection, shadow, vortex.

These are all terms which are partial and suggest certain domains which can be explored but at the same time characterize them in such a way as to suggest that they're not something else. So that when I set up sight versus vision, that, to me, is a false dichotomy insofar as it's taken out of the context of what it is that I'm trying to consider there, and I'm suspicious of it myself.

Chomsky, in *Language and Responsibility*, points out how he feels people in the humanities are particularly caught up with fixing on certain positions because they have so much invested in them. Whereas scientists in his view—a romanticized view of science, I think, but nonetheless I think it's fair to say of him—scientists are willing to totally reverse themselves. Certainly he feels he's totally reversed himself over a twenty-year period. He no longer feels he has to defend or even think in terms of the argument he made in his earlier work.

I think that what happens sometimes is that writers get characterized in terms of their positions. It's very hard; when they change their work they get flak. You have the case of Ashbery who only became accepted in terms of the work of the last ten years. *Self-Portrait in a Convex Mirror* received a great amount of critical attention and prizes and so on. And so it was incumbent upon so many writers in Lehman's *Beyond Amazement* to attack as gibberish portions of *The Tennis Court Oath*, almost like party doctrine. And then one finds Ashbery, in *Crafts of Poetry*, interviews with William Packard, saying he's no longer interested in *The Tennis Court Oath*. And then it becomes incumbent upon me and other people to say, "Well, that's his *best* book." Because, for one thing, it *is* his best book [laughter]. That's a big reason. But *Three Poems* is pretty good. And, of course, Bloom is the big demon in respect to Ashbery. He totally obliterates Ashbery for the early work where he's not dealing with Stevens. But Ashbery himself has capitulated on this score. It's almost as if the poetry *has* to be a development.

MANDEL: But Ashbery lost interest in that work, or had engaged in a self-critique well before he was accepted.

BERNSTEIN: That's right. It might be fairer to say that Ashbery was doing what Chomsky is doing.

WATTEN: You can say that if the words are completely surface words.

MANDEL: You could say it if he'd made more than one such change, perhaps. But you might want to compare him to someone like Wittgenstein, who critiques his earlier work.

BERNSTEIN: Well, yes, you have a lot of artists who progress. But I agree with Barry on Ashbery. On the surface you could say that it seems like early Wittgenstein versus later Wittgenstein, where the later is a psychoanalysis, almost, of the early work, showing the limitations. But it so goes in line with the particular academic characterization of his work in removing it from the context that it exists in that I'm not concerned with John Ashbery as a person or his attitudes toward his work so much as what the politics of the extrapolation and division of his work exist as and how he participates in it and doesn't wish to challenge it.

My own tendency is that it's useful for people not to accept characterizations that are made of them at any level. A poem like "Standing Target" in *Controlling Interests* includes quotes by which I was characterized as a child by my camp counsellors. It quotes them verbatim. It's a poem about my own hostility, my resistance to characterization, to the use of code words that should definitely be attacked.

SILLIMAN: When you finish, will you talk about David DeMotte, and then those other people who are characterizing you in that way?

BERNSTEIN: Well, what was great was I got a letter from Ron that one of his students down in San Diego recognized one of the characters that I have a quote about. I worked for Harcourt Brace Jovanovich. . . . Men who . . . made a gutter art out of publishing. Jovanovich's goal was, rather than be gobbled up by the big companies, that he would become one of the big companies. They publish more magazines—*HairDo Magazine*, *Modern Medicine* was the one I worked for, *Quick Frozen Foods* was right next door. They publish about thirty-five different magazines, that's primarily what their business is. And they had a national circular which included some people who worked, as you shall see, in the San Diego division. As it turned out, Ron's student actually worked for this guy. So was he amused, or . . . ?

SILLIMAN: I don't know if *she* ever gave it to him. Her job was trimming the wings of flamingos.

BERNSTEIN: I'll read parts of "Standing Target".

Deserted all sudden a all
Or gloves of notion, seriously
Foil sightings, polite society
Verge at just about characterized
Largely a base, cups and
And gets to business, hands
Like "hi", gnash, aluminum foil
Plummeting emphatically near earshot
Scopes bleak incontestably at point
Of incompetence, blasting back
Past imperceptible arrogance, islands of
Blown air, overlooked, replies
Startle, stares. . . .
                              . . . So sad
Sitting there. Slows as sense
Descends, very oracular warmth
Would go by maybe years, unnerving.
Redress of slant. Limitless like
Listless. I aim at you, slips
Behind my back, that neither of us
Had told, kept.

. . .

All of a sudden all deserted.

Neurological impairment, speech delay, psychomotor
difficulties with wide discrepancies and
fluctuations, excessive neurotic fears and compulsive
behavior, a diffuse hostile attitude, general
clumsiness, confused dominance, poor fine motor
coordination, asymmetrical reflexes, aggressive,
callous, arrogant, excessive inhibitions,
rebellious, suspicious, attention seeking, erratic
friendship pattern, overexcitable in normal situations.

As President and Chief Executive Officer
of Sea World, Inc., David DeMotte is
responsible for managing all aspects
of the Company's operations at Sea
World parks in San Diego, Aurora,
Ohio, Orlando, Florida, and the Florida
Keys. A native Californian, DeMotte,
and his wife Charlotte, enjoy hunting,
fishing, and tennis in their spare time.

. . .

The end result was a gradual
neurosis superimposed upon a pre-existing
borderline character structure.

Note the exclusive right-side-up feature.

Awkward constellation
points, margins
washed "in good
voice", vanished
in good voice. Delirium
tyrannizes the
approximate moment.
To vanish
outside
the circuit.

. . .

Last spring Charles put himself on record
that he didn't like crafts. We soon
came to understand his feelings
when we worked with him. Charlie

This is not about me, by the way. None of my work is about
me [laughter].

is not strong in manual dexterity. (This
may be part of a mixed dominance
situation Mrs. B. and I discussed in
relation to tying shoes.) Fortunately,
what he lacks in developed skills
he makes up for in
patience, determination, and
knowledge of what he wants as
results.

Charlie has grown to enjoy our organized games.
His interest carries throughout the
period, as a rule. He pulls his share in
team set ups and cheers loudly for
his team. During free time Charlie
has succeeded in busying himself with
friends. Sometimes it's Running
Bases, or digging for coal, or
club meetings in the
"private hideout".

     fatigue
        of   of
            open for
     to   , sees
doubles
    glass   must
       are   for
     in   : they
                         , her
       that it
   watches, leaves,

. . .

> Discussions, fair play, group life—
> Pattern of careless work and sloppy
> Appearance—included is integral,
> Quiet and rather vague, at one period,
> Skills and coordination, enthusiastic business,
> When in actuality the class had merely,
> And often both. He seems to feel depressed
> And unsure of himself. I hoped,
> Holds himself back by doing, this is
> Especially true, omits many times.

BOB PERELMAN: Charles, could you give a close reading of the first section? The way I read it, there's some charged, blunt stuff in the middle that radiates outward, and it's easy to read the poem in terms of a person getting socialized, but the very beginning, before that's set up, how do you hear that?

BERNSTEIN: My sense is that we are characterized insofar as we let ourselves be characterized, that one can resist characterization by becoming conscious of its techniques and its inevitability. We live in a world which communicates through characterization, but we can resist its reification, its finalization, by understanding it as a provisional thing that exists in time for a particular use. Insofar as that use is agreed upon—perceived and acknowledged—in the communication, there may be no problem with characterization. But if it's thought to come from above or it hits you from behind and you don't know that it's happening, it mystifies your conception of your personality. It creates the sense that persons are these objects that exist discretely and outside of time.

I've always been fascinated by the kind of clinical psychological description in the poem; it's the clinical description I find most offensive. And I think it does pop out on the reader because it's very different from other things in my work. But it's not my intention or my reading to have those particular paragraphs stand out over and against other sections.

To me, the key lines are, not so much the opening . . . But, look, you have this opening stanza, "Deserted all sudden a all", which later is echoed in *"All of a sudden all deserted"*. "Gloves of notion" is another kind of characterization of characterization. "Omits"—there's the section which is the most sparse in the poem, which is omitting what would fill out and determine, fix, hold, stamp down like the butterfly in Stein, if you know that in *The Making of Americans* where the boy catches the butterfly and puts it in an album and the father says, "Oh, how could you do that?"

So I think the first part is a comment in general on this issue. "Limitless like / Listless", "Behind my back", "That neither of us has held". But what to me is the key . . . Well, and then there's there's that . . .

PERELMAN: The "like" is confusing, not that that's bad. But before you've been characterized as having your right hemisphere and your left hemisphere battling so you can't tie your shoes, that's what that dominance was about . . .

BERNSTEIN: I suppose. "Mixed dominance" is a concept that this person made up, as far as I'm concerned. "Confused dominance" is what I use in another section, which I think is great. I mean, that's what I would hope for in my work: confused dominance [laughter]. "Limitless like / Listless."

"Limits are what we are inside of." Olson really got that in my ear: a limit. That's what I hear. "Limitless like / Listless": that's like the deterritorializing flows in Deleuze and Guattari for those who have read *Anti-Oedipus* or even for those who haven't. And then there's another stanza about how sad lines—limits—are "crisscrossing / out the hopes of an undifferentiated / experience."

PERELMAN: But "Limitless like / Listless" seems to be saying the opposite. It seems to be validating limits.

BERNSTEIN: I think "Limitless like / Listless" suggests both. I'm interested in statements that you can't take . . . I wrote in "Part Quake", "They ridicule revolutionary theory / and sneer that having a correct / position is sectarian." And Bruce Andrews said, "I'm surprised that you thought that." And I don't think that, actually. That is, I think there are a lot of problems with the sectarianism of taking a correct line. On the other hand, I think it's interesting to struggle to have something that's correct for yourself, but not to have the arrogance of that kind of Stalinist correctness, or many other kinds of correctness. But, nonetheless, the idea of trying to come up with good politics is reasonable, and there's a danger on the left of people being so against coming up with correct lines because of sectarianism that we give up the idea of having any politics at all, which is certainly the case with many of my friends, and what I see out there.

And I think that the problem with Deleuze and Guattari is that they idealize the schizo flow as deterritorializing, where there's just this free flow of energy between people who don't exist in material, historical conditions, and I don't believe that. I believe that everything exists within material, historical situations, within contexts. And that there's nothing wrong with territorializations or characterizations, if we understand them to be provisional contextualizations. In fact, these territorializations and characterizations that we make are our language, are our world. We create these structures with our lives, "taking hands into our history". And so to discount those things as merely arbitrary, to me, is the problem.

And that's why I disagree with the way language is characterized within French structuralist thought from Saussure to Derrida, in which language is thought to be divided in a polarity between the signifier and the signified, as two different things, and that the relation between the sound and the mental image is arbitrary. I don't think that relationship is arbitrary and to characterize it as arbitrary suggests that characterization is purely arbitrary.

WATTEN: But that's two different meanings at two different times. When Saussure wanted to talk about the arbitrariness of the sign what he meant was that it was not mystic. He was trying to get rid of undue concern with etymology in nineteenth century linguistics, and that's exactly what that means, and it doesn't mean *anything else*. I wish somebody would put it on a billboard someplace. Because, absolutely, the arbitrariness of the sign just means he's separating his characterization of language from the historical description of nineteenth century linguistics, that's *all*.

BERNSTEIN: Criticism insofar as it's provisional sets up

terms. And those things do have value within their context, but when they get reified and taken out of their context, then you have this monster which gets created. In every generation the work is summarized, and characterized from one to the next, and this gets compounded when you're dealing with different languages. It gets increasingly reductive and problematic because it embeds basic ideas and dualisms which had a strategic function within the context of the original criticism but become these universal principles which then have to be attacked just in the way Saussure has to attack etymology by proposing his things, just as I could be forced into attacking those things because of the monster that was created from that.

It seems to me that criticism, rather than trying to establish fixed things which are good for everything, in its best exists at a provisional level, and that that provisional quality doesn't need to be masked. But the wrinkle in it is that that masking has social power. If you don't mask it, it doesn't have the impact on an audience.

And, again, I'm going to be ambivalent about this issue, which is certainly something that I should be criticized for.

WATTEN: Okay, Charles, I really think you should purge your vocabulary of phrases like "structuralist linguistics from Saussure to Derrida".

BERNSTEIN: I should purge my . . . ?

WATTEN: You shouldn't allow yourself to say that. And that would be the answer to the whole thing. I mean, if you know better . . .

KIT ROBINSON: Why can't he say that?

WATTEN: Because it's not only a provisional construction, but it's an illusory and unexamined construction that you in fact know better of. And so in fact you can *do* better.

BERNSTEIN: Yes, but I *can't* really. That's the point. I can't make this point sufficiently about how perverse, to me, this particular characterization of language as an arbitrary distinction between the signified and the signifier is, which I think infects a good deal of the criticism that we deal with in the United States. The arbitrariness, this idea of decoding, all this is built in to that notion.

SILLIMAN: But your concept of resistance to characterization reconstructs exactly the kind of structure—to use that term—that you're criticizing Deleuze and Guattari for. That's why I asked about the guy from Sea World in "Standing Target" as distinct from the characterizations of yourself. There's a real question of the social frames that these characterizations occur in. Just as with the Bill Bernbach, which is in fact an ad for an ad company. It's not about Bill Bernbach at all. He's a great excuse to do an ad.

The same kind of social use occurs in a wide range of ways. And you recognize that and say, yes, it's always partial, it's a form of violence, it's manipulative, it socially encodes who we are, and yet this idea of resistance seems to privilege some kind of natural, native proprioceptive sense of self-image. Right now, you're the person who's the speaker here, right? The lights are shining down and you're responding to it with a whole series of different social factors than if you were interviewing one of your doctors for one of those monographs. And you don't get away from that. Yet you seem to be privileging that . . . space between self and self-image, to just use that term roughly.

BERNSTEIN: I actually think that it's the opposite. My sense is that there's no way to get outside of these kinds of characterizations of selves and self, and so it's a blank category to speak of being freed of self-image. But I do want to privilege the role of critique in questioning.

MANDEL: But, let's say, in your treatment of "the treatment of" Bill Bernbach, were you engaging in critique and questioning or were you simply putting it in further frames?

BERNSTEIN: No, I was doing both . . .

MANDEL: Bill Bernbach, whosoever he may have been, could be characterized in a way that would be consonant with some good use of characterization, right? I mean, he was a person, and that's a start. But that's not something you did. Does that pose a problem for you? Is characterization strategic and, if so, is there not some requirement that the strategy be laid bare?

BERNSTEIN: If there is no escape from characterization, then one thing you can do is to try to characterize the characterization, but in characterizing the characterization you're not escaping from the characterization. You're simply, so you're saying, creating another frame around it. It seems to me there is a value in trying to locate that kind of thing.

Characterization

There are two things I want to talk about in respect to this: strategies for criticism, and how you can deal with these things in poetry itself to create a music of contrasting characterizations, so that you can have not only this monoplanar or dyadic movement to characterization, framing the frame, but that you can have lots of different angles in composition so that the whole sounding of the various characterizations gets heard and made palpable.

In editing $L=A=N=G=U=A=G=E$, we were interested in allowing for a space for writing which didn't exist at the level of expository discourse. That's something I've always been sympathetic with. The problem with expository patterns, but also what accounts for their social force, is that they repress some terms or issues because they are complicated or contradictory or just "other" and overfixate on others that fit the "picture" and add to its impact. Certain techniques are used to create a little more dramatic focus—I want to attack Derrida, I don't attack the Yale critics who are easier targets because it's less effective than attacking the more interesting people who are more formidable, and even to mention Saussure, and so on. These kinds of strategic things constantly operate within the realm of criticism. In other words, the expository mode itself forces certain arguments and excludes others.

Actually, the *TV Shopper*, one of my favorite magazines in New York, has this article on Charlotte Curtis who's the editor of the Op-ed page of the *Times*, who says the following: "Our method was to take an issue, decide what we thought should be said about it, and then find an independent writer who would express our point of view" [laughter]. This is why you have to read the *TV Shopper*, it's really an extraordinary [laughter] method.

What I love is that she's really very clear about this. "Our method . . ."—because she's an editor, and she does have a method, "was to take an issue . . . and find an independent writer who would express our point of view. We had no ideology . . ." [laughter].

I'm going to do like in the magic shows, have somebody verify that I'm really reading this [laughter]. This is in contradiction to my theory that I have to make up the quotes because I can make them more outrageous. But Charlotte Curtis has provided me with something better—well, as good as I could have written [laughter].

"We have no ideology; we went issue by issue." And I think one of the claims to power within normative discourse is that claim to nonideology.

I think Silliman runs into a lot of criticism because people think his work is didactic. And it is, hopefully, because it has a method, and that is to elucidate certain issues that he deals with. People say to me, "That Ron, he's such a beautiful poet, why does he have these didactic essays?" And I say that the beauty of Ron's work is that it's not there to fool you into thinking it's this neutral truth. And when you hear the gears of his argument grinding from first to second to third, that's what makes that work important. If it was these seamless webs of the New Criticism, it couldn't do what it's doing.

And it's very hard for us, for me, to get over the desire for this elegant, seamless, logical discourse when writing criticism, because for one thing it has a real power. People all of a sudden start to listen to what you say when you talk in that language. I don't think by any means one should abandon that field. Because I think that to cede that power only to people who want to use it for things that you disagree with is politically foolish.

MANDEL: So what is the function of it? "I don't want to take on the Yale critics. It's more fun to take on people who are more formidable like Derrida himself." There's also a strategics of influence there, too. If you keep taking out hordes of footsoldiers as they approach with their derived and reduced versions of things, you can never really clear away . . .

BERNSTEIN: "The king speaks to the king."

MANDEL: Right. So it's a positioning of the self.

BERNSTEIN: It's positioning where your argument is. And that kind of characterization, especially if you can do it without being noticed, is one of the most powerful social forms. It has a very specific relationship with diplomacy— who you address an argument to, who you leave out. For example, it's a mark of criticism who can understand what it is you're talking about, the references, the nature of the references. Now I didn't actually explain who Derrida was. That's a measure of what I assume people in this audience to understand, but it also has that inherent positioning in it. It's a matter of etiquette—social codes that include by excluding.

MANDEL: So this is exactly what Ron was saying about the Bernbach ad. That ad, while it uses the founder of the agency, actually is designed to characterize Doyle Dane Bernbach and the people there now.

BERNSTEIN: You know it because it was the smallest thing. The smallest thing is obviously what it's an ad for.

SILLIMAN: It's like the Dewar's scotch ad.

BERNSTEIN: You mean the Philip Glass one? "When Phil gets home from a hard day composing . . ." [laughter] and "Twelve notes that revolutionized music". Now there's a characterization of Phil Glass that surely he must *need* to drink a bottle of scotch to get over [laughter]. And he's holding these pictures of notes. And it says, "Phil Glass started out as a typical, derivative young composer." I mean, there's another. I hope they gave him a lot of scotch because . . . In fact, the only difference is that when he started out he didn't have the budget for the big-scale works, didn't have the recognition, the publicity. So he started out as a typically derivative, i.e., not approved by *The New York Times* and Dewar's scotch, young composer, and drove a cab, and then he discovered twelve notes, period. Twelve notes which revolutionized music, period. When Phil gets home from a hard day composing—I'm sure he must have drunk more when he was driving the cab [laughter].

MANDEL: But not Dewar's.

BERNSTEIN: It's a beautiful color picture, too. But we may have the brand wrong.
  But anyway. "We had no ideology. We went issue by issue. Often we'd later run comment by a thinker on the extreme left and extreme right." I've never actually seen an article in *The New York Times* by anybody on the extreme left.

SILLIMAN: Walter Mondale? [laughter]

BERNSTEIN: The extreme right . . .

MANDEL: . . . has not yet been found.

BERNSTEIN: . . . Not by Charlotte Curtis. Now she's talking to the *TV Shopper*, which is not the *New York Magazine* audience or *The Wall Street Journal* audience. They presumably buy *TV Guide*. Or have the Sunday *Times* section. This is the thing you get in the supermarket. And it's mostly ads. I get it in my local xerox store.

"Often we'd later run comment by a thinker on the extreme left or the extreme right. The point was to help readers understand an issue by trying to present all 360 degrees of it." Now somebody should verify that I've read that [laughter]. "All 360 degrees." All of a sudden we have this metaphor of the globe.

I used to feel, being influenced by Stein, that there was no place for straight expository writing. There are poets now, and poets from the previous twenty or thirty years, who were so appalled by the kind of discourse, the kind of positioning that went on in criticism that they simply refused to do it. And I think that was a choice. To simply say, "I'm not going to get involved with that kind of characterizing, because the best thing to do is be silent, apart from the poetry." Another choice was the "Composition as Explanation" mode, which was the one that very much struck me for a long time, that Stein was the great exponent of, and Creeley in his essays, Williams in his imaginitive prose. $L=A=N=G=U=A=G=E$ had a lot of essays in that mode, that weren't expository. Oddly, I have lately found myself writing things that would fit some of the prescriptions that the

MLA, etc., puts forward. And I'm not quite sure why I've done that. Certainly last night was an instance. They're a little bit quirky at times, but the quirkiness is not that great.

PALMER: But also, Charles, there's a way in which what you're saying is quite clear, that there's a functional strategy involved with normative prose that would serve your purposes equally. And I think that it doesn't seem strange at all that at a certain point you would move over there any more than it would seem strange that Barry [Watten] and Lyn [Hejinian] would decide that for *Poetics Journal* they would more or less be emphasizing a version of normative critical discourse to show how certain kinds of thinking can operate in that territory.

BERNSTEIN: That's right. That's exactly the way I can understand that. I think that one of the reasons that I feel the freedom to do that, and even to do this, is the intense distrust I have for normative expository form. But, also, I questioned the hierarchization of style, or mode let's say, that I found myself guilty of. That this particular thing, Poetry, capital P—that Poesy and Expressing yourself is somehow better, whereas when I talk to people, this is pretty much the way I would talk. Ron?

SILLIMAN: I think you're absolutely right. But the other aspect of that, which I find more and more distressing, is the degree to which "Composition as Explanation", if you want to call it that, or artsy criticism might be another characterization of it, is as much an anti-intellectual gesture as is the refusal to speak. Both of them come out of negative reactions to the previous discourse. So when people do actually make those attempts to go in the direction you're talking about, as in *Poetics Journal*—I mean, I've heard from at least two friends that I've completely capitulated to the New Critics by speaking, quote, more plainly than I have on other occasions.

BERNSTEIN: Well, probably in a piece persuasively attacking the New Criticism!

SILLIMAN: But it's clear—and by printing so much of the stuff in $L=A=N=G=U=A=G=E$ is one of the things that makes it clear—that it is absolutely as easy to be manipulative, or to mask confusions using that form . . .

BERNSTEIN: . . . as it is using the regular. I think that's true. To privilege any mode immediately masks certain aspects, that's what I'm saying, which becomes problematic.

   The other thing is—see, I have a very suspicious mind and I feel that what you're saying about this anti-intellectualism, and being silent—if there's some kind of social pressure that makes you feel you can be silent and leave the world and this kind of discourse to them and let them play in that field, I'm too good for it—I'm suspicious of that because it cedes this discourse of power over to those who are willing to use it. I mean, who profits from this attitude exactly, like you "express" and leave the power to us? "But they *like* being marginal"! Still, entering into the discourse of power is painful, if you have ears, because power is crude. So I'm no temperance-preaching ex-alcoholic in this. I don't have a problem with poets who choose not to write criticism, or who choose to write in the composition as explanation style. But I agree with what you're saying nonetheless.

PALMER: Can I disagree? First of all, I don't take either of these gestures as anti-intellectual, necessarily. Remember the place of silence, when and where and how it's used, for example, the contextual use of silence can be an enormously powerful poetical act. It can be an absolutely articulate rejection of the procedures themselves. Also, I'd be reluctant to characterize that Steinian mode of refusal of discursive explanation as anti-intellectual.

BERNSTEIN: I don't. I didn't quite understand Ron to be saying that, either. Look, I love that stuff as much as any other kind of writing. I also published a magazine with Bruce [Andrews] which had hundreds and hundreds of pages of such writing. But I understood Ron to be saying that there's the possibility for an anti-intellectualism within that. Much as I think that rationalism has that same possibility. One of the points I made last night in "Words and Pictures" was that, in talking about Zukofsky and Williams, a lot of people's reaction against the academy tended to cede rationality to—I certainly have done this at times, so I don't mean to exclude myself—have ceded this kind of rationalistic discourse to the academy. That's what I object to. Because I think that unthought, unmethodical, rote, rationalized expository writing is as anti-intellectual as anything's going to be.

WATTEN: What upsets me is this characterization of a form. Because I'm much more interested in positive values of that

Characterization

kind of writing than I'm interested in moving away from
what has been characterized as "composition as explanation
style" in $L=A=N=G=U=A=G=E$. There's a whole tradition
of what I consider expository, and I think it's great, like
Pound and Williams, that wasn't really reached by the
works in $L=A=N=G=U=A=G=E$. In Williams's critical writings he's very thematic, he takes on a question and he writes
about it in a very inspired way. That's what I'd like to see as
values for that rather than "Let's not indulge ourselves with
composition as explanation" and going for some strategic
motivations. There's a constant looking at a form in a static
way in your approach. When I hear strategic . . .

BERNSTEIN: I was saying strategic not referring to what you
were doing. The oddness of my making this point, rather
than someone who doesn't do it, is that I certainly have been
putting forward, to my ability to do so, as straight an
expository work as anyone else in this context. So when I
talk about strategic, I'm talking about impulses within
myself.

I find it hard to put forward Williams in the *Selected
Essays*, —I think that stuff is very strategic. Pound is
incredibly strategic. I don't criticize him for that, but
certainly that's what a lot of that is.

PALMER: He considered it primarily strategic.

BERNSTEIN: And what I'm saying is—and this may be the
disagreement with you [Watten]—that I don't think there's
anything wrong with being strategic, if you're clear about
the fact that you're being strategic, and you understand the

context, because sometimes being strategic is the only thing that's going to get heard.

One has to be aware of the inherent values within, and the inherent limitations of, any kind of mode. I think there's attraction to power that is, for me, disingenuous to deny. I like to get responses when I write things. I got more response to "Three or Four Things I Know about Him" than to anything else I had written up to the time because here it was in this . . . it wasn't expository exactly, it was sort of about working, and it was about . . . I mean, you can't miss those things.

SILLIMAN: A lot of people at first couldn't tell whether that was, quote, a piece, or a piece of criticism.

BERNSTEIN: That's right. Even though it was ambiguous in that way, it nonetheless had chunks that were more normal than other of my works. So I'm just saying it's hard for me as a writer dealing with these things not to be swayed. Various styles have various extrasocial implications which are implicit within them and it's not that the author can control them. By using those modes authors participate in them, and they can try to confuse them or call attention to them, or they can not.

In some ways, there hasn't been that much genuinely straight stuff in *Poetics Journal*. I actually think that it's funny that we may think that. In a lot of ways, that stuff is extremely bizarre. It's only the measure of our own intense, intense bizarreness that we take a slight . . . [laughter]. Certainly "Three or Four Things I Know about Him" is a very bizarre looking thing, but to me that was like my

putting on patent leather shoes. And the distinctions we
make between more or less expository poeticizations are,
while very *real*, and tangible, are to somebody outside all
lumped together, compared to Charlotte Curtis's globe.
This is what the discourse of power is about in the sense that
I mean, not *Poetics Journal*. ". . . and then find an
independent writer who would express our point of view."

But I also wanted to get to poetry, why we should call
criticism "fiction" and save "nonfiction" for poetry. Because
I have been writing poetry that also contains discursive
sentences. And by combining those sentences with other
types of language, the clash in the sounds of the discourses
creates a polyphony that interests me. So for instance I may
not agree with a particular political opinion in a poem, it
may be false from my point of view. But it is the anxiety of
indetermination that is of interest. The political dimension
is not the opinion of any isolated sentence, but the experience
of *hearing* the possibilities of truth and lies and in-between,
and, as readers, *choosing*. Because to read is to choose; I just
want to bring that process to the fore.

I try to create a situation where it's hard for me to know
what I think about something. I like very strong statements;
I like especially statements that first appear to be either false
or true but then begin to destabilize—like a radioisotope.
And that sound . . . I don't want to say . . . I was going to
say it stops being content, but that's false . . . and then once
again . . . see that interests me because I don't know what
that means, I don't know how anything could stop being
content, "and that's false" comes upon it, what gets to
interest me is the sound of "and that's false". And then you
lay down another sound under that or over it. That's what

the process of writing is, dealing with that level of tone and never discounting it. If you focus in on the so-called meaning as divorced from the sound, you have no idea what the meaning is. It's when you start to hear the tonal qualities *as* the meaning of that . . . You hear the tones, which is to hear characterizations, and then resonate them, attach additional possibilities that destabilize, and then work to make that indefiniteness tangible, audible.

LARRY EIGNER: The question is how you get going and how you keep it up. That may be a real mysterious question, especially when you can't do it [laughter]. But you say that the words get destabilized that began as stronger statements. You say the sound becomes the meaning, so you pay more attention to the sound the more doubtful the statement becomes.

BERNSTEIN: And that resonance brings you closer to the meaning of the words. For any given person, the approach to, the hearing of, language is going to be different. We come at this thing we share—our language, our world, what we see, which is in common, but we come at it from different angles. We have different resistances to language that create the different sounds in people's poems or speech or conceptions.

CARLA HARRYMAN: When you say "resistances" do you mean blocks, how am I going to get from this point to this point when all I see is a blank, or resistance to the past, resistance to tradition, or resistance to your mother?

BERNSTEIN: I mean it also in the physical sense—if I go

from here to there air is resistant. Gravity. An impedance, a weight, that you're pressing against and by pressing against it you create "sound". And what you're pressing against is the enormous amount of built-in characterizations that are already there before you characterize anything.

SILLIMAN: In your work, at any given point, there is the meaning of the words immediately in front of you, but it's not necessarily the meaning of the work as a whole—by a long shot. There's one almost abstract, or constructed, sense in which every individual poem, as in fact every individual book, means something, however inarticulable in an individual newspaper phrase it might be. At the same time, at any given point in the book you are so far from that by mechanisms of irony and, in the most neutral sense of the word, distortion that you've set up. In "Substance Abuse" the sentence about "death is the only apparent limit" can be read in about eight different ways and there are few cues as to which the context would edit out. At the same time, the books clearly set up limits.

BERNSTEIN: I don't think I manage to achieve as many different possible interpretations as I might like [laughter]. I'm very limited by what makes sense to me, because of this horribly mistaken but nonetheless ongoing concern for the poem to sound right. I have a desire for an infinitely negative capability, and yet I am always coming upon very concrete forms of stabilization, characterization, that make patterns in respect to one another, which is what you notice at the level of the book.

So there's a desire to push things as far as they will go and the recognition that it doesn't go all that far. But if you don't push, you don't even find out the most obvious relations, the most obvious meanings. The process, to call it destabilization is itself false, ends up creating these tightly woven, webbed formations.

But you say I get at this by irony and distortion. Now, distortion, that's one thing . . . but I've never operated with irony [laughter]. Comedy yes, schticks is more my . . .

ROBERT GRENIER: I did think of "Entitlement" [in *The Sophist*] as serious even though many of the lines are very funny. They wouldn't break you up—the crack would come back to the actuality of what was being said. And I thought that for two reasons. One, because of the inherent nobility of the language used which has this reference to a time in which people didn't break up that way and really inhibits that in part, and also something that happens to me a lot in plays—I take the lives of the people seriously even though they're actors so that even though what they were saying may be hopelessly funny, hopelessly distressing and very funny or something or just very clear—you hear it as being what they say and so it's true in some way and that inhibits the other humor.

BERNSTEIN: It's funny because you can't quite deal with it. It seems ludicrous, sure, but at the same time not more ludicrous than anything else.

GRENIER: It could be the case.

STEPHEN RODEFER: How do you absolve yourself from the

idea of irony in particular in those series of speeches about jobs in "Foreign Body Sensation" [in *The Sophist*]?

GRENIER: I think it isn't ironic because irony presumes some sort of point of view from which some measure of restraint can be applied to such statement by arbitrating in such a way that it seems to be some thing that it's not. And there's no point of view in that sense that would qualify the statement. . . . It's very interesting, the difficulty is trying to identify the point of view in so many different kinds of language use in Charles's stuff. If it were consistent in one or another mode than maybe you could say this is the place that the irony as qualification is coming from.

BERNSTEIN: Yes, I agree with that. See what you may think I . . . I don't have it . . . I as the author, I change what I think . . . There are obviously certain phrases that are what I think but I don't think that what I think is any more . . . I mean I'm interested in the way people take themselves seriously or do these sort of strange things that anyway aren't really strange in "Foreign Body Sensation". What sounds funny to me is probably what I feel outside of. That stuff I find most objectionable probably is involved with some kind of reverse reaction to the way in which I identify myself. So that the stuff that seems the most to be made mock of, when I hear it, is interesting to me because my negative reaction suggests that in my relation to it there's something beyond just that I believe it to be false. Similarly, just disliking or dismissing a statement wouldn't be a motivation to include it in a poem. I include material because it doesn't have that pattern—there's something that comes back that isn't quite settled, that's hard to deny. As opposed to material that's obviously, flatly wrong from my perception.

LYN HEJINIAN: Do you include material that's obviously, flatly right to your perception?

BERNSTEIN: I don't know, if the poem is working, what obviously, flatly right is—or even in saying that. Because, of course, yes, I agree with certain sentiments expressed and disagree with others—which nonetheless are incorporated into this larger context that limits the "flatness" of any asserted truth value, maybe allowing *other* things to emerge as right, or truthful. Which is not to say I—as distinct from the poem—don't have opinions or that I don't believe some or many of them to be true.

SUSAN BEE: But you do use irony.

BERNSTEIN: I don't think of it that way. Even if that appears to be the case in some instances—and it's always deceptive— you have to take into account the context in which the statement appears. And whatever I include I *like*, am fascinated or engaged by, in some way that doesn't reduce simply to irony.

This is not to make the nice-guy distinction between laughing at and laughing with. There's nothing so great as to laugh *at*. But contempt and condescension and right-eousness are not irony either; or we laugh at the arrogance of those attitudes, and so on through a multiple regression of frames. By "resistance" I'm perhaps suggesting something like laughing at, myself included.

My problem with irony is that it is a set-up in which the

"real" meaning is the opposite of the surface meaning. X equals not X. It's just another binary system, like the ambiguity in a drawing of a duck that can also be read as a drawing of a rabbit. It's the difference between a double entendre and Joycean word play. Irony is simple ambiguity: ironic/iconic. What I want is humor that opens out into a multivolitional field destabilizing to any fixed meaning that can be assigned and that persists out of context. Octavio Paz has used the term "meta-irony": "an irony that destroys its negation and, hence, returns in the affirmative." But I wouldn't want to stop at that flip back to the affirmative but to go beyond yes and no. Humor as destabilizing not only the negation to mean affirmation but the affirmation also— the idea of a perpetual motion machine that never stops pinging and ponging off the walls, ceilings, floors. So returns to . . . let's say "the absolute", maybe the in- effable—everywhere said, nowhere stated. But then I wouldn't want to make humor into too serious a business.

ACKNOWLEDGEMENTS

Many of these works have been revised for this collection.
Only first publication is listed. Note that some of the
punctuation of this text departs from conventional American
practices; this is intentional.

ONE/ THE SECRET OF SYNTAX

"Three or Four Things I Know about Him" (1977). *A Hundred Posters* No.
26 (Boston: 1978).

"Semblance". A contribution to Ken Edwards's symposium on recent
American poetry, "Death of the Referent?", *Reality Studios* 2:4 (London:
1980).

"Stray Straws and Straw Men" (1976). A contribution to Steve McCaffery's
symposium, "The Politics of the Referent", *Open Letter* 3:7 (Toronto:
1977).

"A Particular Thing" (1975). *Red M* No. 1 (New York: 1977).

"Style". Coauthor: Susan Bee. *L=A=N=G=U=A=G=E* No. 6 (1978).

"The Dollar Value of Poetry". A contribution to the "Politics of Poetry"
issue, *L=A=N=G=U=A=G=E* No. 9/10 (New York: 1979).

"Thought's Measure" (1980). Notes from a series of eleven workshops at
St. Mark's Poetry Project, New York. *L=A=N=G=U=A=G=E* Vol. 4 (1981),
published simultaneously as *Open Letter* 5:1 (Toronto: 1982).

TWO/ FILM OF PERCEPTION

"Frames of Reference". Presented as part of "Image Talks" at the
Collective for Living Cinema, New York, in March 1982. Thanks to
Abigail Child, curator of the series. *Southern Humanities Review* 19:3
(Auburn, AL: 1985).

"Words and Pictures". Presented as part of a residency at 80 Langton
Street, San Francisco, in January 1983. Thanks to Susan Howe, Nick
Piombino, Madeline Gins, and Joan Snitzer. *Sagetrieb* 2:1 (Orono, ME:
1983).

THREE/ READING, PERSON, PHILOSOPHY

"The Objects of Meaning" (1979). *boundary 2* IX:2 (Binghamton, NY:
1981).

"Meaning the Meaning" (1981). Coauthor: Susan Bee. *Beauty and Critique*,
ed. Richard Milazzo (New York: Mussman-Bruce, 1982).

463

464   Acknowledgements

"The Stadium of Explanation" (1981). *Code of Signals*, ed. Michael Palmer, *Io* No. 30 (Berkeley: 1983).

"On Theatricality" (1981 and 1979). *Wch Way* No. 4 (Albany and Los Angeles: 1982).

"G—/" (1975). Tape transcription. *The Big House*, ed. Michael Slater (New York: Ailanthus, 1978).

"Writing and Method" (1981). Written in conjunction with a series on "Poetry and Philosophy" conducted with Edmund Leites at the St. Mark's Poetry Project, New York. *Poetics Journal* No. 3 (Berkeley: 1983).

FOUR/ CONSPIRACIES

"Introduction". *The Paris Review* No. 86 (New York: 1982).

"The Academy in Peril". Presented at "Poets' Centennial Tribute to William Carlos Williams", Modern Language Association convention, New York, on December 29, 1983. *Sulfur* No. 10 (Pasadena: 1984).

"Jackson at Home". *Paper Air* 2:3 (Blue Bell, PA: 1980).

"Maintaining Space" (1975). "A Symposium on Clark Coolidge", ed. Ron Silliman, *Stations* No. 5 (Milwaukee: Membrane, 1978).

"Making Words Visible". *L=A=N=G=U=A=G=E* No. 5 (1978).

"The Alphabet of Stride". *L=A=N=G=U=A=G=E* No. 3 (1978).

"Counting and Uncounting". *Poetry Project Newsletter*, July 1978 (New York).

"Writing Against the Body". Written on the occasion of a memorial reading for Ted Berrigan at St. Mark's Church, November 15, 1983. *Exquisite Corpse* 2:1 (Baltimore: 1984).

"Hejinian's Notes". *Reality Studios* 3:2 (1980).

"I Think I Understand Alan Davies" (1981 and 1983). *Jimmy and Lucy's House of K*, No. 2 (Oakland: 1984).

"With Words". An introduction to an exhibition, curated with Susan Bee, at Ugo Carrega's Mercato del Sale gallery in Milan during March 1979. *A Critical Assembling: Assembling* No. 9/ *Precisely* Nos. 6/7/8/9 (New York: 1979).

"Hearing 'Here'". *Sagetrieb* 1:3 (1982).

"Narrating Narration". *The Difficulties* 2:2 (Kent, OH: 1984).

"Undone Business". *Credences* III:2 (Buffalo: 1984).

"The Telling". *Poetry Project Newsletter*, January 1977.

"The Conspiracy of 'Us'". Originally part of a dialogue with Michael Lally. *L=A=N=G=U=A=G=E* No. 8 (1979).

Five/ Flesh

"Blood on the Cutting Room Floor". Presented at 11th Alabama Symposium on English and American Literature, "What Is a Poet?", University of Alabama, Tuscaloosa, on October 19, 1984. Thanks to Christopher Dewdney and his "Parasite Maintenance" in *Alter Sublime*. Excerpt in *Poetry Project Newsletter*, January 1985. *What Is a Poet?*, ed. Hank Lazer (Tuscaloosa: University of Alabama, 1986).

"Living Tissue / Dead Ideas". Presented at the Third Annual Conference, The Humanities Institute, "Theory and Methods: The Idea of Poetry and the Poetry of Ideas", Jerome J. McGann (Director), at Alumni House, University of California, Berkeley, on October 13, 1984.

Six/ Catechesis

"An Interview with Tom Beckett" (1981). Written responses to Beckett's questions. *The Difficulties* 2:2 (1982).

"Socialist Realism or Real Socialism?". Edited transcript of a presentation at the Institute for Policy Studies in Washington, D.C., in December 1981. It was the last of eight sessions on politics and language. *New Critical Perspectives*, ed. Bruce Boone, *Soup* No. 4 (San Francisco: 1985).

"Characterization". Edited and transcribed by Bob Perelman from a talk and discussions during a residency at 80 Langton Street, San Francisco, in January 1983. *Writing/Talks*, ed. Perelman (Carbondale: Southern Illinois University, 1984).

Special acknowledgement, and thanks, to Susan Bee for numerous editorial comments that are incorporated into many of these works.

SUN & MOON CLASSICS

The Sun & Moon Classics is a publicly supported, nonprofit program to publish new editions, translations, or republications of outstanding world literature of the late nineteenth and twentieth centuries. Through its publication of living authors as well as great masters of the century, the series attempts to redefine what usually is meant by the idea of a "classic" by dehistoricizing the concept and embracing a new, ever changing literary canon.

Organized by the Contemporary Arts Educational Project, Inc., a nonprofit corporation, and published by its program Sun & Moon Press, the series is made possible, in part, by grants and individual contributions.

This book was made possible, in part, through matching grants from the National Endowment for the Arts and from the California Arts Council, through an organizational grant from the Andrew W. Mellon Foundation, through a grant for advertising and promotion from the Lila B. Wallace/ Reader's Digest Fund, and through contributions from the following individuals:

Charles Altieri (Seattle, Washington)
John Arden (Galway, Ireland)
Jesse Huntley Ausubel (New York, New York)
Dennis Barone (West Hartford, Connecticut)
Jonathan Baumbach (Brooklyn, New York)
Guy Bennett (Los Angeles, California)
Bill Berkson (Bolinas, California)
Steve Benson (Berkeley, California)
Charles Bernstein and Susan Bee (New York, New York)
Sherry Bernstein (New York, New York)
Dorothy Bilik (Silver Spring, Maryland)
Bill Corbett (Boston, Massachusetts)
Fielding Dawson (New York, New York)
Robert Crosson (Los Angeles, California)
Tina Darragh and P. Inman (Greenbelt, Maryland)
David Detrich (Los Angeles, California)
Christopher Dewdney (Toronto, Canada)
Philip Dunne (Malibu, California)
George Economou (Norman, Oklahoma)
Elaine Equi and Jerome Sala (New York, New York)
Lawrence Ferlinghetti (San Francisco, California)
Richard Foreman (New York, New York)
Howard N. Fox (Los Angeles, California)

Jerry Fox (Aventura, Florida)
In Memoriam: Rose Fox
Melvyn Freilicher (San Diego, California)
Miro Gavran (Zagreb, Croatia)
Peter Glassgold (Brooklyn, New York)
Barbara Guest (New York, New York)
Perla and Amiram V. Karney (Bel Air, California)
Fred Haines (Los Angeles, California)
Fanny Howe (La Jolla, California)
Harold Jaffe (San Diego, California)
Ira S. Jaffe (Albuquerque, New Mexico)
Alex Katz (New York, New York)
Tom LaFarge (New York, New York)
Mary Jane Lafferty (Los Angeles, California)
Michael Lally (Santa Monica, California)
Norman Lavers (Jonesboro, Arkansas)
Jerome Lawrence (Malibu, California)
Stacey Levine (Seattle, Washington)
Herbert Lust (Greenwich, Connecticut)
Norman MacAffee (New York, New York)
Rosemary Macchiavelli (Washington, DC)
Beatrice Manley (Los Angeles, California)
Martin Nakell (Los Angeles, California)
Toby Olson (Philadelphia, Pennsylvania)
Maggie O'Sullivan (Hebden Bridge, England)
Rochelle Owens (Norman, Oklahoma)
Marjorie and Joseph Perloff (Pacific Palisades, California)
Dennis Phillips (Los Angeles, California)
David Reed (New York, New York)
Ishmael Reed (Oakland, California)
Janet Rodney (Santa Fe, New Mexico)
Joe Ross (Washington, DC)
Dr. Marvin and Ruth Sackner (Miami Beach, Florida)
Floyd Salas (Berkeley, California)
Tom Savage (New York, New York)
Leslie Scalapino (Oakland, California)
James Sherry (New York, New York)
Aaron Shurin (San Francisco, California)
Charles Simic (Strafford, New Hampshire)
Gilbert Sorrentino (Stanford, California)
Catharine R. Stimpson (Staten Island, New York)
John Taggart (Newburg, Pennsylvania)

Nathaniel Tarn (Tesuque, New Mexico)
Fiona Templeton (New York, New York)
Mitch Tuchman (Los Angeles, California)
Wendy Walker (New York, New York)
Anne Walter (Carnac, France)
Arnold Wesker (Hay on Wye, England)

If you would like to be a contributor to this series, please send your tax-deductible contribution to The Contemporary Arts Educational Project, Inc., a non-profit corporation, 6026 Wilshire Boulevard, Los Angeles, California 90036.

*First American publication
**Revised edition